Lecture Notes in Computer Science   11753

Pau Fonseca i Casas · Maria-Ribera Sancho ·
Edel Sherratt (Eds.)

System Analysis and Modeling

Languages, Methods, and Tools for Industry 4.0

11th International Conference, SAM 2019
Munich, Germany, September 16–17, 2019
Proceedings

 Springer

Editors
Pau Fonseca i Casas ⓘ
Universitat Politècnica de Catalunya
Barcelona, Spain

Maria-Ribera Sancho ⓘ
Universitat Politècnica de Catalunya
Barcelona, Spain

Edel Sherratt
Aberystwyth University
Aberystwyth, UK

ISSN 0302-9743   ISSN 1611-3349   (electronic)
Lecture Notes in Computer Science
ISBN 978-3-030-30689-2   ISBN 978-3-030-30690-8   (eBook)
https://doi.org/10.1007/978-3-030-30690-8

LNCS Sublibrary: SL2 – Programming and Software Engineering

This Springer imprint is published by the registered company Springer Nature Switzerland AG
The registered company address is: Gewerbestrasse 11, 6330 Cham, Switzerland

Preface

This book constitutes the refereed proceedings of the 11th International Conference on System Analysis and Modeling (SAM 2019), held during September 16–17, 2019, in Munich, Germany.

This year's edition of SAM was under the theme "Languages, Methods, and Tools for Industry 4.0."

In 1784, industry was characterized by the combined use of three elements, the steam engine, the use of coal as a fuel, and the use of iron. From 1870, major changes to industry were driven by new sources of energy – gas, oil, and electricity – along with new materials, new systems of transportation, and the rise of telephone and radio use. Since 1969, industry has been characterized by greater utilization of the renewable energy sources, development of rechargeable batteries, of hydrogen batteries, and of other new energy storage technologies, such as the intelligent grid or electric power distribution network "smart" (smart Grid). Increased use of transport based on electric vehicles (all-electric vehicles, as well as fuel cells), using renewable electricity as a propulsion power, has also played a major role. But remarkably, and related to the context of this conference, during this period we see the rise of electronics, telecommunications, and computers, raising in the programmable logic controllers (PLCs) and robots.

Now Industry 4.0 represents a qualitative leap in the organization and control of the entire value chain throughout the life cycle of the manufacture and delivery of the product. The exponential expansion of this fourth revolution is mainly caused by the possibility of merging the technology, breaking the limits between the physical and the digital worlds. This produces a paradigm shift in society. There are plenty of different technologies that individually have a great impact on the production processes, but more interestingly, when those technologies act together, they create an increased force that accelerates the generation of news processes on the industrial frame. The mainstream adoption of technologies and processes that will soon lead the upcoming production methods will change the face of the industry in a broad spectrum.

Several consulting firms with the goal to establish a clear definition of what is Industry 4.0 agree that there is a set of technologies that will lead this revolution, like Simulation, Cloud computing, 3D printers, among others. The key concept of the digital twin, a copy of the system that defines the main elements that drive the behavior of the system along with the system evolution, is to serve as the glue between all the elements that exist on this system.

A digital twin is a model, and by definition a model uses formal languages and tools that supports description and the adoption of the model vision in all spheres of the industry to achieve a holistic approach. In this sense, conferences like SAM 2019 provide an excellent opportunity to depict the main concerns and solutions regarding the modeling process that will lead the upcoming industrial (r)evolution.

The 12 regular papers (maximum 20 pages) and the 2 work-in-progress papers (maximum 12 pages), were carefully reviewed and selected from 28 submissions. Each submission was reviewed by at least 2, and on average 2.9, Program Committee members.

We had two keynote presentations, from two strong researchers and practitioners of the area: Antoni Guasch i Petit from the InLab FIB, a research institution of the Universitat Politècnica de Catalunya, who presented interesting examples and experiences learned from the use of conceptual modeling in critical projects; and Thomas Weigert, Chief Technology Officer and Vice President at UniqueSoft. This second keynote presentation contextualized the current trends in model-driven engineering and was also included in this volume.

As is the usual at SAM conferences, the papers describe innovations, new trends, and interesting experiences in modeling and analysis of complex systems mainly focused on ITU-T's Specification and Description Language (SDL-2010) and Message Sequence Chart (MSC) notations, but also including system design languages like UML, ASN.1, TTCN, SysML and the User Requirements Notation (URN). This edition includes software engineering technologies related to Industry 4.0, such as distributed applications, interoperability, social and environmental modeling, concurrency, data integrity, software verification and validation, and automated code generation.

SDL Forum Society

The SDL Forum Society is a not-for-profit organization that, in addition to running the System Analysis and Modelling (SAM) conference series of events, also:

- Runs the System Design Languages Forum (SDL Forum) series
- Is a body recognized by ITU-T as co-developing system design languages in the Z.100 series (SDL), Z.120 series (MSC), Z.150 series (URN), and other language standards
- Promotes the ITU-T System Design Languages

For more information on the SDL Forum Society, see http://www.sdl-forum.org.

July 2019   Pau Fonseca i Casas
Maria-Ribera Sancho
Edel Sherratt

Organization

Program Committee

Shaukat Ali	Simula Research Laboratory, Norway
Daniel Amyot	University of Ottawa, Canada
Ludovic Apvrille	Telecom ParisTech, France
Tibor Csöndes	Ericsson, Hungary
Juergen Dingel	Queen's University, Canada
Joachim Fischer	Humboldt University of Berlin, Germany
Antoni Fonseca	Polyhedra Tech S.L., Spain
Pau Fonseca i Casas	Universitat Politècnica de Catalunya, Spain
Emmanuel Gaudin	PragmaDev, France
Abdelouahed Gherbi	École de Technology Supérieure, Université du Québec, Canada
Reinhard Gotzhein	University of Kaiserslautern, Germany
Jens Grabowski	Georg-August-University of Göttingen, Germany
Jameledine Hassine	KFUPM, Saudi Arabia
Oystein Haugen	Østfold University College, Norway
Steffen Herbold	Universität Göttingen, Germany
Ferhat Khendek	Concordia University, Canada
Gabor Kovacs	Budapest University of Technology and Economics, Hungary
Finn Kristoffersen	Cinderella ApS, Denmark
Gunter Mussbacher	McGill University, Canada
Ileana Ober	IRIT, University of Toulouse, France
Iulian Ober	IRIT, University of Toulouse, France
Xavier Pi	Universitat Oberta de Catalunya, Spain
Andreas Prinz	University of Agder, Norway
Rick Reed	TSE, UK
Cristina Ruiz	Carleton University, Canada
Maria-Ribera Sancho	Universitat Politècnica de Catalunya, Spain
Edel Sherratt	University of Wales Aberystwyth, UK
Ernest Teniente	Universitat Politècnica de Catalunya, Spain
Maria Toeroe	Ericsson, Canada
András Vörös	Budapest University of Technology and Economics, Hungary
Gabriel Wainer	Carleton University, Canada
Man Zhang	Kristiania University College, Norway

Additional Reviewer

Weber, Dorian

Acknowledgements

Organizing a conference is a large undertaking that cannot be carried out alone. The program co-chairs would like to recognize the dedicated work and the contributions of many people and organizations. We wish to thank the keynote speakers, the members of the Program Committee (PC), the members of the SDL Forum Society Board, and the many postgraduate students and support staff who made this conference possible.

Furthermore, we thank the MODELS Organizing Committee for the effective support during the preparation and smooth realization of the SAM conference.

We thank Springer for once again publishing the conference proceedings in their LNCS series.

Finally, and most importantly, we would like to thank the authors of the papers that provided the content for this conference.

Many thanks to all the speakers, attendees, PC members, and the SDL Forum Board for making this event a success.

Contents

Keynote Talk

Generating Test Suites to Validate Legacy Systems

Thomas Weigert[3]([✉]), Alexander Kolchin[2], Stepan Potiyenko[2], Oleg Gurenko[1],
Aswin van den Berg[3], Valentyn Banas[1], Roman Chetvertak[1],
Roman Yagodka[1], and Vlad Volkov[2]

[1] ISS, Kyiv, Ukraine
[2] V.M. Glushkov Institute of Cybernetics of the NAS of Ukraine, Kyiv, Ukraine
[3] Uniquesoft LLC, Palatine, IL, USA
thomas.weigert@uniquesoft.com
http://www.uniquesoft.com

Abstract. Testing of modernized legacy systems is difficult due to
that typically requirements specifications do not exist and that detailed
knowledge of the architecture and design of the system may have been
lost. In this paper we present an approach which derives test suites for
a modernized legacy systems from the legacy code. We extend our earlier presented approach deriving test suites from use case map (UCM)
specifications of a system by transforming the legacy code into a UCM
model. We further discuss enhancements to the test generation process
required to operate on the large models obtained from realistic legacy systems and to assure that the generated tests are meaningful to the tester.
This approach has been used to validate the modernization of large (in
excess of 20 million lines of code) mainframe applications implemented
in COBOL.

Keywords: System testing · Test generation · Legacy modernization ·
State space reduction

1 Testing Is Hard

While who writes the code for software products often gets all the glory, testing those products is often much harder than producing them in the first place.
When creating tests, the tester must be able to envision the sequences of states
the execution of the software may traverse during its execution. By the state of a
software system we mean the conjunction of the values of all its explicit variables
(the variables that the code defines) as well as all its implicit variables (the variables that the code induces when executing in the context of its environment).
We refer to a sequence of such states as a trace. A trace that leads from an entry
point into the system to its termination or to points in the program where the
trace keeps repeating represents a possible behavior of the system. The complete
behavior of the system is represented by the sum of all such traces.

© Springer Nature Switzerland AG 2019
P. Fonseca i Casas et al. (Eds.): SAM 2019, LNCS 11753, pp. 3–23, 2019.
https://doi.org/10.1007/978-3-030-30690-8_1

Even for simple systems, it is not easy to envision all possible traces. When a system interacts with other agents in its environment, in particular in an asynchronous manner, the number of possible traces explodes rapidly due to the interleaving of its interactions. Nevertheless, a good tester must be able to envision such traces, especially where these may lead to undesired behaviors.

At some states, the system will require inputs which will determine its subsequent behavior. Such inputs may come from other agents (such as users or other systems that the system under test interacts with) or they may come from databases or otherwise reflect persistent data that is obtained. For each trace, the tester must be able to determine the inputs that are required to trigger this trace and arrange that during execution of the test these inputs are provided. If such inputs come from persistent data, the tester must arrange for the data source to be configured to provide exactly that data.

At other states, the system will produce outputs to its environment which one can observe. The tester must be able to predict what output the system will produce at each such state, given the preceding inputs. As such output may be the result of complex computation, a tester may need to rely on an oracle to determine the desired outputs.

A test is a sequence of inputs to the system which trigger its execution and outputs observable during its execution. A test suite is a set of such tests. Much research has gone into determining criteria that would establish the quality of a test suite, that is, a measure of the trust we can place in the system to execute correctly and error-free if all the tests in a test suite have passed (that is, the predicted outputs were indeed observed when the system was stimulated with the given inputs). These criteria are usually referred to as coverage criteria. Finding a test suite that includes all possible traces through the system will usually be prohibitively large or even theoretically impossible. Coverage criteria help us to determine whether a test suite covers a sufficiently large subset of the state space for us to place trust in the software system. It is difficult for the tester to envision all the important consequences of the system behavior. In practice, we often find that tests tend to cover some regions of the state space many times over, while other regions are barely visited or not visited at all. The history of software engineering provides a seemingly endless stream of examples where testers failed to envision traces present in the state space leading to disastrous consequences.

Tests as discussed so far establish that the system behaves as intended with respect to its functionality, that is: Does the system produce the expected outputs given a set of predetermined inputs. Developers are also concerned with non-functional characteristics of the system, such as how quickly it will produce these outputs, how many other agents it can interact with before its performance will become unbearably slow, its resilience when the environment changes in unexpected ways or when the environment does not provide desired inputs, and many more. In this paper, we shall not further be concerned with testing for non-functional system properties.

A number of languages have been developed to specify test suites [1–5]. In earlier papers, we have described an approach we have developed to derive tests from an abstract specification of system behavior [6–9]. In that approach, we describe system behavior through use case map (UCM) specifications [10,11]. A use case map is a graphical or textual description of the system behavior in a simple and easy to understand notation. Use case maps have been successfully used to specify systems in many domains, from telecommunications to industrial control. Our approach reasons over a formal model derived from UCM specifications and generates a set of traces that cover the specification, according to chosen coverage criteria [8]. We rely on reachability analysis of the formal model, and thus are subject to the theoretical limits of this technology. Nevertheless, leveraging well-known techniques as well as our own recently developed methods of reducing the size of the induced state space, we have been able to achieve impressive practical results [12–14,39]. Tools which have implemented our approach have been successfully used to derive test suites for communications network elements developed by Motorola and Samsung. We have reported on the results of applying these tools to industrial projects elsewhere [6,8].

Testers will then execute the developed test suites, that is, stimulate the system under test with the inputs specified in a test, and observe the outputs that result and compare them to the behavior the test had predicted. Much engineering work has gone into developing tools that execute test suites against a system under test. (In industry terminology, "test automation" confusingly refers to test execution, not to the automation of producing tests.) In particular in the information technology space, support for test execution has converged on widely used frameworks, such as Cucumber [5] and Robot [15]. These systems provide notations to express tests and are able interact with the system under test to stimulate it and observe its behavior. We will not further discuss test execution in this paper. Our approach produces test suites that can be executed by such frameworks.

2 Testing of Modernized Systems

The modernization of legacy systems brings additional challenges for the tester. For older systems, in particular for legacy mainframe applications which now are increasingly migrated to Linux client-server systems or to cloud-based systems, often requirements descriptions do not exist. If any description of system behavior exists, it usually covers only the expected or "sunny-day" scenarios, but is silent on error or "rainy-day" scenarios.

Therefore, legacy modernization carries a substantial level of risk. Not only are such systems written in languages which are not familiar to the majority of today's programmers (e.g., COBOL), but also these languages usually lack the abstraction capabilities of modern programming languages which prevent many software defects. The consequent extensive usage of global variables and/or the complex control flow mediated through goto constructs make such systems hard to understand. The architectures imposed by mainframe middleware such as CICS and IMS, by older storage technologies such as VSAM files or hierarchical databases, and the need for optimizations imposed by limitations of past hardware solutions also contribute to the difficulty in analyzing legacy systems. Alas, the legacy systems that are still in operation today are usually business critical, representing the heart of the operation of many organizations, from financial institutions to manufacturing. Any failure of a modernized system would be unacceptable. To no surprise, there is great reluctance to embark on such modernizations, even if it promises dramatic reductions in operating and maintenance expenses.

When testing a modernized system, we need not establish that it satisfies its requirements. By definition, the legacy system is correct. The main concern for a modernized system is whether it faithfully reproduces the behavior of the legacy system, modulo any changes due to the changed operating environment. This change of focus offers an opportunity: we merely need to establish that the traces of the modernized system match the traces of the legacy system. The most reliable source for traces of the legacy system is its code. If there was a way of inferring the traces from the code of the legacy system and derive a test suite, then we could subject the modernized system to this test suite and establish that its behavior matches the behavior of the legacy system. While in ordinary system development basing tests on the code itself would be a rather silly undertaking, for legacy modernization it may prove the most viable route.

In order to apply the test case derivation approach discussed earlier [6–8] to generate test suites for legacy systems, we transform the legacy code into a model represented as use case maps. This transformation maps the semantics of the programming language to the means of expression afforded by UCM. We have augmented the standard UCM syntax with an expression language which models the update to state variables of the system. For some legacy languages, such as COBOL, this mapping is complicated due to the possible overlap between data entities due to constructs such as redefinition or group entities. The use case map model reduces the computations of the legacy system to either updates to the system state or to abstract computations summarizing their effect on the system state.

The state space induced by the code of any realistic legacy system will be enormous and thus we had to develop further techniques to deal with very large state spaces. We further found that it is important for the derived traces to reflect understandable behaviors. Reachability analysis does not consider the causal relationships that may exist between different states and chooses its traversal of the state space either randomly or determined by optimizations applied. Often such traces, while representing admissible behaviors, surprise the tester as they do not represent system scenarios the tester would normally encounter. Scenarios that a tester expects might be absent, when they do not further increase coverage beyond what has already been achieved. It is therefore important to enhance reachability analysis so that traces are not arbitrarily selected to achieve the desired coverage level, but that traces reflect well-understood usage scenarios.

In the following, we will discuss the process we realized to derive system test suites from legacy code. Section 3 discusses the transformation of the legacy code to a UCM model. We shall restrict our discussion to legacy systems implemented in COBOL. The details of the transformation need to reflect the legacy language but the approach is independent of the language modernized. Section 4 presents enhancements we developed to handle the enormous state spaces induced by legacy systems when deriving test cases from a UCM model. We further discuss a strategy that assure that the derived test cases are meaningful to a tester.

3   Obtaining a Model from Legacy Code

We begin with the observation that for system testing we are usually concerned with the business logic of the system, that is, the part of the system behavior that relates to realizing the business purpose of the system. In most systems, the business logic is only a, sometimes small, subset of the code. Much software has to be written to implement the business logic in the computational environment the system executes in. There is code which will obtain the inputs to the system, which will format and create the outputs from the system, and which ties the system to the underlying middleware and operating system. There further is much code handling errors that could arise from erroneous or incorrect inputs or from undesired behavior of the computing environment. Cross-cutting concerns may provide other system services not related to the business logic proper, such as authentication, logging, monitoring, and so on. Isolating the business logic from the rest of the code will dramatically reduce the state space that needs to be analyzed.

Next we observe that even throughout the business logic there are aspects that are of greater interest to the tester than others. Often, when examining the outputs of the system, we can find parts that are not as important as others. From their interaction with the legacy systems, testers tend to be aware of the "important" results of the system. If we focus on the traces of the system which lead to those "important" results, we will reduce the state space further.

Tests relate stimuli to the system under test to observed outputs. Starting at the observed outputs, we analyze all exit points from a program to identify the data that is passed out of the program. Having separated the business logic from other code of lesser interest, we separate the data output into data that is "interesting" and such that is not. We can then reduce the set of all possible execution traces to the set of all possible traces which lead to the selected points of interest and effect the "interesting" data. The remainder of the code can be ignored. This code is eliminated through program slicing [16]. We extend slicing with techniques to separate the business logic implemented in the program from other code which shall be ignored. The resultant slices are then converted into a UCM model.

3.1   Control Flow and Data Flow Dependencies

A program slice consists of the statements of a program which have a potential effect on the values computed at some points of interest; these points of interest are referred to as the slicing criterion. Static slicing [17] is independent of possible input values of the program, while dynamic slicing [18] is triggered by specific input values. A slice is computed by analyzing control flow and data flow dependencies and collecting statements and conditions during traversal of the program, starting at a statement which satisfies a slicing criterion. Slices could be computed by traversing the program forward or backward. In this paper, we rely on backward slicing from points of interest to entry points of the program. We consider the slicing criterion to select as "interesting" either output statements, i.e., statement that pass data from the current program to its environment (e.g., display data on the screen or write it to persistent storage) or termination statements, i.e., statements which terminate the execution of the current program and pass control to another program or to the caller.

Control flow and data flow dependencies are represented in a program dependency graph (PDG). A PDG is a directed graph which contains a node for each statement or control predicate in the program, and edges between nodes indicating possible flow of control or data between these nodes [19,20].

Control flow dependencies are defined in terms of postdominance. A PDG node n is postdominated by node n' if all paths from n to the end node pass through node n'. Node n' is directly control flow dependent on node n if n is not postdominated by n' and there is a path between n and n' such that any other node on this path is postdominated by n'.

To compute data flow dependencies, for each node n in the PDG two sets $defs(n)$ and $uses(n)$ are calculated, where $defs(n)$ is a set of variables defined/written at n, and $uses(n)$ is a set of variables used/read at n. These sets are calculated using effects analysis, which includes the direct read/write effect of a statement or control predicate with respect to the semantics of the specific programming language and points-to analysis based on the context-insensitive Andersen algorithm [21] with optimizations taken from the Ant and Grasshopper algorithms [22]. Taking into account the specifics of the COBOL programming language, read and write effects are defined in terms of a memory model with start points and offsets. Given $defs(n)$ and $uses(n)$ sets, a node n' is directly data flow dependent on node n if there is a variable $v \in defs(n) \wedge v \in uses(n')$, and there is a path between n and n' without intervening definitions of v.

3.2   PDG-Based Slicing Method

The slicing criterion is typically defined as a pair $\langle n, vars(n) \rangle$ where n is a node in the PDG, and $vars(n)$ is the set of all variables defined or used at n. Control and data flow dependencies are transitive and introduce dependency chains. A slice S is computed by collecting all nodes that affect n through a control or data flow dependency chain. The computation of slices must preserve the reachability of the slicing criterion: If the slicing criterion is reachable in the original program, it must be reachable in a program slice. Conversely, if the slicing criterion is not reachable in the original program, it must not be reachable in a program slice.

Our slicing algorithm is shown in Fig. 1. We improve the precision of the slice by, instead of considering all effects of each node, narrowing the slicing criterion to $\langle n, vars_r(n) \rangle$, where $vars_r(n) \subseteq vars(n)$. Correspondingly, we reduce data

```
1   Given slicing criterion ⟨n, vars_r(n)⟩ in program P
2     slice S = {n}
3     until the start point is reached do
4         for all new nodes n ∈ S, analyzing dependencies for variables from
5             the set of visited nodes uses_r(n) do
6             let N be the set of nodes corresponding to reaching definitions
7             for all variables v ∈ vars_r(n)
8             S = S ∪ N
9             let M be the set of nodes corresponding to control dominators
10            of n, considering only business related control predicates in n
11            S = S ∪ M
```

Fig. 1. PDG-based slicing algorithm

flow dependencies to the nodes which directly or indirectly affect the variables from $vars_r$, ignoring all other data flow dependencies (lines 6–8). At lines 9–10, we collect nodes corresponding to dominators of control predicates. Each such node n introduces an additional set of variables $uses(n)$ which, in turn, adds the corresponding reaching definition nodes to the slice, significantly increasing the size of the slice. We divide the control predicates of the legacy program into two sets: business related control predicates which operate on business variables and non-business control predicates which do not. Assuming that non-business control variables do not create business-relevant branches in the path, these nodes do not have a direct effect on the result of the variables from $vars_r$ and can be ignored. If there are multiple slicing criteria then perform lines 1–11 for each slicing criterion and form the union of all resultant slices.

The reduced sets $defs_r(n)$ and $uses_r(n)$ for each PDG node n are calculated during backward liveness data flow analysis with respect to the reduced set $vars_r$ from the slicing criterion such that $uses_r(n) \subseteq uses(n)$ and for every variable $x \in uses_r(n)$, there is a variable $y \in defs_r(n)$, such that y is calculated from x. Calculating the reduced sets and the mapping between the sets $defs_r$ and $uses_r$ is not trivial and is specific to a programming language. However, any narrowing of the effects greatly reduces the number of dependencies and improves the precision of the resulting slice. For COBOL, we calculate such mapping with bytewise precision.

3.3 Interprocedural Data Flow Analysis

The algorithm from Fig. 1 focused on intraprocedural data flow analysis. COBOL, as many other programming languages, allows the control and data flow of called procedures to be affected by the calling procedure and vice versa. Interprocedural slicing obeys control and data flow dependencies between statements from different programs or procedures and preserves statements in the calling or called procedures. The effect of called procedures may be different for each unique call due to their context. Computing the slice separately for each procedure as in [23] gives rise to the "calling context" problem [24] which may introduce nonexistent execution paths which enter a procedure Q from a procedure P and exit Q to a procedure different from P. Replacing recursive calls iteratively by instances of the procedure body does not suffer from the calling context problem [25]. A slice is recomputed for each iteration until no new statements are added to the slice. However, this algorithm is exponential in the number of procedures and thus cannot be effectively applied to large systems.

To compute interprocedural static slices we build an extended PDG, similar to the system dependency graph proposed in [24]. As COBOL procedures (paragraphs, sections, and nested programs) do not have their own parameters and all data is global to the program, we do not need to map between formals and actuals, other than for external program calls. We limit interprocedural slicing to sections, paragraphs, and nested programs in the scope of a standalone COBOL program. In addition to intraprocedural dependency edges, the extended PDG also contains interprocedural dependency edges. Control flow dependency are extended with an edge between each call node and the entry node of the corresponding called procedure. Interprocedural data flow dependencies are calculated by interprocedural liveness data flow analysis with respect to the variables listed in a slicing criterion. This analysis is iterative based on the intraprocedural analysis solved for each procedure for specific interesting variables, analyzing definition-use dependencies as discussed earlier. With the help of the extended PDG, interprocedural slicing can be performed using the algorithm in Fig. 1.

Analysis of procedure P starts at the location identified by its reduced slicing criterion. If P contains a call to procedure Q, and this call is reached during backward traversal of P, we interrupt the analysis of P and compute the intraprocedural liveness analysis of Q starting from its return node, where a variable is live if it holds a value that is needed to compute the value of a variable in the list of used variables collected as a result of the liveness analysis before the call of Q in P was reached. After analysis of Q, we return to P, taking the result of liveness analysis from the start node of Q as the result of the procedure call. The analysis is recomputed at each iteration of the data flow analysis, extending the results from the previous iterations until a fixed point is reached, i.e., until no new variables are added to the set of a live variables for any node. In the worst case, all variables defined in the program are considered live. To avoid the calling context problem, we perform a recursive traversal collecting a call stack, which consists of all procedures we entered, but have not yet returned from. Each call node with its specific call stack is considered as a unique call node, and liveness analysis for the corresponding called procedure has to be recalculated. This call stack is also used to avoid infinite recursion of procedure calls. This analysis can be sped up using memoization: we do not recompute the analysis for a called procedure, if we have already computed it for the same procedure with the same input data. Instead, we reuse the results of the previous computation.

3.4   Abstraction of Non-business Procedures

Programs typically contain much code besides their business logic. Separating business and non-business logic allows to narrow the scope of analysis and reduce the size of the resulting slice. Unfortunately, in many situations we cannot completely ignore the non-business logic, as it will affect the results of a business computation. For example, a program may perform authentication to determine whether a user is permitted to execute this program. While the system test is not interested in the details of the authentication, whether the user was authorized or not is essential as further processing depends on it. Thus, while we can remove the computation of authentication, we cannot remove its effect. Similarly, utility routines often are called to obtain values from input and updating variables that are used in the business logic. We may not be interested in the details of how the data was obtained, but the business logic critically depends on which variables in the business logic were updated by the input.

To exclude the unnecessary details of non-business routines, we abstract them by replacing their calls with their effects. After the computation of the interprocedural slice, we can summarize the effects of each procedure P into two sets: the set $mod(P)$ of variables that are modified by P, and the set $uses(P)$ of variables that are used by P, taking into account any procedures called by P. Then, each call of P can be replaced by a set of assignments, where each modified variable from $mod(P)$ is assigned in the call of an abstract procedure that takes corresponding variables from $uses(P)$ as input parameters to produce the new value of the updated variable.

Such effects can be calculated using the results of interprocedural liveness analysis computed for slicing, in combination with a reachability analysis computed for each procedure P separately, when for every variable $x \in uses(P)$, there is at least one node n in P, where the reaching definition for variable x is the start of P, i.e., its definition is somewhere outside of the program and for every variable $y \in mod(P)$, at the end of P, there is at least one node in P which is a reaching definition for variable y that is not the start of P and y is live in the slice after the call of P. If the summarized effect of P determines that $mod(P)$ is empty, this procedure can be safely ignored. Since each call of a procedure P in each specific context is treated as a unique call, we are able to perform this analysis separately for each call, taking into account the liveness results for each specific call which results in more precise summarized effects.

3.5   Conversion to Model

After abstraction, each slice contains only nodes representing guards, assignments of effects to variables, and abstract functions. It is straightforward to translate the control flow of such slices into UCM models. In order to reason about this model, we represent it formally as an attributed transition system.

An *attributed transition system* is a tuple $\langle C, c_0, E, V, T \rangle$, where C is a set of flow locations, $c_0 \in C$ is the initial location, E is a set of events, V is a finite set of attributes (variables) with finite value domains and T is a finite set of

```
level-number [data-name-1 | FILLER]
    [REDEFINES data-name-2]
    [IS EXTERNAL]
    [IS GLOBAL]
    [[PICTURE | PIC] IS character-string]
    [[USAGE IS] [BINARY | COMPUTATIONAL | COMP | DISPLAY | INDEX |
        PACKED-DECIMAL]]
    [[SIGN IS] [LEADING | TRAILING] [SEPARATE CHARACTER]]
    [OCCURS integer-2 TIMES
        [[ASCENDING | DESCENDING] KEY IS [data-name-3] ... ] ...
        [INDEXED BY [index-name-1] ...] |
      OCCURS integer-1 TO integer-2 TIMES DEPENDING ON data-name-4
        [[ASCENDING | DESCENDING] KEY IS [data-name-3] ... ] ...
        [INDEXED BY [index-name-1] ...]]
    [[SYNCHRONIZED | SYNC] [LEFT | RIGHT]]
    [[JUSTIFIED | JUST] RIGHT]
    [BLANK WHEN ZERO]
    [VALUE IS literal-1].

66  data-name-1 RENAMES data-name-2 [[THROUGH | THRU] data-name-3].

88  condition-name-1 [VALUE IS | VALUES ARE]
    [literal-1 [[THROUGH | THRU] literal-2]] ... .
```

Fig. 2. Data definitions in COBOL

transitions. A *transition* is represented as a tuple $\langle c, g, t, a, c' \rangle \in T$, where $c \in C$ is the source location and $c' \in C$ is a destination location, g is a precondition over V, $t \in E$ is an event, and a is a postcondition. Preconditions (guards) are first order predicate calculus formulae. Postconditions contain assignments to attributes from V. A *state* is a tuple $\langle c, m \rangle$ where $c \in C$ and m is a mapping from V to values and their definition locations.

A *state transition* $\langle c, m \rangle \xrightarrow{t} \langle c', m' \rangle$ is possible if for a transition $\langle c, g, t, a, c' \rangle \in T$ the guard g is satisfied for the valuation of m, and the result of updating m according to a is m'. The semantics of transitions is analogous to Dijkstra's guarded commands: if the precondition of some transition t is satisfiable in some state s, then the model can perform this transition and moves to a new state that differs from the previous state by the values of attributes which where assigned in the postcondition. Attributes may be of integer, boolean, or enumerated type, or may be arrays of these types.

The emulation of COBOL data, see Fig. 2, is more challenging. Level numbers from 1 to 49 define a hierarchy of data elements. A data element (analogous to a variable) can be elementary or a group entities (analogous to a structure which contains all entities defined below it with a greater level number continuing to an entity with the same or lower level number). Level 66 defines an alternative name to a memory area containing another entity or alternative names for sequences of data entities. Level 77 entities must always be elementary. Level 88 introduces data values that may be present in the memory denoted by the entity preceding it (its "parent" entity) along with "condition names" that can be used to set or test for the presence of these values. Level 88 entities are transformed as follows: First, all occurrences of level 88 names with unique values are converted to operations comparing the parent entity with this value or to a corresponding assignment. If a level 88 entity represents a set of values, it represents a disjunction of comparisons between the parent entity and one of the values and assignments are performed only for the first value in the set. While data entities are not typed in the modern sense, they must be either numbers in a chosen binary representation or alphanumeric (analogous to strings). In this discussion, we will focus on integer data and ignore floating point types.

Every enumerated type is an unordered set of constants with equality and disequality operations. Both arguments must have the same type. To convert variables into enumerated types, we collect all variables associated through operators requiring strong type correspondence (assignment, comparison) and all their values. These variables are merged into "type groups". All variables in a type group will be given the same type; their values form elements of this shared type. Variables which do not fulfill the restrictions required for enumerated types described below or are used in arithmetic and comparison operations are represented as integer attributes or are processed bytewise as described below.

Integer variables in binary representation (BINARY, COMPUTATIONAL, or COMP) are represented as integer attributes. COBOL defines an integer variable with a PICTURE description of four or fewer digits as occupying 2 bytes; five to nine digits occupy 4 bytes, and 10 to 18 digits occupy 8 bytes. Integer variables with a PICTURE description 9(N) or S9(N) are converted to integer attributes in the same way as binary integers. If all integer variables from a type group satisfy the restrictions on enumerated types, we transform these integer values to enumerated type elements and construct a new enumerated type.

Bytewise Representation. COBOL defines a number of operations which prevent an attribute to be represented as discussed above. For such attributes, we represent the memory of the COBOL program as an array of integers. Each element corresponds to a byte in program memory. The following COBOL constructs require bytewise representation. (i) Redefinitions allow variables to overlap in memory. Only in trivial cases, where the length of the intersected variables coincides these can be translated to enumerated attributes, but this situation is rare in practice. (ii) Reference modification allows access to an arbitrary subsequence of bytes in memory. (iii) Concatenation combines values into a single larger variable. (iv) Any variable, even non-numeric variables, can be compared. (v) Assignments and comparison are possible between different group entities or between a group entity and an elementary entity. In the general case, each variable or field can be split to make associated variables consistent. After splitting, we can compare or assign structures field by field and use enumerated types if the individual fields satisfy above restrictions. In the worst case, variables can be split into one-byte fields reducing to bytewise representation. We choose heuristically between bytewise representation and variable splitting. (vi) When variables associated by assignment or comparison have different lengths, different constants are converted to different elements of the enumerated type. However, when these variables match due to COBOL semantics, the bytewise representation must be used. Considering each individual byte in data flow analysis (discussed later in Sect. 4.1) is inefficient and leads to unreasonable redundancy. Therefore, we detect blocks of bytes in COBOL memory which possess the following property: if some statement defines a value for any byte in a particular block, then this statement defines values for all bytes in that block. We refer to such blocks as synchronized and treat them as single variables.

4   Deriving Test Suites from Legacy Code

We can apply the method from [8] to derive tests from the UCM model obtained through the process presented in Sect. 3. However, the large size of the UCM model generated from the code presents a challenge. [8] relies on reachability checking to identify the tests required to achieve its coverage criterion. As the state space for models derived from code is significantly larger than for requirements models, efficient state space traversal is of vital interest to automated test development [12, 13, 26–35].

Problems with decidability and performance are the main obstacles for reachability analysis, and many different approaches were invented to deal with these shortcomings: random and combinatorial methods are easy to implement and have good performance, but result in poor coverage and high redundancy [26, 28]; search-based methods [29] attempt to minimize the "distance" between the generated test population and the desired test coverage objectives measured by approximation functions. Systematic methods such as model checking or symbolic execution [30–35] extract constraints on program paths through code analysis, and obtain test data that direct the execution of the program following these paths. In [36], data dependency is expressed via temporal logic formulae, which allows to perform test generation using model checking approaches, inheriting related difficulties. Search heuristics can guide program exploration to the most promising paths in the program [26–29, 31, 37]. For example, chopped symbolic execution [33] prunes irrelevant paths with respect to defined points of interest. However, search heuristics often produce incomplete results. Path merging [34] combines paths within a function into a summary that can be reused at subsequent invocations which may reduce the number of paths explored exponentially, but merely shifts the cost to a constraint solver. In contrast to random or combinatorial methods, search-based and systematic methods can produce test suites based on small data sets, but algorithms often get stuck enumerating paths without increasing coverage [31, 33].

4.1   Data-Flow Coverage Criteria

Selecting test cases typically relies on structural coverage critera [26, 27]. Control-flow based coverage criteria (such as statement and branch coverage) are too weak for defect detection, while path coverage is too time-consuming and usually not realizable: The number of paths grows exponentially with the number of branches and may become infinite in programs containing loops. Data-flow coverage may be a reasonable compromise [37, 38].

It is also critical that generated traces be meaningful to the tester. If derived tests are completely unintuitive, testers are not likely to trust a test suite. Generated test suites that satisfy statement coverage or branch coverage often result in unintuitive traces as it is only important that all statements or branches be covered, but not that they be covered in any manner that is meaningful to the tester. Tests generated following these coverage criteria are often long execution sequences or stop after a region of the code is encountered that has already been covered. For a test to be meaningful, it should observe outputs which bear some clearly recognizable relation to the test stimuli. Relationships interpreted as meaningful by a tester are often causal. While causality is not typically expressed in code, considering data flow often provides a reasonable approximation. Rapps and Weyuker [38] classify each occurrence of a variable as a definitional occurrence (the variable is assigned a new value) or a usage occurrence (in a computation use, the variable is used in computing the value of some other variable or itself; in a predicate use the variable is used in a condition that affects which path the program takes). A DU-path with respect to a variable is a path starting from the definition of the variable and ending at a usage of this variable. A DU-path is def-clear with respect to a variable if it does not contain a redefinition of this variable.

[38] defines a number of test criteria: A test suite satisfies the *all-defs criterion*, if the test cases include a def-clear path from every definition of a variable to some use of this variable. A test suite satisfies the *all-p-uses* or *all-c-uses criterion*, if the test cases include a def-clear path from every definition of a variable to all of its predicate or computational uses, respectively. A test suite satisfies the *all-uses criterion*, if the test cases include a def-clear path from every definition of a variable to every use of that variable. A test suite satisfies the *all-du-paths criterion*, if the test cases include all DU-paths for every variable defined. A test suite satisfies the *all-paths criterion*, if the tests cases include all paths of the program.

Ordered by the coverage achieved, the all-paths criterion is the strongest and the all-defs, all-p-uses, and all-c-uses criteria are the weakest. All-uses subsumes statement and branch coverage. We choose the all-uses criterion as the most practical since the number of paths required by all-du-paths or all-paths is too big or even infinite due to possible loops.

We rely on the model of attributed transition systems introduced in Sect. 3.5: A *path* is a sequence of states $\langle c_0, m_0 \rangle \xrightarrow{t_0} \langle c_1, m_1 \rangle \xrightarrow{t_1} \ldots$ starting from the initial state $\langle c_0, m_0 \rangle$. A state $\langle c_i, m_i \rangle$ is reachable if there is a path from $\langle c_0, m_0 \rangle$ to $\langle c_i, m_i \rangle$. The sets $defs(c)$ and $uses(c)$, where c is a location, denote the set of all variables defined and used (either for computing a value or in a guard), respectively. The expression $s.v.def$ denotes the live definition location of variable v at state s. The set DU denotes the set of all DU pairs required to be covered; each pair is denoted as $[D : U]_v$, where D is a definition location and U a use location of a variable v. The expression $s.loc$ denotes the location referenced by state s.

A direct data flow dependency $[D : U]_v \in p$ exists if $\exists i, j, k : p = \{s_0 \xrightarrow{t_0} s_1 \xrightarrow{t_1} \ldots \xrightarrow{t_{k-1}} s_k\} \wedge D = s_i.loc \wedge U = s_j.loc \wedge i < j \wedge v \in defs(D) \wedge v \in uses(U) \wedge 0 \leq i < k \wedge 0 < j < k \wedge (i < n \leq j \implies v \notin defs(s_n.loc))$. A direct control flow dependency $[D : U]_v^{v'} \in p$ exists if $\exists i, j, k : p = \{s_0 \xrightarrow{t_0}$

1   WAIT:=$\{s_0\}$, where s_0 is the initial state
2   VISITED:=$\emptyset$; TRACES:=$\emptyset$; G:=$\emptyset$;
3   while WAIT $\neq \emptyset$ do
4   select s from WAIT;
5   if $[d:u]_v \in DU \wedge [d:u]_v \notin G \Rightarrow \exists s_i : s_i \in$ VISITED $\wedge$
6           $restrict(s) \subseteq restrict(s_i) \wedge s_i.v.def = s.v.def$ then
7   continue;
8   add s to VISITED;
9   for all $v : v \in uses(s.loc) \wedge [s.v.def : s.loc]_v \in DU$ do
10   add $[s.v.def : s.loc]_v$ to G;
11   add $(s, [s.v.def : s.loc]_v)$ to TRACES;
12   for all $t, s' : s \xrightarrow{t} s'$ do
13   for all $v : v \in V$:
14   if $v \in defs(s'.loc)$ then $s'.v.def:=s'.loc$;
15   else $s'.v.def:=s.v.def$;
16   add s' to WAIT;
17 return G and TRACES;

Fig. 3. Naive algorithm search(DU)

$s_1 \xrightarrow{t_1} \dots \xrightarrow{t_{k-1}} s_k\} \wedge D = s_i.loc \wedge U = s_j.loc \wedge v \in defs(D) \wedge v' \in uses(U) \wedge i < j \wedge 0 \leq i < k \wedge 0 < j < k \wedge \exists c_1, c_2 : c_1 = succ(D) \wedge c_2 = succ(D) \wedge c_1 \neq c_2 \wedge c_1$ is postdominated by $U \wedge c_2$ is not postdominated by U. A DU-chain $chain(D, v, U, v') \in p$ exists if $\exists i, j, k : p = \{s_0 \xrightarrow{t_0} s_1 \xrightarrow{t_1} \dots \xrightarrow{t_{k-1}} s_k\} \wedge D = s_i.loc \wedge U = s_j.loc \wedge i < j \wedge ([D : U]_v \in p \wedge v = v' \vee [D : U]_v^{v'} \in p \vee \exists U', v'' : chain(D, v, U', v'') \in p \wedge chain(U', v'', U, v') \in p)$.

Figure 3 depicts a naive algorithm to generate all-uses coverage. In essence, this algorithm performs reachability analysis and uses two data structures WAIT and VISITED to hold states waiting to be examined and states already examined, respectively. Initially VISITED is empty and WAIT holds the initial state s_0. Lines 4–16 are repeated until WAIT is empty. At line 4 a state is taken from WAIT, at lines 5–6 it is compared against states encountered earlier, and, if the state is new, it is placed into VISITED (line 8) to avoid needless further examination; lines 12–16 generate the successor states. The result sets G and TRACES are updated at lines 10 and 11 if the current path satisfies the desired coverage criteria. A well-known problem with the naive algorithm in Fig. 3 is the large state space explored [13,32,39], which has a size proportional to the number of model states multiplied with the number of DU pairs.

4.2   Improved Algorithm for DU-Chain Coverage

In [32], test generation is performed using a coverage criterion in the form of a set of items to be covered and introduces the notion of coverage subsumption, which allows to truncate the exploration of a path if it does not cover more items than were previously generated. The method proposed in [35] truncates exploration of a path as soon as the analysis can determine that continued execution will

```
 1  s_0.prev := ∅; s_0.used := ∅; s_0.chained := ∅; s_0.idems := ∅;
 2  WAIT:={s_0}, where s_0 is the initial state;
 3  VISITED:=∅; TRACES:=∅; G:=∅;
 4  while WAIT ≠ ∅ do
 5      select s from WAIT;
 6      if [d : u]_v ∈ DU ∧ [d : u]_v ∉ G ⇒ ∃s_i : s_i ∈ VISITED ∧
 7      restrict(s) ⊆ restrict(s_i) then
 8          if u ∈ s_i.used then propagate_use(⟨v, u⟩, s);
 9          if u ∈ s_i.chained then propagate_chain(⟨v, u⟩, s);
10          if s_i.v.def = s.v.def ∨ u ∉ s_i.used ∨ u ∉ s_i.chained then
11              add s to s_i.idems;
12              continue;
13      add s to VISITED;
14      for all v : v ∈ uses(s.loc) do
15          if [s.v.def : s.loc]_v ∈ DU then
16              propagate_use(⟨v, s.loc⟩, s);
17          if s.loc ∈ OUTPUTS then
18              propagate_chain(⟨v, s.loc⟩, s, s);
19      for all t, s' : s --t--> s' do
20          s'.used := ∅; s'.chained := ∅; s'.idems := ∅;
21          s'.prev := s;
22          for all v : v ∈ V do
23              if v ∈ defs(s'.loc) then s'.v.def:=s'.loc;
24              else s'.v.def:=s.v.def;
25          add s' to WAIT;
26  return G and TRACES;
```

Fig. 4. Improved algorithm: du_chain_search(DU)

produce effects that have already been seen. This approach collects the set of all read-accessed (live) variables during the search and compares only states up to those variables. However, in order to identify the read-set for some state, the approach requires complete depth-first traversal of all paths after that state.

In [36], data flow-based testing is extended to consider control flow dependencies; this approach allows to make the effect of coverage items observable if the DU-chain completes at a statement with an observable effect of the coverage item (e.g., a statement where this item is output to the environment or written to persistent storage). Following this approach we prolong all generated paths with respect to a DU-chain. This will guarantee that all generated traces will be meaningful to the tester by reflecting the dependency chain.

In previous work we presented an algorithm that efficiently computes all-uses coverage without requiring observability [39]. In this paper, we introduce a novel on-the-fly algorithm to generate test cases through model-based reachability analysis aimed to cover DU-chains. The algorithm guarantees completeness of the search, yet avoids exhaustive state-space exploration by applying a specialized decision procedure enabling early termination of path unfolding, which limits exploration to states which might increase coverage. Our search algorithm

27 while $s.prev \neq \emptyset$ do
28   if $\langle v, loc \rangle \notin s.used$ then
29   for all $i : i \in s.idems$ do add i to WAIT; remove i from VISITED;
30          $s.idems := \emptyset$;
31      $s.used := s.used \cup \langle v, loc \rangle$;
32   if $v \in defs(s.loc)$ then break;
33      $s := s.prev$;

Fig. 5. Improved algorithm: propagate_use($\langle v, loc \rangle, s$)

34 while $s \neq \emptyset$ do
35   for all $v : v \in uses(s.loc) \wedge [s.v.def : s.loc]_v \in$ DU do
36   add $[s.v.def : s.loc]_v$ to G;
37   add $(o, [s.v.def : s.loc]_v)$ to TRACES;
38   if $\langle v, loc \rangle \notin s.chained$ then
39   for all $i : i \in s.idems$ do add i to WAIT; remove i from VISITED;
40          $s.idems := \emptyset$;
41      $s.chained := s.chained \cup \langle v, loc \rangle$;
42   if $v \in defs(s.loc)$ then
43   for all $z : z \in uses(s.loc)$ do
44   propagate_chain($\langle z; s.z.def \rangle, s, o$);
45          $cfg\_loc := control\_dominator(s.loc)$;
46   for all $z : z \in uses(cfg\_loc)$ do
47   propagate_chain($\langle z, s.z.def \rangle, s' : s'.loc = cfg\_loc, o$);
48   break;
49      $s := s.prev$;

Fig. 6. Improved algorithm: propagate_chain($\langle v, loc \rangle, s, o$)

aims to recognize duplication in state exploration early. It is based on dynamic abstraction [12], which applies early-terminated, yet complete, search with on-the-fly refinement to the variables of a model and its control flow locations. This method relies on the fact that if a state has no reachable usage of some variable or has no reachable observable effect of a required DU pair, then its definition location does not affect the search for coverage, and consequently, the exploration of any state that only differs in the definition location provably will not increase coverage and therefore can be pruned from the search. Our approach also advances [13], where the state refinement procedure is used for control-flow based cumulative model behavior analysis and [39], where the state-space reduction technique is applied for DU pairs coverage. The path termination condition is extended to avoid the unfolding of states which do not increase coverage: for each state, the algorithm will store information about reachable usages and observability (i.e., reachability of a statement at which the effect can be observed) of the considered DU pairs. The algorithm relies on auxiliary attributes of the state representing used variables (for the DU pair and its chain to an observable location). These sets will be computed on-the-fly but at the moment of state comparison it is unknown whether each set can be enlarged. Nevertheless, a decision regarding path termination must be made. Therefore, the algorithm uses a state refinement procedure which may resume a search that was previously terminated at a state and continue its unfolding. Thus, the state structure is extended to a tuple $\langle loc, val, used, chained, idems, prev \rangle$. Given a state s, $s.loc$ and $s.val$ are location and valuation as above. The sets $s.used$ and $s.chained$ store information about the prospect of the search, the set $s.idems$ keeps track of identical states and is used for resuming terminated paths, and $s.prev$ holds the previous state on the current path.

Our algorithm consists of three procedures, du_chain_search (Fig. 4), propagate_use (Fig. 5), and propagate_chain (Fig. 6). The key change is the extension of state comparison: The current state will be terminated if it cannot contribute to the coverage because it (presumably) cannot reach the required usage or observable effect (lines 6–11). However, this termination is not irreversible: The set $idems$ is examined later by propagate_use and propagate_chain at lines 8, 9, 16, and 18 which may place a terminated state into the WAIT set again (lines 29 and 39, respectively) in order to maintain completeness. OUTPUTS is a set of observable points of interest used as slicing criterion as described in Sect. 3.1. The procedure propagate_use propagates detected uses of variables bottom-up to their redefinition along the current path, and also adds every encountered state in $idems$ for which its use has not been propagated into the WAIT set. Similarly, propagate_chain propagates detected observations (i.e., the reachability of output locations) bottom-up to the initial state using reverse dependencies and updates the WAIT set with every encountered state in $idems$. Let S denote the set of reachable states and P the set of feasible paths. This algorithm has the following main properties:

1. Termination. Asymptotic time is $O(max(|T|, |S|) \times |DU|)$.
2. Soundness. The set G will consist only of DU-pairs which belong to feasible paths leading to an observable effect: $[D : U]_v \in G \implies \exists p : p \in P \wedge p = \{s_0 \xrightarrow{t_0} s_1 \xrightarrow{t_1} \ldots \xrightarrow{t_{k-1}} s_k\} \wedge [D : U]_v \in p \wedge \exists v' : chain(D, v, s_k.loc, v') \in p \wedge s_k.loc \in$ OUTPUTS
3. Completeness. At termination, the set G will include all DU-pairs which belong to feasible paths leading to an observable effect: $\exists p : p \in P \wedge p = \{s_0 \xrightarrow{t_0} s_1 \xrightarrow{t_1} \ldots \xrightarrow{t_{k-1}} s_k\} \wedge [D : U]_v \in DU \wedge [D : U]_v \in p \wedge \exists v' : chain(D, v, s_k.loc, v') \in p \wedge s_k.loc \in$ OUTPUTS $\implies [D : U]_v \in G$

The search can easily be tuned to different strategies. For example, selection of the state from WAIT could consider the path depth to realize breadth-first or depth-first traversal. Note that terminating a path explored by the improved algorithm results in a large gain, as the number of new paths spawned from the discarded state can be exponential in the number of reachable branches encountered in its unfoldings.

5   Summary

This paper described our approach to validating the modernization of legacy systems. When modernizing a legacy system, their source code may be translated into a different programming language and the application will usually be migrated from the original computational environment (often mainframes) to a more modern environment, such as client/server or cloud environments. Validation of a modernized system must establish that the new system behaves exactly as the original system, ignoring any changes required due to the change in operating environment. As legacy systems often lack descriptions of their requirements, we derive a test suite to validate the modernized system from the legacy code.

We have earlier presented an approach to derive test suites from use case map specifications [6–8]. To apply this approach to the generation of test suites for legacy systems, we needed the capability to derive a UCM model from the legacy code and we needed our reachability analysis to have sufficiently high performance to cope with the very large state space induced by the source code of legacy systems. We presented our approach in the context of the modernization of COBOL legacy applications.

To transform the legacy code into a UCM model requires the separation of the code into low-level code and code which is otherwise not of interest to system validation and the code that implements the main business logic of the legacy system. We presented an interprocedural slicing algorithm which, starting from outputs of the system deemed "interesting" for testing, extracts only those parts of the source code that impact the interesting outputs. Slicing together with an abstraction that reduces non-business logic procedures to their effect allows to represent the legacy code in terms of assignments to attributes of a labelled transition system and abstract functions over these attributes. Such program slices can easily be converted to UCM specifications. The COBOL data model can be represented through attributes of enumerated types, integers, and byte strings.

This paper further presented a new efficient on-the-fly algorithm for tests generation to cover all feasible DU pairs in a system. Space exploration-based methods suffer from the exponential growth of the search space. This algorithm stores and dynamically refines knowledge about coverage items reached from each state to prune paths from the remaining exploration, so that a state will not be explored until it is determined that doing so may increase coverage. The exploration of a postponed state can later be resumed if such would augment coverage. This characteristic helps avoid unnecessary exploration and speeds up termination by several orders of magnitude. While the asymptotic complexity is not improved and memory consumption is even increased, in many practical cases this algorithm terminates much earlier.

This algorithm also assures that the derived traces are meaningful to the tester by producing traces that lead to the observable points of interest that had been selected as criteria for slicing during business logic isolation.

This approach is compatible with dynamic abstraction methods [12] which reduce the state-space using relaxed checking of state equivalence as well as with partial order reduction methods for redundant interleaving elimination [40]. The approach was successfully applied to the analysis of legacy code and the generation of test suites [14]. We have used the presented approach in the validation of COBOL mainframe applications exceeding 20 million lines of code.

References

1. European Telecommunications Standards Institute. TTCN-3: Core Language. ES 201 873–1 4.11.1 (2019)
2. International Telecommunications Union. Message Sequence Charts Z.120 (2011)
3. Letichevsky, A.A., Kapitonova, J.V., Kotlyarov, V.P., Volkov, V.A., Letichevsky, A.A., Weigert, T.: Semantics of message sequence charts. In: Prinz, A., Reed, R., Reed, J. (eds.) SDL 2005. LNCS, vol. 3530, pp. 117–132. Springer, Heidelberg (2005). https://doi.org/10.1007/11506843_8
4. Chelinsky, D.: The RSpec Book. The Pragmatic Bookshelf (2010)
5. Wynne, M., Hellesoy, A.: The Cucumber Book. The Pragmatic Bookshelf (2012)
6. Baranov, S., Kotlyarov, V., Letichevsky, A.: An industrial technology of test automation based on verified behavioral models of requirement specifications for telecommunication applications. In: Proceedings of the Region 8 IEEE EUROCON 2009 Conference 2009, pp. 122–129 (2009)
7. Baranov, S., Kapitonova, J., Letichevsky, A., Volkov, V., Weigert, T.: Basic protocols, message sequence charts, and verification of requirements specifications. Comput. Netw. **49**(5), 661–675 (2005)
8. Baranov, S., Kotlyarov, V., Weigert, T.: Verifiable coverage criteria for automated testing. In: Ober, I., Ober, I. (eds.) SDL 2011. LNCS, vol. 7083, pp. 79–89. Springer, Heidelberg (2011). https://doi.org/10.1007/978-3-642-25264-8_8
9. Kolchin, A., et al.: An approach to creating concretized test scenarios within test automation technology for industrial software projects. Autom. Control Comput. Sci. **47**(7), 433–442 (2013)
10. Buhr, R.: Use Case Maps for Object-Oriented Systems. Pearson, London (1995)
11. International Telecommunications Union. User Requirements Notation Z-151 (2018)
12. Kolchin, A.V.: An automatic method for the dynamic construction of abstractions of states of a formal model. Cybern. Syst. Anal. **46**(4), 583–601 (2010)
13. Kolchin, A.V.: Interactive method for cumulative analysis of software formal models behavior. In: Proceedings of the 11th International Conference on Programming UkrPROG2018, CEUR-WS, vol. 2139, pp. 115–123 (2018)
14. Guba, A., et al.: A method for business logic extraction from legacy COBOL code of industrial systems. In: Proceedings of the 10th International Conference on Programming UkrPROG2016, CEUR-WS, vol. 1631, pp. 17–25 (2016)
15. Robot Framework User Guide. http://robotframework.org/robotframework/#user-guide
16. Tip, F.: A survey of program slicing techniques. J. Program. Lang. **3**, 121–189 (1995)
17. Weiser, M.: Program slices: formal, psychological and practical investigations of an automatic program abstraction method. Ph.D. thesis, University of Michigan, Ann Arbor (1979)

18. Korel, B., Laski, J.: Dynamic program slicing. Inf. Process. Lett. **29**(3), 155–163 (1988)
19. Ottenstein, K., Ottenstein, L.: The program dependence graph in a software development environment. In: Proceedings of the ACM SIGSOFT/SIGPLAN Software Engineering Symposium on Practical Software Development Environments, pp. 177–184 (1984)
20. Aho, A., Ullman, J.: Compilers: Principles, Techniques, and Tools. Addison-Wesley, Boston (2007)
21. Andersen, L.: Program analysis and specialization for the C programming language. Ph.D. thesis, DIEM, University of Copenhagen (1994)
22. Hardekopf, B., Lin, C.: The ant and the grasshopper: fast and accurate pointer analysis for millions of lines of code. In: Programming Language Design and Implementation (2007)
23. Weiser, M.: Program slicing. IEEE Trans. Softw. Eng. **10**(4), 352–357 (1984)
24. Horwitz, S., Reps, T., Binkley, D.: Interprocedural slicing using dependence graphs. ACM Trans. Program. Lang. Syst. **12**(1), 26–61 (1990)
25. Hwang, J., Du, M., Chou, C.: Finding program slices for recursive procedures. In: Proceedings of the 12th Annual International Computer Software and Application Conference, Chicago (1988)
26. Su, T., et al.: A survey on data-flow testing. ACM Comput. Surv. **50**, 5 (2017)
27. Dssouli, R., et al.: Testing the control-flow, data-flow, and time aspects of communication systems: a survey. Adv. Comput. **107**, 95–155 (2017)
28. Volkov, V., et al.: A survey of systematic methods for code-based test data generation. Artif. Intell. **2**, 71–85 (2017)
29. Campos, J., Ge, Y., Fraser, G., Eler, M., Arcuri, A.: An empirical evaluation of evolutionary algorithms for test suite generation. In: Menzies, T., Petke, J. (eds.) SSBSE 2017. LNCS, vol. 10452, pp. 33–48. Springer, Cham (2017). https://doi.org/10.1007/978-3-319-66299-2_3
30. Beyer, D., Gulwani, S., Schmidt, D.A.: Combining model checking and data-flow analysis. Handbook of Model Checking, pp. 493–540. Springer, Cham (2018). https://doi.org/10.1007/978-3-319-10575-8_16
31. Cadar, C., Sen, K.: Symbolic execution for software testing: three decades later. Commun. ACM **56**(2), 82–90 (2013)
32. Hessel, A., Petterson, P.: A global algorithm for model-based test suite generation. Electr. Notes Theor. Comput. Sci. **190**, 47–59 (2007)
33. Trabish, D., Mattavelli, A., Cadar, C.: Chopped symbolic execution. In: Proceedings of ICSE 2018 (2018)
34. Kuznetsov, V., et al.: Efficient state merging in symbolic execution. ACM SIGPLAN Conference on Programming Language Design and Implementation, pp. 193–204 (2012)
35. Boonstoppel, P., Cadar, C., Engler, D.: RWset: attacking path explosion in constraint-based test generation. In: Ramakrishnan, C.R., Rehof, J. (eds.) TACAS 2008. LNCS, vol. 4963, pp. 351–366. Springer, Heidelberg (2008). https://doi.org/10.1007/978-3-540-78800-3_27
36. Hong, H.S., Ural, H.: Dependence testing: extending data flow testing with control dependence. In: Khendek, F., Dssouli, R. (eds.) TestCom 2005. LNCS, vol. 3502, pp. 23–39. Springer, Heidelberg (2005). https://doi.org/10.1007/11430230_3
37. Kolchin, A., Potiyenko, S., Weigert, T.: Challenges for automated, model-based test scenario generation. In: Proceedings of the 25th International Conference on Information and Software Technologies, 12 p. (2019)

38. Rapps, S., Weyuker, E.: Data flow analysis techniques for test data selection. In: Proceedings of the International Conference of Software Engineering, pp. 272–277 (1982)
39. Kolchin, A.: A novel algorithm for attacking path explosion in model-based test generation for data flow coverage. In: Proceedings of the IEEE 1st International Conference on System Analysis and Intelligent Computing, SAIC (2018)
40. Maiya, P., Gupta, R., Kanade, A., Majumdar, R.: Partial order reduction for event-driven multi-threaded programs. In: Chechik, M., Raskin, J.-F. (eds.) TACAS 2016. LNCS, vol. 9636, pp. 680–697. Springer, Heidelberg (2016). https://doi.org/10. 1007/978-3-662-49674-9_44

Distributed Applications, Metamodeling and Protocols

Deriving Distributed Design Models from Global State Machines Requirements

Mohammad F. Al-hammouri$^{(\boxtimes)}$ and Gregor V. Bochmann$^{(\boxtimes)}$

School of Electrical Engineering and Computer Science (EECS),
University of Ottawa, Ottawa, ON, Canada
{m.alhammouri,bochmann}@uottawa.ca

Abstract. This paper deals with deriving a distributed design model from a global requirements model written in the notation of Hierarchical State Machines (HSMs). In this paper, we extend the UML notation of HSMs to describe the roles (components) that participate in the actions of each state of the global behaviour. A simple state represents some local actions, while a hierarchical state usually represents a collaboration between several roles (system components). Our global HSM requirements model describes the sequencing of collaborations and local actions. We compare this notation with other notations such as UML Collaborations, Hierarchical Message Sequence Charts (HMSC), Activity Diagrams, Partial-Order(PO)-Charts and others. Then we explain how a distributed design model, including all required coordination messages between the different system components, can be automatically derived from a global requirements model. We consider the following sequencing constraints between different collaborations: weak or strict sequence, alternatives, weak or strict while loop, and concurrency.

Keywords: Distributed applications · Hierarchical state machines ·
Global requirements model · Distributed design models

1 Introduction

Various kinds of modelling notations can be used during the development process of distributed systems. In this paper, we are concerned with the transformation from a global requirement model, which describes the system behaviour abstractly (defined in terms of local actions to be performed by different system components), to a distributed design model which describes the behaviour of each role (component) separately.

Different notations were proposed for describing requirements models. Alur [1] used Message Sequence Charts (MSCs), and Hierarchical Message Sequence Chart (HMSC), Castejon [2] proposed the concept of Collaborations and Activity Diagrams, and PO-Charts in [3].

In this paper, we propose to use the concept of UML Hierarchical State Machines (HSMs) [4] for modelling the requirements model since it is a well-known notation and directly supports concurrency (which is not supported by

© Springer Nature Switzerland AG 2019
P. Fonseca i Casas et al. (Eds.): SAM 2019, LNCS 11753, pp. 27–43, 2019.
https://doi.org/10.1007/978-3-030-30690-8_2

some of the above notations). In many aspects, the HSM formalism is similar to HMSC and PO-Charts. A composed state defines a partial order of actions, very similar to the notation of partial orders of Pratt [5] and Gischer [6]. We introduce certain extensions to HSMs in order to describe the different roles that may be involved in the actions performed within one (composed) state, and for distinguishing between strict and weak sequencing [7].

For deriving a distributed design model from a global requirements model, an algorithm was described in [8] which assumes that the requirements are given in the form of a collaboration which consists of several sub-collaborations that are ordered by strict or weak sequence, alternatives, concurrency, or strict or weak while loop. The algorithm introduces flow messages (if required) for the coordination of actions related by a strict sequence as proposed in [9,10]. It also introduces a choice indication message (*cim*) to inform a role that does not participate in some alternative when this alternative is chosen. In order to solve a problem of race conditions during the termination of a weak loop, it introduces an additional parameter in all messages of the loop body containing a sequence number which indicates the number of times the loop has been executed. We have shown in [11] that in many cases the loop does not exhibit any termination race, and, in addition, the sequence number is not needed in all messages within the loop when a termination race exists.

In this paper, we follow these ideas and show how a distributed design model can be derived from a global requirement model written in our notation of extended HSMs. The distributed design model obtained by our algorithm contains, for each identified system component, a HSM which contains the local actions of that component identified in the global requirements and the sending and reception of the coordination messages generated by our derivation algorithm. These local HSM can be easily implemented by any suitable tool that generates implementation code from UML HSMs.

We also show in this paper how the general condition for the absence of a termination race in weak loops can be checked when the global requirements are given in the form of a HSM.

The paper is organized as follows: In Sect. 2, we present the different concepts which were proposed for describing the behaviour of a distributed system in a global view, like collaboration, MSC-Graphs and Hierarchical MSC (HMSC), Partial Order Charts, and our proposed notation of Hierarchical State Machines (HSMs). In Sect. 3, we discuss the algorithm for deriving local design models for the different system components from the requirement model written in HSMs notation. Section 4 is the conclusion.

2   Describing Distributed Systems in a Global View

Different concepts have been proposed for describing the behaviour of a distributed system in a global view, which is sometimes referred to as *choreography*, in contrast to *orchestration* which represents a centralized view of the behaviour [12].

2.1   Review of Notations for Describing Global Requirements

2.1.1   Collaborations

The UML collaborations concept is proposed by [2] for modelling the global requirements (behaviour of the distributed system from a global point of view). A collaboration determines different roles in a distributed environment and different actions executed by those roles. However, this concept does not describe the dynamic form of the behaviour. For describing the behaviour dynamically, they propose a decomposition of a collaboration into several sub-collaborations (each may involve two or more roles), and identify their execution order using the sequencing primitives of Activity Diagrams: (1) The dynamic behaviour of a collaboration is represented by an Activity Diagram, where each activity represents a sub-collaboration which could involve several roles (or system components). (2) For each activity, the initiating roles (performing a local action which is not preceded by another action of this activity) are indicated by a solid circle, and the terminating roles (performing a local action not followed by an action of this activity) are indicated by a solid square. (3) Sequencing between activities is either strict or weak.

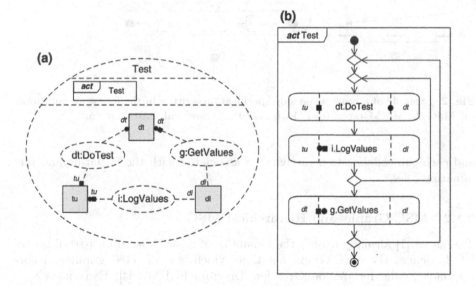

Fig. 1. Example of a medical test modelled by (a) a UML Collaboration and (b) an Activity Diagram.

The example in Fig. 1 (taken from [2]) presents the model of a medical test. The UML collaboration of Fig. 1(a) shows three roles: doctor terminal (dt), test unit interfacing the patient (tu), and data logger (dl). The dynamic behaviour is shown in Fig. 1(b). As we see, the test starts with the DoTest sub-collaboration,

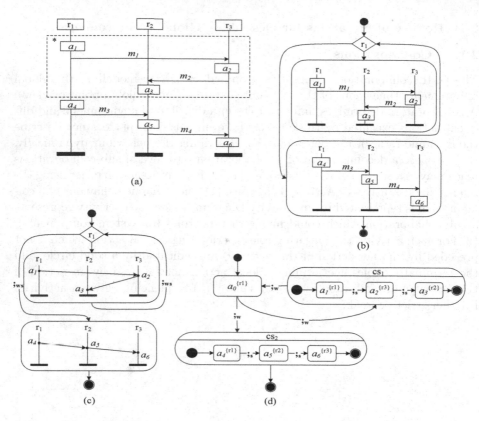

Fig. 2. Example of a weak while loop specification written in the following notations: (a) MSC (b) MSC-Graphs (c) PO-Charts (d) Hierarchical State Machine

and each sub-collaboration (activity) is associated with the initiating and terminating roles.

2.1.2   MSC-Graphs and Hierarchical MSC

The paper [1] formally defines the semantics of a MSC based on partial orders [5]. It defines the MSC-Graph notation, which is a directed graph and corresponds to the Interaction Overview Diagram in UML [4]. Each node in a MSC-Graph represents an MSC, and each edge represents the sequential execution between two MSCs. It is assumed that all edges in a MSC-Graphs represent either strict sequence (called synchronous concatenation) or weak sequence (called asynchronous concatenation). The paper also defines Hierarchical MSC (written HMSC) as an extension of MSC-Graphs, where a node contains either a MSC or another MSC-Graph and can be used for modelling complex system specifications.

2.1.3 Partial Order Charts (PO-Charts)

PO-Charts are proposed by [3] for modelling the specification of distributed systems. Each PO-Chart is similar to HMSC, except that each node of a PO-Chart contains a partial order of events (which we call actions) and the roles that perform these actions. Such partial order is similar to the one in MSC; however, the arrows between events represent a partial order dependency between local actions and not necessarily message exchanges like in MSC. See for instance Fig. 2 which shows (a) an MSC and (b) MSC-Graph (c) the equivalent PO-chart. The actions (a_1 through a_6) in the MSC are executed locally by the roles (r_1, r_2 or r_3) to determine some parameters before messages are sent or to store locally some received information. These actions correspond to the events in the PO-charts where their ordering relationships are defined.

In PO-Charts, both weak and strict sequences can be used for representing the sequential execution between two nodes (each of them is a partial order with roles). Strict sequence ("ss") means the initiating roles of the second node can't start until the last actions of the terminating roles of the first node have occurred. Weak sequence ("ws") enforces the execution order for each role separately. However, in HMSC, only one type of sequencing is allowed in one figure, and therefore, the notation for sequencing was not included. See, for instance, Fig. 2(b). In this paper, we extend the notation of PO-Charts by indicating which role does a choice (see for instance the role r_1 in the choice node in Fig. 2(c)). This is useful when comparing PO-Charts with our proposed notation of HSM (see Sect. 2.2).

2.2 Using Hierarchical State Machines (HSMs) for Describing the Global Requirements

The state machine concept is a powerful modelling formalism for describing the behaviour of a part of a system [4]. Hierarchical state machines enable the modelling of complex system behaviour concisely; each state is either a simple state or a composite state which represents another state machine. Hierarchical state machines formally define the syntax and semantics of concurrency and nesting concepts which are not allowed by simple state machine [13]. In this paper, we assume that a local action (as introduced above) is executed as a "do-action" of a simple state, and we extend the UML hierarchical state machine notation in order to define the role that performs the do-action of a simple state. Therefore a simple state is associated with a single role. This allows us to calculate, for a composite state, the set of initiating, terminating and participating roles (which is important for the derivation of a distributed design, as explained in Sect. 3). This extension of adding roles to the states make it possible to derive a distributed design model from the given requirements.

Figure 2(d) is an example of a HSMs, which is equivalent to the PO-Chart in Fig. 2(c). In our notation, we assume that the do-action in a simple state (if it exists) is the same as the state name. For example, the event a_1 in the PO-chart is realized as a do-action a_1 in the HSMs (Fig. 2(d)). We use a notation where the role of a simple state is between curly brackets. A composite state could have multiple initiating, participating, and terminating roles (written as IR, PR and TR, respectively). The transitions between states are "completion transitions" (in the sense of UML) which means they are executed as soon as the actions of the state have been completed. They represent either strict or weak sequencing, written as ";$_s$" or ";$_w$", respectively.

Figure 3 shows global specifications for different behaviours written in the HSMs notation. Figure 3(a) shows an example of a weak sequence between two simple states: a_1 and a_3, which have r_1 and r_3 as participating roles, respectively. The composite state "cs_1" in Fig. 3(b) has IR=$\{r_1, r_2, r_3\}$ and the TR=$\{r_1, r_2, r_3\}$. Note that the initiating, terminating, and participating roles of composite states are calculated based on the rules presented in Table 2 in [8].

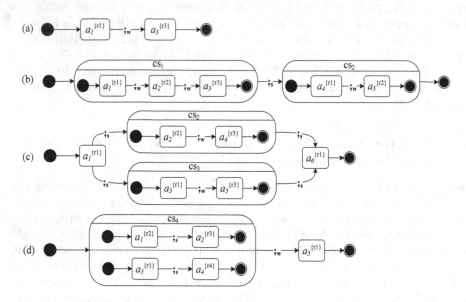

Fig. 3. Global specification for different behaviour expressions written in HSMs notation: (a) Weak Sequence composition (b) Strict Sequence (c) Alternatives with Strict Sequence (d) Concurrency

We prefer the notation of extended HSMs for modelling the global system requirement because the standard HSM are well-known and the derived distributed design model consist, for each system component, of a standard HSM model which is relatively easy to implement.

In fact, our notation is similar to Gischer work [6]; he proposed a state diagram to model the behaviour of collaborations that consist of several partial orders. He used the term "process" which corresponds to a composed state in our notation. He used the same sequencing operators as in our notation, except the weak sequence. Gischer notation does not show the roles or components involved in a process. Also, its alternatives are well-structured (see [14]) which is not the case for the branching structure of state machines.

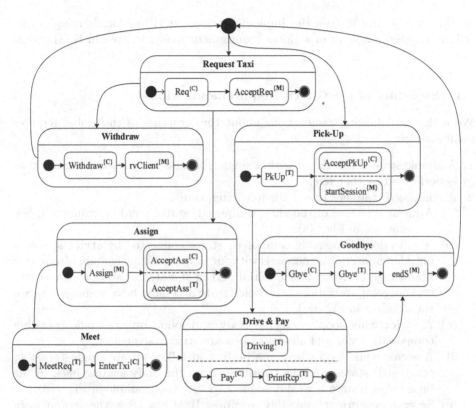

Fig. 4. Taxi example written in Extended HSMs notation and involving three roles: Manager {M}, Client {C}, and Taxi {T}.

2.3 Example of Using the Notation of Extended HSMs

The example in Fig. 4 shows a requirements model of a taxi application. It defines the global behavior of a taxi session involving the Manager {M}, a Client {C}, and Taxi {T}. For all simple states, we show the role involved in curly bracket (as we discussed above). The taxi application involves a single manager who deals with many clients and many taxis. He establishes a session with a client and a suitable taxi during the *Assign* collaboration. The figure shows one of these sessions. The client can request a taxi by activating the *Request Taxi* collaboration or pick up a taxi on the street using the *Pick-Up* collaboration. The client may cancel a request using the *Withdraw* collaboration. When the client reaches his destination, the taxi session is terminated through the *Goodbye* collaboration, and the taxi becomes free for another session.

3 Deriving Distributed Design Models

In this section, we discuss the implementation algorithm for deriving a distributed design model from a global requirement model written in HSMs notation.

3.1 Structure of the Global Requirements Model

We make the following assumptions about the structure of the global requirements model:

1. A simple state is associated with a single role and contains a do-action that is performed by that role.
2. A composed state has one of the following forms:
   (a) A linear sequence of (possibly composed) states **weakly** sequenced. See the example in Fig. 3(a).
   (b) A collection of (possibly composed) states connected by **strict** sequencing, the connection structure is without loops, but may contain alternative branching. There are single initial and final states. A state that has several outgoing transitions is a choice state and must be a simple state. See the example in Fig. 3(c).
   (c) A **strict** while loop where the body and follow-up are single (possibly composed) states and all transitions are strictly sequenced.
   (d) A **weak** while loop where the body and follow-up are single (possibly composed) states, and the transition from the body leading back to the initial choice state is weakly sequenced. See the example in Fig. 2(d).
   (e) Several concurrent (possibly composed) states. See the example in Fig. 3(d).

Comments:

- We do not allow for a linear sequence of (composed) states with mixed strict and weak sequencing, since strict and weak sequencing are not associative [15] and such a sequence could have an ambiguous meaning.
- We assume that all choices are local, that is, are performed by a single role. Choices are associated with strict sequencing to ensure consistent choice propagation [16].

– The important difference of the weak while loop, as compared with loops with strict sequencing, is the fact that it may have a termination race [11] (see also Sect. 3.7.1) and that it may lead to an unbounded number of messages in transit [1].

3.2 Algorithm for Deriving a Design Model from HSMs Requirements

In the following, we define an algorithm that derives a design model for a given role r_n from a requirement model which is represented by the function $genDM(StateMachine\ sm, role\ r_n)$. The inputs for the function are an HSM sm describing the global requirement model, and the target role r_n. The algorithm returns a design model for that role.

The algorithm distinguishes the cases 1 through 2e above (see Sect. 3.1) and invokes for each case a specific operation which is explained in the following subsections. The function "genDM" is first applied to the whole global requirements model and is then recursively applied to all its composed states and substates.

For the generation of a design model for a given role (or system component) from the global requirements, a technique of projection has often be used [2,8, 10,17]. Different notations have been used for the requirements and the local design model. Using projection, the design model for a role r is obtained by projecting the global requirement model onto role r, that means, deleting all events (states) associated with other roles $r' \neq r$. A design model obtained by projection without any coordination messages is called **basic implementation** [11].

In the presence of weak sequencing, this projection approach is usually combined with the use of a message reception pool which allows the component to wait for the reception of specific types of messages [8,17], thus avoiding *race conditions* [18] because the other types of messages will be stored in the reception pool until they are (later) requested by the local implementation.

In the following sections, we discuss in details, the operations of "genDM" in each case above.

3.3 Simple State

In the case of simple states, the algorithm keeps the state as is if the role r_n participate in that state, and otherwise replaces it by a dummy state. There is no recursive call for genDM in the case of the simple state.

3.4 Weak Sequence

The distributed design model for weakly sequenced behaviour does not need any coordination messages and is only based on the local sequencing by each role (see, for instance, Fig. 3(a)). Therefore the basic implementation provides a correct design model.

The function "genDM" in the case of weak sequence will, therefore, operate as follows. It will generate a state sequence corresponding to the states in sm by recursively applying "genDM" to the states in which the role r participates and replacing the other states by dummy states (denoted dms, without any local actions). The resulting state machine will be the design model for r_n, and it will have the same state structure as in the global design. Figure 5(a) is the generated design model for r_1 in Fig. 3(a). Before generating an implementation from the design model, we may optimize the resulting model by deleting the dummy states.

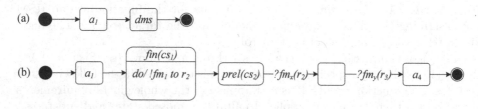

Fig. 5. Local design models for r_1 derived from the requirement models: (a) weak sequence in Fig. 3-a (b) strict sequence in Fig. 3-b

3.5 Strict Sequence and Alternatives

The problem of deriving a local design model from a global behaviour expression that contains a strict sequence was discussed in [8,9,19]. Coordination messages (called flow messages (fm) in [8]) were introduced for a strict sequence $(C_1 ;_s C_2)$ to ensure that all actions in C_1 are completed before any actions in C_2 can start. Besides, since these flow messages must be distinguished to avoid ambiguities, a parameter x is added to each flow messages (fm_x) to differentiate between them. The derivation of a local design model from a global requirements model containing alternatives has been studied by many authors [8–10,17]. In all these references, the local choice is assumed, i.e., the choice decision is always made by a single role. In a non-local choice, several roles are involved in a choice [20]. Different algorithms were proposed for solving non-local choice in a distributed environment, e.g., a circulating token. Different forms of competing initiatives were discussed in [2]. Gouda proposed to give different priorities to the different initiatives to solve this problem [21]. In the following, we assume that all choices are local. Note that for non-local choice, certain proposals could be easily integrated with our derivation algorithm to solve this problem. We note that the semantic definition of choice, as given in [16], explicitly shows that the choice must be followed by a strict sequence. Therefore we discuss here the design model for strict sequence and alternatives. In the following, we discuss a basic algorithm for deriving a design model for a given role (component) from the global requirements in the form of a single sequence of strictly sequenced states, and then discuss how choices can be integrated into this context.

Basic derivation algorithm for role r_n in the case of a linear strict sequence of states:

1. Create a local state s_l in the local design model for each state s_g in the global requirements. Call the generation function "genDM" to establish the design model for each local state s_l according to the corresponding global state s_g. Calculate for s_g the sets of initiating roles (IR), terminating roles (TR), and participating roles (PR).
2. For each global state s_g, except the last state in the sequence, consider the outgoing transition t (directed from s_g to the next state s_{next}). If $r_n \in TR_s$, a flow message should be sent to each role in IR of the next state (written IR_{snext}) except r_n, written as $(IR_{snext} - \{r_n\})$, see [8]. For this purpose, a new state called **"final state of s"** (written fin(s)), is be created (in the local design model) containing as do-actions the sending of these flow messages. A completion transition is created from s to **fin(s)**. We use the term **"outflow state of s"** to designate the final state of s, if it exists, or s itself.
3. For each global state s_g, except the first state in the sequence, consider the incoming transition t (from s_{prev} to s_g). If $r_n \in IR_s$, a flow message should be received from each role in TR of the previous state except r_n, written as $(TR_{sprev} - \{r_n\}))$, see [8]. For this purpose, a new state called **"preliminary state of s"** (written prel(s)), is created (in the local design model) containing no do-action but having an outgoing transitions which is triggered by the reception of one of the flow messages to be received. If more than one flow messages are to be received, an additional intermediate state is created for each additional flow message with an outgoing transition to receive the corresponding flow message. These additional states are linked sequentially (in an arbitrary order – since the reception pool allows the receiving component to determine in which order it wants to receive these messages) to finally lead to the state s_l. We use the term **"inflow state of s"** to designate the preliminary state of s, if it exists, or s itself.
4. For each local state s_l in the design model, except the last state in the sequence, create a completion transition from the outflow state of s_l to the inflow state of s_{next}.

Figure 5(b) shows the generated design model for r_1 in the linear strict sequence in Fig. 3(b). The simple states a_1 and a_4 is the remaining states (after deleting the dummy states) from the composite states cs_1 and cs_2, respectively. What we explained above for the derivation of strict sequence can also be applied in the case of alternatives where a choice state (node) may have two or more outgoing transitions. Consider the requirement model in Fig. 3(c) which contains alternatives and strict sequence. Based on the derivation rules above and considering the alternatives, the local design model for r_1 is shown in Fig. 6.

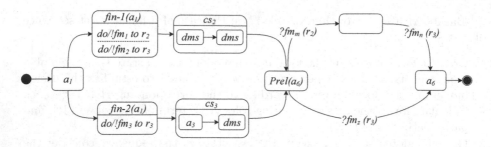

Fig. 6. Local design model for r_1 derived from the requirement model in Fig. 3(c)

As we see in the figure, for any composite state, the global function "genDM" is called recursively to evaluate the design model for that state, see for instance the composite states: cs_2 and cs_3. For the outgoing transitions from the choice node, each one will be treated separately based on the rules described before. In the first alternative, the coordination messages fm_1 and fm_2 are sent to $IR_{cs2} = \{r_2, r_3\}$ in the first final state of a_1 (denoted $fin-1(a_1)$) (see concurrent do-actions), and fm_3 is sent to the $IR_{cs3} = \{r_3\}$ in the second alternative (see state $fin - 2(a_1)$). At state a_6 (executed by r_1) where the two alternatives are combined, r_1 receives coordination messages from the terminating roles (TR) of the previous state (in each alternative) in any order. $Prel(a_6)$ is the preliminary state of a_6; the receiving of flow messages starts after this state.

It is important to note a problem with choice propagation related to "inactive choice nodes". These are (dummy) choice states generated by our algorithm for the roles that have to follow the choice made by the role executing the choice node. If the inactive choice node is followed by dummy states (where the role does not perform any actions), the role may not know which choice should be taken. An example is shown by the example design model of in Fig. 7(a), where the role does not know which choice to follow. In certain cases the elimination of dummy states is sufficient to solve the problem. For instance, eliminating the first dummy state in the right alternative allows the role to follow the right choice, as shown in Fig. 7(b).

In general, we propose to solve this problem with choice indication messages (cim). These messages were proposed in [8] for the case that a role does not participate in one of the choices and this choice is taken, as in the choice within the composed state cs_2 of in Fig. 7 (see cim_2 message in Fig. 7(b)). In general, the transitions from an inactive choice state must contain the reception of a message. If this situation cannot be realized by the elimination of dummy states, the transition in question should be the reception of an additional choice indication message, as in the left choice in Fig. 7(b) where cim_1 must be received.

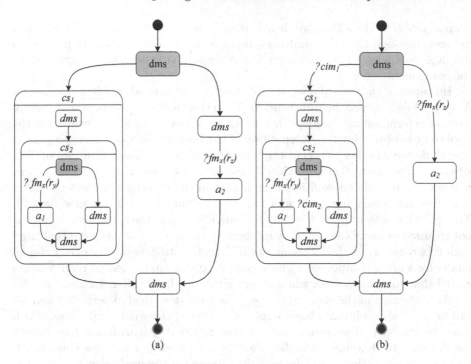

Fig. 7. (a) Incorrect local design model for the role r_n (b) correct design model for r_n (includes the addition of choice indication messages)

3.6   Concurrency and Strict While Loop

The generation of a design model for a composed state that contains several concurrent substates is systematic. Since there is no interaction between the activities of the different concurrent substates, the design model for a particular component r is constructed by creating a composed state for component r that contains concurrent substates that contain the design model (for r) for each concurrent substate of the global requirement model in which component r participates.

The generation of a design model for a composed state that contains a strict while loop is also systematic. It is sufficient to apply the rules explained in the previous section to the occurrences of strict sequences and the alternative which make up the strict while loop.

3.7   Weak While Loop

The derivation of the design model from a requirement model, including a weak while loop, was studied by many authors [2, 8, 11, 22]. Most of this research was in the context of requirement models defined in terms of Interaction Diagrams or MSC. Because of the weak sequencing between subsequent MSCs, the messages received by a given component could arrive in an unexpected order which is called a *race condition* [18]. This problem is usually resolved by making a distinction between message reception and consumption: a received message is put into a message pool where it is stored until it is consumed in the order requested by the component.

However, in the case of a weak while loop, an additional problem may occur. A weak while loop may be **unbounded** [1]. In this case, a component may receive a message terminating the loop when there are still some messages waiting in the pool to be consumed within a repetition of the body of the loop. The component cannot decide whether to accept the terminating message for consumption. This situation was called **Termination Race** [11]. To solve this problem, it was proposed to include an additional parameter in the messages of the loop which indicates how often the body was repeated to date (see for instance, [8,22]). This solution was improved in [11] by indicating that the sequence number is not required in many cases, and by minimizing the number of messages that need such a parameter. In the following, we discuss how to generate a correct design model for a given component r_n for a composed state in the global requirements model that contains a weak while loop, written in the HSMs notation.

As in the case of the strict while loop, the rules described in Sects. 3.4 and 3.5 can be applied to obtain a basic implementation of the weak while loop, which must be modified if sequence numbers are required. Algorithm 1 (see below) can be used to determine whether there is a termination race for this role. If there is a termination race, the first flow messages received by r_n in the loop body and in the follow-up part should contain a sequence number (written as $?fm_x(seq)$). Also, the roles that send these messages to r_n (in the loop body and in the follow-up part) should include these sequence numbers in the send actions ($!fm_x(seq)$). These roles, as well as r_n, need a local counter n to record the number times that the loop was executed. As explained in [11], there are two ways to implement, in component r_n, the consumption of the next message with the correct sequence number. If the interface to the pool allows the component to request the consumption of a message with a particular sequence number, then the component may simply ask for a message of the body with number $(n + 1)$ or a message of the follow-up with sequence n. For the case that the pool interface does not allow this choice (but only a choice based on the message types), an alternate implementation is described in [11,22].

3.7.1   Check for Termination Race

In this section, we determine whether the termination race could happen for a role r_n in a given weak while loop. Based on the results in [11], there is no termination race for role r_n if the first event of r_n in the loop body is before the last event of the loop initiator (r_i) inside the loop body. To check the termination race, we evaluate the function $precede(r_1, r_2, s)$ (see Algorithm 1). We know that no termination exists if the result is true, since the meaning of $precede(r_1, r_2, s)$ is the following: An action of r_1 precedes an action of r_2 during the execution of the behaviour of the composed state s.

The function $precede(r_1, r_2, s)$ is evaluated according to the different forms that the composed state s may take according to the cases mentioned in Sect. 3.1.

Algorithm 1: *precede* Function

---

1 **Function** *precede(* r_1 *,* r_2 *,* s *)*
2   **switch** s **do**
3   **case** *(1) linear strict sequence of states* $s_{1,s}\, s_{2,s} \ldots ,_s s_k$ **do**
4             $precede(r_1\,,\,r_2\,,\,s) = (\exists\, i \in [1:k] : precede(r_1, r_2, s_i))$ **OR**
            $(\exists\, i,j \in [1:k] : i < j,\ r_1 \in PR_{si}\ and\ r_2 \in PR_{sj})$;
5   **case** *(2) strict sequence with alternatives* **do**
6             $precede(r_1, r_2, s) = (\forall\ \text{linear sequences } ls \text{ allowed by } s, \text{ we}$
            have $\text{precede}(r_1, r_2, ls))$;
7   **case** *(3) several concurrent substates of the form* $ccs_1 \parallel ccs_2 \parallel \ldots$
        $\parallel ccs_k)$ **do**
8             $precede(r_1, r_2, s) = (\exists\, i\ in\ [1:k] : precede(r_1, r_2, ccs_i))$
9   **case** *(4) strict or weak while loop with body and follow-up* **do**
10             $precede(r_1, r_2, s) = precede(r_1, r_2, s.\text{follow-up})$ **OR**
11             $(r_1$ is the loop initiator (r_i) and $r_2 \in PR_{s.follow-up})$
12   **case** *(5) linear weak sequence of states* $s_{1,w}\, s_{2,w} \ldots ,_w s_k$ **do**
13             $precede(r_1, r_2, s) = (\exists\, i \in [1:k] : precede(r_1, r_2, s_i))$ **OR**
14             $(\exists\, r_{x1}, r_{x2}, \ldots r_{xm} \in PR_s$ with $r_{x1} = r_1$ and $r_{xm} = r_2$ and
15   a number of states $s_{y1}, s_{y2}, \ldots s_{y(m-1)}$ with $yi < y(i+1)$ for
            $i = 1, \ldots m - 2$ such that $precede(r_{xi}, r_{x(i+1)}, s_{yi})$ for $i = 1, \ldots$
            $m - 1)$

We give in the following a reasoning for the evaluation of the function $precede(r_1, r_2, s)$ in the different cases:

- Case (1) – strict sequencing: The function is true if there is a state s_i in the sequence for which *precede* is true or if role r_1 participates in one of the states and role r_2 in a subsequent state.
- Case (2) – alternatives: Different linear strict sequences of states are possible. Since we do not know which one will be executed, *precede* must be true for all of them.
- Case (3) – concurrent substates: Since all concurrent substates will be executed, it is sufficient that *precede* be true for one of them.
- Case (4) – while loop: The body may not be executed, while the follow-up will always be executed.
- Case (5) – weak sequence: Like for strict sequencing, *precede* may be true because it is true for one of the substates s_i. The second possibility relates to intermediate roles. In the case that $m = 3$, we have the roles r_1, r_2 and an intermediate role r_{x2}. Suppose that $y1 = 2$ and $y2 = 5$ (and $k = 6$). Then the formula states that $precede(r_1, r_2, s)$ is true if $precede(r_1, r_{x2}, s_2)$ and $precede(r_{x2}, r_2, s_5)$ are both true. The actions of r_{x2} in state s_2 are before those in state s_5 because of the weak sequencing relationship.

4   Conclusion

This paper deals with deriving a distributed design model from a global requirements model written in the notation of Hierarchical State Machines (HSMs). In this paper, we extend the UML notation of HSMs to indicate the roles (components) that participate in the actions of each state of the global behaviour. A simple state represents some local actions, while a hierarchical state usually represents a collaboration between several roles (system components). Our global HSM requirements model describes the sequencing of collaborations and local actions. We compare this notation with other notations such as UML Collaborations, Hierarchical Message Sequence Charts (HMSC), Activity Diagrams, PO-Charts and others. Then we explain how a distributed design model, including all required coordination messages between the different system components, can be automatically derived from a global requirements model. We consider the following sequencing constraints between different collaborations: weak or strict sequence, alternatives, weak or strict while loop, and concurrency.

The local design model generated by our algorithm, for each component, is an HSM which represents the local actions identified in the requirement model and executed by this component, and the exchange of the coordination messages which are generated by our proposed algorithm. These local state machines can be easily implemented by any suitable tools that generate code from a design model written in UML HSM. We plan to implement this generation algorithm in the context of the Umple development environment [23] using the distributed implementation environment described in [24].

References

1. Alur, R., Yannakakis, M.: Model checking of message sequence charts. In: Baeten, J.C.M., Mauw, S. (eds.) CONCUR 1999. LNCS, vol. 1664, pp. 114–129. Springer, Heidelberg (1999). https://doi.org/10.1007/3-540-48320-9_10
2. Castejón, H.N., von Bochmann, G., Bræk, R.: On the realizability of collaborative services. Softw. Syst. Model. **12**(3), 597–617 (2013)
3. von Bochmann, G.: Conformance testing with respect to partial-order specifications. In: Wotawa, F., Nica, M., Kushik, N. (eds.) ICTSS 2016. LNCS, vol. 9976, pp. 3–17. Springer, Cham (2016). https://doi.org/10.1007/978-3-319-47443-4_1
4. Object Managment Group: UML 2.5.1 Specification. Technical report (2017)
5. Pratt, V.: Modeling concurrency with partial orders. Int. J. Parallel Program. **15**(1), 33–71 (1986)
6. Gischer, J.L.: The equational theory of pomsets. Theoret. Comput. Sci. **61**(2–3), 199–224 (1988)
7. Mauw, S., Reniers, M.A.: High-level message sequence charts. In: SDL 1997: Time for Testing, pp. 291–306. Elsevier (1997)
8. Bochmann, G.V.: Deriving component designs from global requirements. In: CEUR Workshop Proceedings, vol. 503, pp. 55–69 (2008)
9. Khendek, F., von Bochmann, G., Kant, C.: New results on deriving protocol specifications from service specifications. In: Proceedings of the ACM SIGCOMM 1989, pp. 136–145 (1989)

10. Gotzhein, R., von Bochmann, G.: Deriving protocol specifications from service specifications including parameters. ACM Trans. Comput. Syst. **8**(4), 255–283 (1990)
11. Al-hammouri, M.F., Bochmann, G.: Realizability of service specifications. In: Khendek, F., Gotzhein, R. (eds.) SAM 2018. LNCS, vol. 11150, pp. 127–143. Springer, Cham (2018). https://doi.org/10.1007/978-3-030-01042-3_8
12. Barros, A., Dumas, M., Oaks, P.: Standards for web service choreography and orchestration: status and perspectives. In: Bussler, C.J., Haller, A. (eds.) BPM 2005. LNCS, vol. 3812, pp. 61–74. Springer, Heidelberg (2006). https://doi.org/10.1007/11678564_7
13. Badreddin, O., Lethbridge, T.C., Forward, A., Elaasar, M., Aljamaan, H., Garzon, M.A.: Enhanced code generation from UML composite state machines. In: 2014 2nd International Conference on Model-Driven Engineering and Software Development (MODELSWARD), pp. 235–245. IEEE (2014)
14. Wikipedia contributors: structured programming, the free encyclopedia (2019). https://en.wikipedia.org/wiki/Structured_programming. Accessed 4 July 2019
15. Bochmann, G.: Associativity between weak and strict sequencing. In: Amyot, D., Fonseca i Casas, P., Mussbacher, G. (eds.) SAM 2014. LNCS, vol. 8769, pp. 96–109. Springer, Cham (2014). https://doi.org/10.1007/978-3-319-11743-0_7
16. Toqeer, I.: Modeling and performance analysis of distributed systems with collaboration behaviour diagrams. Ph.D. thesis, University of Ottawa (2014). http://hdl.handle.net/10393/30950
17. Mooij, A., Romijn, J., Wesselink, W.: Realizability criteria for compositional MSC. In: Johnson, M., Vene, V. (eds.) AMAST 2006. LNCS, vol. 4019, pp. 248–262. Springer, Heidelberg (2006). https://doi.org/10.1007/11784180_20
18. Alur, R., Holzmann, G.J., Peled, D.: An analyzer for message sequence charts. In: Margaria, T., Steffen, B. (eds.) TACAS 1996. LNCS, vol. 1055, pp. 35–48. Springer, Heidelberg (1996). https://doi.org/10.1007/3-540-61042-1_37
19. Bochmann, G.V.: Deriving protocol specification from service specifications. In: Proceedings of the SIGCOMM 1986, pp. 144–156 (1986)
20. Ben-Abdallah, H., Leue, S.: Syntactic detection of process divergence and non-local choice in message sequence charts. In: Brinksma, E. (ed.) TACAS 1997. LNCS, vol. 1217, pp. 259–274. Springer, Heidelberg (1997). https://doi.org/10.1007/BFb0035393
21. Gouda, M.G., Yu, Y.T.: Synthesis of communicating finite-state machines with guaranteed progress. IEEE Trans. Commun. **32**(7), 779–788 (1984)
22. Mustafa, N.M.F., Bochmann, G.V.: Transforming dynamic behavior specifications from activity diagrams to BPEL. In: Proceedings - 6th IEEE International Symposium on Service-Oriented System Engineering, SOSE 2011, pp. 305–311 (2011)
23. Umple, v 1.29.1 (2018). http://www.umple.org
24. Zakariapour, A.: Model-driven development of distributed systems in umple. Master's thesis, University Of Ottawa (2018). http://hdl.handle.net/10393/37143

Generic Graphical Navigation for Modelling Tools

Hyacinth Ali, Gunter Mussbacher$^{(\boxtimes)}$, and Jörg Kienzle

McGill University, Montreal, Canada
hyacinth.ali@mail.mcgill.ca, {gunter.mussbacher,joerg.kienzle}@mcgill.ca

Abstract. To describe the characteristics of software systems, model-driven engineering (MDE) advocates the use of different modeling languages and multiple views that modellers need to navigate in the models' editors to understand and modify the system under development. This paper introduces a generic navigation mechanism that facilitates navigation within a model, from one model to other linked models potentially expressed in a different language, as well as for feature-based development and across reuse hierarchies. Furthermore, a proposed navigation bar visually indicates to the modeller the place of a model in this structure. To make a modelling language navigable, a language designer enhances the modelling language at the metamodel level with our generic navigation capabilities, which include the ability to filter language elements based on attribute values. We present evidence that the proposed generic navigation mechanism comprehensively supports model navigation by analyzing the navigation facilities offered by popular UML modelling tools and a feature-based modelling tool.

Keywords: Navigation · Domain-specific language · Multi-view modelling · Features · Reuse · Model-driven engineering

1 Introduction

Model-driven engineering (MDE) [1] advocates the use of different modelling languages and multiple views to *describe* the characteristics of software systems as well as to *prescribe* their structure and behaviour. The software development process that is being used establishes conceptual and causal links between models, potentially crossing different levels of abstraction. While several works have focused on describing and enforcing these relationships [2–4], graphical navigation support for the user of a modelling tool within and across models has received only limited attention. This is the case even though studies have shown the importance of good visualization and navigation mechanisms in both software usage and during development [5–7].

With the proliferation of domain-specific modeling languages (DSMLs) [8], one cannot assume anymore that a fixed set of modeling languages is used to develop software systems. Rather, a flexible modeling environment needs to be

© Springer Nature Switzerland AG 2019
P. Fonseca i Casas et al. (Eds.): SAM 2019, LNCS 11753, pp. 44–60, 2019.
https://doi.org/10.1007/978-3-030-30690-8_3

provided that allows sets of languages to be integrated as the needs arise. Consequently, the corresponding set of models needs to be navigated. This navigation is not about generic navigation of models with the Object Constraint Language (OCL) or similar languages, but rather the navigation of models by the modeller in the models' editors.

In this paper, we present a generic approach for language designers and modelling tool developers to specify navigation mappings within a model, from one model to other linked models potentially expressed in a different language, as well as for feature-oriented development and across reuse hierarchies. We show how these mappings can be used to populate a navigation bar with navigation links that make it easy for a user to traverse models and navigate to related model elements. We use different colour highlighting to help the user find model elements within large models, and to inform the user when navigation links cross model boundaries. We explain how we encoded our generic approach in a metamodel targeting modelling languages and tools developed as part of the Eclipse Modelling Framework (EMF), and illustrate intra-model, inter-model, and inter-language navigation by means of a small example. We further demonstrate how our navigation approach can be used in a reuse-context and to filter language elements. Furthermore, we analyze popular UML modelling tools and a feature-oriented modelling tool with respect to their navigation capabilities. For each tool, we explain which navigation capabilities they support and show that the navigation concepts in our proposed metamodel are sufficient to handle them.

In the remainder of this paper, Sect. 2 presents generic language navigation by means of a running example. Section 3 elaborates our navigation metamodel and Sect. 4 discusses the navigation capabilities of several UML modelling tools. We briefly review related work in Sect. 5. The conclusion in Sect. 6 provides a summary and discusses future work.

2   Generic Language Navigation

MDE advocates the use of models expressed in different languages to capture the many characteristics of systems. This set of models needs to be navigated to understand the system under development. In this section, we first motivate our proposed generic navigation facility with the help of four examples, each representing a typical navigation situation.

2.1   Single Model Navigation

The first situation concerns the navigation of a single model, i.e., intra-model (and hence also intra-language) navigation. A complex model may consist of many model elements, and it is hence desirable to have a concise and easy-to-use way to find important model elements or navigate model element relationships.

For example, Fig. 1 depicts a class diagram of a bank system and our proposed navigation bar. Clicking the drop-down arrow under *BankClassDiagram* pops up the *Classes* of the model, listed under the tab *Classes*. Clicking on a class

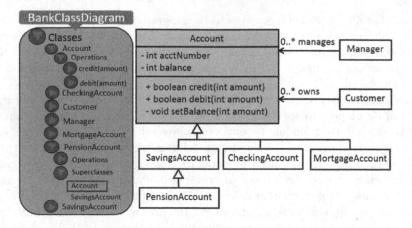

Fig. 1. Bank class diagram

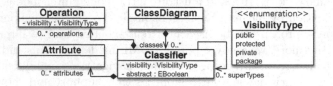

Fig. 2. Class diagram metamodel, *(an excerpt)*

reveals the operations and superclasses of the class in the navigation bar. In this example, we navigate from the class diagram to the class, `PensionAccount`, and then to its superclass, `Account`. Once a class is selected, the background of the class is highlighted in yellow in the model and centred on the screen, if needed, for easier identification.

To realize this navigation, several *navigation mappings* have to be specified on the class diagram metamodel shown in Fig. 2. The first navigation mapping has the `ClassDiagram` metaclass as its source and the `classes` reference as its target. The second and third mappings have the `Classifier` as their source and the `operations` rsp. `superTypes` reference as their target. A reference is used as the target instead of a metaclass, because one metaclass may have several relationships with another metaclass.

These three navigation mappings each consist of one *hop*. However, it may sometimes be necessary to skip intermediate elements and, e.g., define a navigation that goes from a class diagram directly to all the operations defined in the diagram without listing all the classes first. Such a navigation requires multiple hops, e.g., first from the `ClassDiagram` to the `classes` reference and then on with the `operations` reference.

The navigation mapping from `Classifier` to `superTypes` is different compared to the other mappings, because it is useful to not only show the direct

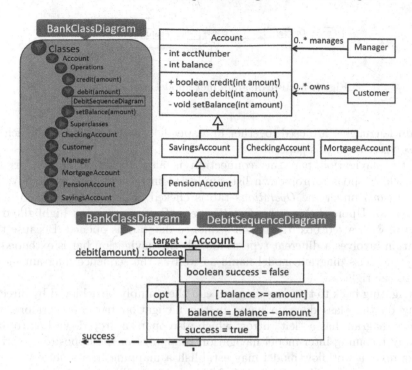

Fig. 3. Bank class diagram and sequence diagram of debit operation

superclass of a class, but instead the complete hierarchy of superclasses. For these situations we provide a *closure* flag that can be set.

2.2   Multi-view Navigation

The second situation concerns multi-view modeling, i.e., inter-model navigation. The navigation may involve models of the same type, i.e., intra-language navigation, or models from different languages, i.e., inter-language navigation. An example of inter-model, intra-language navigation is a sequence diagram that defines the behaviour of an operation, which sends messages to invoke other operations. In this case, one may want to navigate from the invocation message in the first sequence diagram to another sequence diagram showing the detailed behaviour of the invoked operation. This navigation can be handled the same way as single model navigation, with the *from* element being the message and one *hop* to its sequence diagram reference. In this case, though, the reference points to a model element in a different model.

An example for inter-model, inter-language navigation is a class diagram, where one may want to navigate from an operation declaration in a class to a sequence diagram defining the behaviour of the operation as shown in Fig. 3. In this situation, the two languages – the class diagram language and the sequence

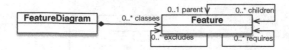

Fig. 4. Feature diagram metamodel, *(an excerpt)*

diagram language – are used together in a specific way for a purpose, which we term *perspective* in this paper.

In the navigation bar, this connection is also visualized as the "right" arrow, which opens a drop-down list similar to intra-model navigation. When *debit(amount)* under the *Operations* tab is clicked, a list of other linked models pops up. Upon clicking the *DebitSequenceDiagram* tab, as highlighted in the figure with a red box, the linked sequence diagram is opened. Because this navigation involves a different type of model, the navigation bar is extended to display the class diagram model name as well as the sequence diagram model name to the right.

Navigating back to the class diagram can then simply be achieved by directly clicking on the class diagram name in the navigation bar. Furthermore, the sequence diagram has a "left" arrow which also opens a drop-down box to navigate any incoming inter-model navigation mappings in the opposite direction. For example, a workflow model may establish a mapping from one of its steps to the same sequence diagram. The "left" arrow then allows navigating from the sequence diagram to the class diagram or to the workflow model.

We also need to take into account that it is possible to directly open any model using a file browser. When the above sequence diagram is opened directly with a file browser (and not through navigation starting with a class diagram), the navigation bar should still show that the sequence diagram depicts behaviour that is best understood in the context of the class diagram or workflow model. To determine which model should be shown in the navigation bar, the boolean attribute (*default*) of one of the incoming inter-model mappings is set to true.

The main difference to the intra-language navigation mappings described in the previous section is that there exists no prior link between the metamodel of the class diagram language and the metamodel of the sequence diagram language (assuming that these two metamodels have been developed independently). Consequently, an inter-language mapping involves a *from* metaclass and a *to* metaclass instead of reference hops.

2.3   Software Product Line Navigation

The third situation involves Software Product Line (SPL) development, which groups related model artifacts with commonalities and variabilities for a given family of products [9]. In SPL, a *feature* designates a user-relevant functionality or system quality that can be present or not in a product. A feature diagram describes the relationships among features, i.e., the set of feature configurations that produce valid products.

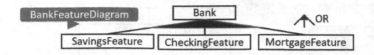

Fig. 5. Feature diagram of a bank system

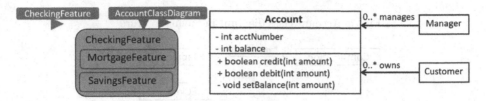

Fig. 6. Account class diagram in CheckingFeature

Figure 4 depicts a metamodel for feature diagrams. A `FeatureDiagram` basically has a list of `Features` with parent/children relationships among them. Some of these features may be optional, while others are mandatory, and define *requires* and *excludes* relationships to other features. Figure 5 shows an example feature model for a bank system supporting different kinds of bank accounts. The features *SavingsFeature*, *CheckingFeature*, and *MortgageFeature* are in an OR relationship, meaning that at least one of them must be selected in order to create a valid configuration.

In model-driven SPLs, the structural and behavioural properties of features are described with models linked to these features. In additive variability, each feature is realized by one or several models, and to derive a product the realization models corresponding to the chosen features are composed with each other. In negative variability, a so-called 150% model describes the system with all features enabled. Each feature is linked to model elements related to the feature, and to derive a product the model elements that are not linked to any chosen features are removed from the model.

While negative variability requires a highlighting feature similar to what is shown in Fig. 1, positive variability requires navigation among models. To illustrate feature-oriented navigation, we split the bank account class diagram from Fig. 1 into four smaller class diagrams. These class diagrams can then be composed (i.e., merged) to produce a bank model with the desired features.

Clicking on the "right" arrow under *BankFeatureDiagram* first shows the features and then the models realizing a feature (similar to the sequence diagrams of operations). Selecting a feature highlights the feature in the feature diagram, while selecting a model of a feature takes the modeler to the model associated with this feature as illustrated in Fig. 6.

Figure 6 shows the class diagram that contains the common structure used by *all* bank account features. At this time, though, the developer is currently working on the class diagram in the context of the *CheckingFeature*. This focus is depicted in the navigation bar by displaying the name of the *CheckingFeature* in

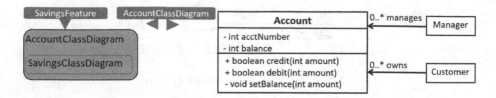

Fig. 7. Account class diagram in SavingsFeature

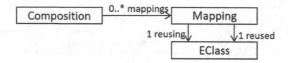

Fig. 8. Reuse metamodel, *(an excerpt)*

the navigation bar instead of the *BankFeatureDiagram*. The "right" arrow under *CheckingFeature* allows navigating to the models associated with the feature, i.e., the shared *AccountsClassDiagram* and the *CheckingClassDiagram* (which shows the generalization of the `CheckingAccount` class). The "left" arrow under the *AccountClassDiagram* shows a drop-down list with all other features that also use this class diagram. For example, when the "SavingsFeature" is clicked, the name "CheckingFeature" in the navigation bar is changed to "SavingsFeature", i.e., a context switch, and clicking the arrow under the "SavingsFeature" shows the models associated with it as shown in Fig. 7.

In terms of navigation mappings, feature-oriented navigation does not introduce any new kind of mapping. The mappings between a feature diagram and its features are intra-model mappings already discussed in Sect. 2.1. The mappings from features to class diagrams are inter-model, inter-language mappings already discussed in Sect. 2.2. However, since a feature is treated differently than other model element in terms of how it is displayed in the navigation bar, a `fromIsNavigationKey` flag needs to be set in its navigation mapping.

2.4 Navigation of Reusable Artifacts

The final situation discussed here concerns the use of reusable artifacts during software development. Consider the sequence diagram for `debit(amount)` in Fig. 9 and assume that a reusable artifact for authentication exists with a sequence diagram as shown in Fig. 10. When the `debit(amount)` sequence diagram reuses the *Authentication* sequence diagram, the body of the reusing sequence diagram replaces the box labeled with * in the reused sequence diagram. Consequently, the authentication check is performed before the body of the reusing sequence diagram. To specify this reuse, a composition specification needs to be provided that links the `debit(amount)` sequence diagram with the *Authentication* sequence diagram as defined in the metamodel for reuse specifications (see Fig. 8). The reuse metamodel captures the links between *reused*

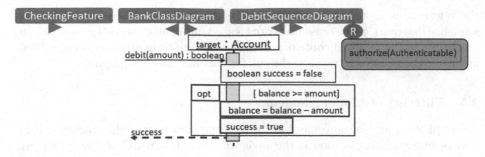

Fig. 9. Reuse of authentication

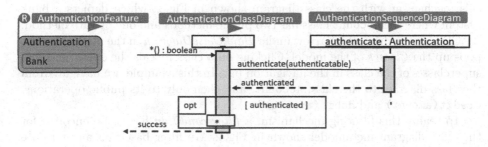

Fig. 10. Authentication reuse hierarchy

elements and *reusing* elements with a mapping. In our example, a mapping is established between the instance of the *SequenceDiagram* metaclass representing the `debit` operation to the *SequenceDiagram* metaclass instance representing the `authentication` operation. Once such a mapping in the reuse specification is established, it should be possible to navigate this composition link with the help of the proposed navigation bar.

To support this navigation, an "R" is displayed under the *DebitSequenceDiagram* in Fig. 9. Clicking on it shows all reuses of this model (or individual model elements of the model). Once a reuse is selected, the modeler is taken to the reusable artifact. This involves a context switch, which results in the navigation bar showing the reused sequence diagram with its default parent (i.e., its class diagram) and the default parent of the class diagram (i.e., its feature). As shown in Fig. 10, an "R" at the left of the navigation bar indicates the reuse hierarchy that is currently explored (e.g., the reusable artifact *Authentication* and the *Bank* that is reusing it). Clicking on an element in the reuse hierarchy results in direct navigation to that level.

In terms of navigation mappings, an intra-language mapping needs to be established (e.g., from the reusing sequence diagram to the reused sequence diagram). This navigation mapping requires a `from` element. Furthermore, two hops are required, which are references. The first hop is identified by the `reusing` reference and the second hop is identified by the `reused` reference. Note, however, that the `reusing` reference needs to be traversed in the reverse direction, because the reference is at the side of the source element of the hop (i.e., the reusing sequence diagram). Since reuse links are treated differently than other navigation links (due to the required context switch from the reusing artifact to the reused artifact), the `reuse` flag needs to be set for this navigation mapping.

2.5   Filtering of Model Elements

A complex model diagram may have a large number of model elements, which may be overwhelming to show in the navigation bar. To streamline navigation, we support filtering of model elements. E.g., a modeler may want to find all classes in a system and show only the *public* operations of each class. We demonstrate this mechanism with the class diagram shown in Fig. 1, which depicts a bank system where the `Account` class has two public methods and one private method.

Clicking the drop-down arrow under *BankClassDiagram* in the navigation bar pops up the *Classes* of the model. Clicking on a class reveals the operations and superclasses of the class in the navigation bar. In this example, we navigate from the class diagram to the class, `Account`, and then only to its public operations, `credit(amount)` and `debit(amount)`.

To realize this filtering mechanism, a *filter condition* has to be encoded for the class diagram metamodel shown in Fig. 2. We filter based on an attribute value of the relevant model element. For example, the filter condition could be *abstract classes*, *public classes*, etc. In Fig. 1, the result based on filtering *public operations* is shown. To achieve this, the filter condition specifies the attribute of the metaclass that the filter should consider (i.e., the `visibility` attribute of the `Class` metaclass), the comparison value (i.e., the enumeration literal `public`), and a comparison operator (i.e., `EqualTo`).

To allow a modeler to dynamically configure which navigation mappings and associated filters the navigation bar uses to populate its content, it is possible to activate navigation mappings at runtime through preference settings.

3   Navigation Metamodel

This section describes our navigation metamodel that the designer of a language or modelling tool can use to define navigation mappings that configure our generic navigation bar. We elaborate our metamodel in the context of the Eclipse Metamodelling Framework (EMF), in which all metamodels are expressed using the metametamodelling language ECore. As such, any model element that is part of a language metamodel and could be selected as the source of a navigation link is encoded as an instance of the class `EClass`.

As explained with the examples above, for each `Perspective`[1] there are two broad categories of navigation, namely intra-language and inter-language navigation, which are indicated by two metaclasses (`IntraLanguageMapping`

---

[1] Recall that a *perspective* represents a purpose for using models expressed in one or several modelling languages during software development.

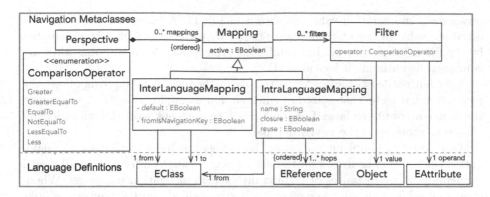

Fig. 11. Navigation metamodel

and `InterLanguageMapping`) in Fig. 11. In intra-language, we navigate *from* a model or one of its model elements (represented as `EClass`) to one or several elements of the same language by following references. In language metamodels defined with Ecore, these references are instances of `EReference`. Since navigation might involve traversing several references, every `IntraLanguageMapping` therefore defines an ordered collection of `EReference` called *hops*.

Furthermore, each intra-language mapping has the following three attributes: `name`, `closure`, and `reuse`. The string attribute `name` allows the tool designer to specify the text that should appear in the navigation bar for this navigation. The boolean `closure` attribute can be set for any `IntraLanguageMapping` where the *from* `EClass` is identical to the model element referred to by the last *hop*. In this case, the navigation bar will traverse this mapping recursively and display all reached target model elements. In our example, `closure` is set when navigating from a class to its superclasses in order to display the entire superclass hierarchy in the navigation bar. The boolean `reuse` identifies an intra-language navigation mapping that requires a context switch.

In case of inter-language mappings, the navigation involves models of different software languages, e.g., navigating from an operation definition in a class diagram to the sequence diagram specifying the behaviour of the operation. Hence, for `InterLanguageMappings`, the *from* and *to* are always instances of `EClass`, and each mapping is a 1-to-1 relationship. Finally, the `default` attribute specifies whether the source of an inter-language navigation mapping identifies the default parent of a target model. The `fromIsNavigationKey` attribute identifies key model elements (e.g., a feature) that need to be shown in the navigation bar instead of their model name.

To support filtering of language elements, we attach a `Filter` to the `Mapping` metaclass, which is the superclass of the `InterLanguageMapping` and `Intra-LanguageMapping` navigation mappings. Filtering is always applied on the `to` elements in the case of inter-language filtering, or to the elements designated by the `EClass` referred to by the last `hop` in the case of intra-language filtering. The `operator` attribute specifies the comparison operator for the filtering using pre-defined enumeration values as shown in Fig. 11. A filter then compares the attribute value of the operand EAttribute with the value Object designated by the filter. When several filter conditions are specified for a mapping, they are combined by an implicit logical AND.

Last but not least, the active attribute in the metaclass Mapping allows the navigation bar to be customized at runtime. For example, a modeller can toggle the active attribute to false if at some point he does not wish the operations of classes to show up in the navigation bar.

Our prototype implementation of the navigation bar ensures that the navigation information is always up-to-date by registering as a listener to all model elements that are instances of EClass involved in navigation mappings. Whenever a model is changed, the navigation bar is notified and the navigation links are adjusted according to the occurrences of the mappings in the model.

4   Evaluation

The Unified Modelling language (UML) [10] is a widely accepted standard for modelling software intensive systems. In its current version it defines 13 different diagrams. UML modelling tools facilitate the specification of systems at different levels of abstraction and from different points of view.

In this section, we analyse the navigation facilities of several popular modelling tools and evaluate whether our navigation metamodel covers them. We performed a Google search for "most popular UML tools". From the obtained list we investigated the top 4, namely: ArgoUML (free), StarUML (free), Visual Paradigm Enterprise (commercial), and MagicDraw (commercial). We also selected Papyrus, as a representation of a popular modelling tool based on EMF, and finally TouchCORE [11], as a representative of a UML modelling tool that explicitly supports software product line modelling and model reuse. In each tool, we specified a class diagram, and defined the behavior of some operations using sequence diagrams or state machines. We then explored how the tools support navigation. We organize our findings under the topics of intra-language and inter-language navigation, filtering, element highlighting, navigation of inheritance hierarchy, feature-oriented navigation, and navigation across reuse boundaries.

ArgoUML is an open source tool supporting all UML 1.4 diagrams [12]. *Intra-Language Navigation* in ArgoUML is done with the model explorer, which shows the list of diagrams and their contained elements. *Inter-Language Navigation* is limited, but clicking on an element in a diagram in the model explorer opens the corresponding diagram and highlights the selected element. ArgoUML supports different kinds of *filtering* using their own notion of *perspective*. Each perspective specifies the kind of model elements to be shown in the explorer. The tool allows modelers to define their own perspectives using existing rules by combining existing filter conditions from a provided library. When a model element is selected in the model explorer, the element is *highlighted* in blue in the editor, if it is currently visible on screen. The model explorer can also list all the model classes and their subclasses to explore the *inheritance hierarchy*.

Our proposed generic navigation approach can support all the navigation facilities that ArgoUML offers. The perspectives of ArgoUML can be represented as a filter condition in our generic mechanism. For example, the Class-Centric perspective lists only diagrams and classes in the model explorer. With our approach, this can be done by setting the `active` flag of `Mapping` for all instances of `Class` (see Figs. 2 and 11), and deactivating all other mappings.

StarUML is a modelling tool compatible with the UML 2.x standard and supporting 11 types of diagrams [13]. The tool partially supports *intra-language navigation* in the model explorer by right-clicking on a model element and choosing *Select In Diagram*. The tool supports *inter-language navigation* using the model explorer: clicking on a class shows the contained operations. Clicking on the operation displays the list of associated sequence diagrams, if any. StarUML has no support for filtering. Each model element in the currently displayed diagram can be *highlighted* in blue by selecting it in the model explorer. StarUML partially supports navigation of the *inheritance hierarchy* in class diagrams by navigating from a subclass to its parent class. However, it is not possible in StarUML to visualize the complete inheritance hierarchy of a given class.

Our proposed generic navigation approach can express all the navigation facilities that StarUML provides. Additionally, our approach supports filtering and displaying of the entire inheritance hierarchy.

MagicDraw [14] supports all UML diagrams. MagicDraw provides a structured containment tree which facilitates *navigation* from a model element to its related elements. Clicking on a model element displays it in the diagram editor, switching diagrams if necessary. However, just like in StarUML, the containment tree in MagicDraw displays the model element definitions separately from the diagrams in which they are used in. MagicDraw provides full support for *inter-language navigation*. A sequence diagram or activity diagram that is linked to an operation in a class diagram can be navigated to directly from the model element in the model editor. The tool has several *filter* conditions under three different categories, namely: *List*, *Inheritance*, and *Structural*. Each category has multiple options that can be turned on or off, e.g., Class, Actor, or Association. When a filter condition is enabled, the corresponding model elements are hidden in the containment tree. In the containment tree of the model explorer, a *superclass* can be navigated to by clicking a plus (+) tab before its subclass.

Our generic approach supports the navigation facilities of MagicDraw. The filtering in MagicDraw is at the granularity of model element types, i.e., every model element of a given type is either shown or not shown. Our generic mechanism supports this using the `active` flag in `Mapping` (see Fig. 11). Unlike our approach, MagicDraw does not support filtering based on attribute values, e.g., to define a filter that displays only abstract classes.

Visual Paradigm Enterprise supports UML 2 and SysML modelling [15]. Visual Paradigm has full support for *intra-language navigation* within the *diagram navigator* similar to MagicDraw. The tool also provides excellent support for *inter-language navigation*. E.g., when an operation in a class diagram has a linked sequence or state diagram, an icon is displayed with the class that can be

Table 1. Navigation support of UML tools

Tool	Intra-language	Inter-language	Attribute filtering	Activation filtering	Element highlighting	Inheritance hierarchy	SPL	Model reuse
ArgoUML	Yes	Yes	No	Yes	Yes	Yes	No	No
StarUML	Partial	Yes	No	No	Yes	Partial	No	No
MagicDraw	Yes	Yes	No	Yes	Yes	Partial	No	No
Visual Paradigm	Yes	Yes	No	No	Yes	Partial	No	No
Papyrus	Yes	Yes	No	Yes	Yes	Partial	No	No
TouchCORE	Yes	Yes	No	No	Yes	No	Yes	Yes

clicked to navigate to the linked diagrams. Visual Paradigm does not support filtering. A modeler can right-click an element in the explorer or diagram navigator and choose *Select In Diagram*. This takes the modeler to the diagram containing the element with the element being *highlighted* in bold, switching the current view if necessary. The tool only partially supports *inheritance navigation*, as a modeler can only navigate from a class to its direct superclasses.

Papyrus is a UML modelling tool based on EMF that supports many UML diagrams. The tool supports *navigation* of elements within a model in the model explorer, including traversing from a diagram to its elements. Papyrus uses *hyperlinks* to establish relationships between two diagrams, e.g., between a class and an activity diagram or a state diagram. The tool displays these *inter-language links* under the corresponding model elements in the model explorer. The contents for every model element shown in the diagram editor can be selectively hidden or shown by enabling or disabling *filter* options. For example in a class diagram, classes can be visualized with or without their attributes. Selected model elements in the model explorer, are *highlighted* in the diagram editor. Navigating from the model explorer to an element opens up the diagram containing the element in case it was not previously shown. Papyrus supports navigating from subclasses to direct *superclasses* only.

TouchCORE is a modelling tool for concern-oriented software design [11, 16], focussing specifically on feature-driven modularisation as required in SPLs. It also has explicit support for model reuse, and ships with a library of reusable models. The tool supports Feature Models, Goal Models, Class Diagrams, State Diagrams, and Sequence Diagrams. When selected in the model explorer, model elements in the current diagram are *highlighted* in orange. The model explorer allows the modeller to *navigate*, e.g. from an operation defined in a class diagram to an attached sequence diagram. TouchCORE does not support filtering of model elements nor navigation of the inheritance hierarchy. Since TouchCORE was designed to specifically support SPL, there is excellent support for *feature-oriented navigation*, e.g., navigating from a feature in a feature diagram to the associated realization model(s). Conversely, when visualizing a model in the model editor, the associated features are displayed and can be navigated to easily. The tool keeps track of reuse dependencies between models. A modeler can navigate from a current model to the *reused models* via the model explorer.

Evaluation Summary. Table 1 shows a summary of each tool's navigation capabilities. Each of the investigated tools has a model explorer, which corresponds to our navigation bar. Our proposed generic mechanism covers all the navigation means provided by the surveyed tools. No tool offers complete support for all navigation features provided by our proposed navigation mechanism. Only one tool supports the navigation of closures: ArgoUML supports the navigation of the entire inheritance hierarchy in a class diagram. Attribute-based filtering is not supported in any of the surveyed tools. However, we decided to include this feature in our proposed metamodel, because many development environments for programming languages have the ability to filter, e.g., by public elements. Of course, our proposed metamodel could easily employ a general query expression language for navigation purposes (e.g., OCL). However, the goal of this work is to provide the modeller with a *succinct* set of concepts needed for navigation in modelling editors instead of offering the full capabilities of languages such as OCL, which are not needed in this context according to our analysis of popular UML modelling tools. For the same reason, our proposed metamodel only supports conjuntive filters and not disjunctive filters.

5   Related Work

Navigation is an important mechanism to traverse, search, and retrieve information. Many studies have been done on how to improve navigation in software applications and web sites.

dos Santos et al. [7] investigate the effects of different types of menus in web site navigation, assessing the usability as well as performance of 8 different navigation mechanisms, each with distinctive properties. The study concludes by putting forward a horizontal menu, which is the base structure of the navigation bar presented in this paper. Burrel and Sodan [17] analyze six different types of menus contained in web pages of institutions. Considering the factors layout, ease of use, clarity of information, and ease of learning, they determine that navigation consisting of tabs, side navigation bars at the top and vertical menus on the left are the most favourite. We considered these insights when developing the navigation bar proposed in this paper. Finally, Muneo Kitajima et al. [18] present *CoLiDeS* (Comprehension-based Linked model of Deliberate Search), which is a model-based design methodology that website developers can follow to design better navigation for webpages. The main objective is to improve the user's success rate while searching for information on typical web sites.

To the best of our knowledge, there has been no prior work specifically on navigation for graphical modelling tools. Programming IDEs typically offer contextual menus that allow a developer to navigate within and across source code modules, e.g., from a method call to the method declaration. These relationships are typically inferred from static source code analysis. The following works target advanced navigation in programming IDEs, and as such can also be applied for navigation in textual modelling languages.

Mylyn is a task and application lifecycle management (ALM) framework for the Eclipse IDE [19,20]. In Mylyn, a developer can define tasks and declare which tasks he is currently working on. Mylyn then keeps track of code elements that are being looked at, created, or modified for each task. The developer can then use this information for task-based navigation.

Similarly, the FEAT plugin for Eclipse [21] allows the developer to define a high-level conceptual unit called *concern*, e.g., a feature, a nonfunctional requirement, a design idiom, or an implementation mechanism. When coding, a developer can deliberately associate code elements to the concern, slowly building up a concern graph that relates code elements that are scattered throughout multiple source code modules. Subsequently, the developer can use the concern graph for highlighting and navigation purposes.

6   Conclusion

Model-driven engineering is a conceptual development framework where models of the system under development are created and manipulated using different formalisms at different levels of abstraction. Separation of concerns is further promoted when working with multi-view modelling, software product lines, and domain-specific modelling languages. While this separation into many interrelated models has many benefits, it also makes it harder for the developer to determine the relevant context when looking at a model, and to navigate from one model to related ones.

We propose a metamodel that covers two categories of navigation, intra-language and inter-language navigation. The metamodel allows the designer of a modelling tool to generically capture the relevant navigation links between model elements in a set of models manipulated for a given purpose. It is done by establishing inter-language and intra-language mappings designating the relevant metaclasses and references in the metamodels of the involved languages. We illustrate the effectiveness of our navigation metamodel by examples that involve feature models, class diagrams, and sequence diagrams, but our approach can be applied to any modelling language that is defined by a metamodel.

We furthermore show how this generic information can be used to visualize the current context of a model with a navigation bar, and how to populate the navigation bar with navigation links. When a navigation link is clicked, we either highlight the chosen model element if that element is located in the current model, or we navigate to the model that contains the model element and update the navigation bar to reflect the new context.

We validate that our generic navigation approach covers the navigation facilities provided by current modelling tools by conducting a survey of 6 popular UML modelling tools.

Our approach is not tool specific and can be applied to any language and modelling environment that uses metamodels. The main benefit is that if a modelling environment adopts our generic navigation approach, setting up navigation when adding a new language to an environment becomes greatly simplified. In that case, language designers do not have to implement intra-navigation support from scratch during language design, but can customize the navigation bar simply by creating the appropriate intra-language mappings. To link the new models with models expressed in other languages already supported by the modelling environment, the corresponding inter-language mappings must be defined. With the increased adoption of Domain-Specific Languages (DSLs), this approach gives language designers essential support to rapidly define navigation within models expressed in the DSL as well as across model boundaries.

As future work, we are planning to examine the navigation facilities of non-UML modelling tools to ensure that our generic navigation approach can cover them. Furthermore, we will carry out an empirical user study to evaluate the usability of the navigation facilities offered by our navigation bar. Finally, we are planning to integrate our current navigation bar implementation with a modelling tool that supports language plug-ins.

References

1. Brambilla, M., Cabot, J., Wimmer, M.: Model-Driven Software Engineering in Practice. Morgan & Claypool Publishers, San Rafael (2012)
2. Pfeiffer, R.-H., Wąsowski, A.: TexMo: a multi-language development environment. In: Vallecillo, A., Tolvanen, J.-P., Kindler, E., Störrle, H., Kolovos, D. (eds.) ECMFA 2012. LNCS, vol. 7349, pp. 178–193. Springer, Heidelberg (2012). https://doi.org/10.1007/978-3-642-31491-9_15
3. Di Ruscio, D., Lämmel, R., Pierantonio, A.: Automated co-evolution of GMF editor models. In: Malloy, B., Staab, S., van den Brand, M. (eds.) SLE 2010. LNCS, vol. 6563, pp. 143–162. Springer, Heidelberg (2011). https://doi.org/10.1007/978-3-642-19440-5_9
4. Cicchetti, A., Di Ruscio, D., Eramo, R., Pierantonio, A.: JTL: a bidirectional and change propagating transformation language. In: Malloy, B., Staab, S., van den Brand, M. (eds.) SLE 2010. LNCS, vol. 6563, pp. 183–202. Springer, Heidelberg (2011). https://doi.org/10.1007/978-3-642-19440-5_11
5. Beard, D.V., II, J.Q.W.: Navigational techniques to improve the display of large two-dimensional spaces. Behav. Inf. Technol. **9**(6), 451–466 (1990)
6. Mackinlay, J.D., Robertson, G.G., Card, S.K.: The perspective wall: detail and context smoothly integrated. In: Proceedings of the SIGCHI Conference on Human Factors in Computing Systems, pp. 173–176. ACM (1991)
7. dos Santos, E.P., de Lara, S., Watanabe, W.M., Fortes, R.P., et al.: Usability evaluation of horizontal navigation bar with drop-down menus by middle aged adults. In: Design of Communication Conference, pp. 145–150. ACM (2011)
8. Combemale, B., DeAntoni, J., Baudry, B., France, R.B., Jézéquel, J., Gray, J.: Globalizing modeling languages. IEEE Comput. **47**(6), 68–71 (2014). https://doi.org/10.1109/MC.2014.147
9. Pohl, K., Böckle, G., van Der Linden, F.J.: Software Product Line Engineering: Foundations, Principles and Techniques. Springer, Heidelberg (2005). https://doi.org/10.1007/3-540-28901-1
10. OMG: Unified Modeling Language, 2.5.1, p. 802 (2007)
11. TouchCORE (2018). http://touchcore.cs.mcgill.ca/
12. ArgoUML - Free, opensource UML engineering tool. http://argouml.tigris.org/index.html
13. StarUML. http://staruml.io/

14. No Magic Inc.: MagicDraw. https://www.nomagic.com/products/magicdraw
15. Ideal Modeling & Diagramming Tool for Agile Team Collaboration. https://www.visual-paradigm.com/
16. Alam, O., Kienzle, J., Mussbacher, G.: Concern-oriented software design. In: Moreira, A., Schätz, B., Gray, J., Vallecillo, A., Clarke, P. (eds.) MODELS 2013. LNCS, vol. 8107, pp. 604–621. Springer, Heidelberg (2013). https://doi.org/10.1007/978-3-642-41533-3_37
17. Burrell, A., Sodan, A.C.: Web interface navigation design: which style of navigation-link menus do users prefer? In: Proceedings of the 22nd International Conference on Data Engineering Workshops, pp. 42–42. IEEE (2006)
18. Kitajima, M., Blackmon, M.H., Polson, P.G.: A comprehension-based model of web navigation and its application to web usability analysis. In: McDonald, S., Waern, Y., Cockton, G. (eds.) People and Computers XIV-Usability or Else!, pp. 357–373. Springer, London (2000). https://doi.org/10.1007/978-1-4471-0515-2_24
19. Kersten, M., Murphy, G.C.: Using task context to improve programmer productivity. In: Proceedings of the 14th ACM SIGSOFT International Symposium on Foundations of Software Engineering, pp. 1–11. ACM (2006)
20. EMF Website. Mylyn. https://www.eclipse.org/mylyn/
21. Robillard, M.P., Murphy, G.C.: Representing concerns in source code. ACM Trans. Softw. Eng. Methodol. 16(1), 3 (2007)

Protocol Syntax Development Using Domain Specific Modeling Languages

Goran Rajić[1](✉) 🆔 and Vlado Sruk[2](✉) 🆔

[1] Research and Development, Ericsson Nikola Tesla,
Krapinska 45, 10000 Zagreb, Croatia
goran.rajic@ericsson.com
[2] Faculty of Electrical Engineering and Computing, University of Zagreb,
Unska 3, 10000 Zagreb, Croatia
vlado.sruk@fer.hr

Abstract. Traditionally telecommunication protocols were developed by the use of the ITU languages such as SDL, ASN.1, and ECN. Recently, many parts of protocols are more and more being developed using model-driven development tools such as UML. However, in these cases, the syntax of protocol needs to be developed in separate tools creating issues of interfacing, integration, and maintenance. Additionally, the majority of today protocols are developed in a way that formal ASN.1 specifications of its syntax are not provided.

This paper presents domain-specific modeling language (DSML) used for the specification and development of syntax for a family of Diameter protocols. We are proposing the use of dedicated DSML tools for the protocols or family of protocols and its integration with the rest of the protocol development tool chain. Creating a protocol family-specific DSML enables more efficient development of protocol syntax since developers use the syntax for describing protocols that are very close to the notation used in protocol specification documents, exploit semi-automatic importers from informal formats and benefit from developed integration with UML and SDL languages.

Keywords: Communication protocols · Protocol syntax specification · Domain-specific modeling languages · Model driven engineering · ASN.1

1 Introduction

Many new communication applications and their functional requirements lead to new protocol definitions and their standardization. At the same time, legacy protocols, many of them considered as basic infrastructure, often need reimplementation on new target platforms. Such scenarios deal with an artifact base that should be highly reusable, grounded on a number of platform-dependent customizations and extra-functional requirements mapping. Today's competitive market-driven economies dictate engineering process requirements that have

© Springer Nature Switzerland AG 2019
P. Fonseca i Casas et al. (Eds.): SAM 2019, LNCS 11753, pp. 61–77, 2019.
https://doi.org/10.1007/978-3-030-30690-8_4

time-to-market and quality as their main components. These two requirements are usually being satisfied with the use of software engineering tools and processes that properly address variability, scalability, and maintainability of software artifacts in question. Such a situation positions protocol stack implementation as one of the more important tasks in the network infrastructure development as well as the development of other types of distributed systems.

Protocol stack development can be roughly divided into two areas: message content and format development and protocol semantics development. In line with the usual computer science and language engineering terminology [4], abstract content, structure and physical format of protocol messages can be denoted more commonly as syntax. Consequently, a set of valid messages of a protocol corresponding to the usual notion of a formal language. Syntax of the language or valid messages of a protocol can be further divided into the concrete syntax (CS) and abstract syntax (AS). CS describes the physical representation of a message in terms of a set of symbols making-up an alphabet of this protocol/formal language. AS represents a more structured domain that reflects actual language abstract content in terms of how small message entities can make-up compete valid sentences (messages). The semantics of a protocol is determining actions to be taken by that protocol entity. Actions can be triggered by events on internal interfaces of a protocol entity or as a response to the received valid or invalid messages over the communication interface. Results of actions can range from a change of state of protocol user executed over internal software interface of protocol entity, change of internal state of protocol entity itself, creating and sending a message to one or more peer entities as well as any combination of these activities. Due to the state controlling interpretation of protocol semantics, in this paper, protocols semantics is commonly referred to as control part of a protocol.

Historically, the control part of protocol development received comparatively more attention than the syntax part. This was probably due to perceived and experienced bigger challenges in the early development procedures of the control part of protocols. Consequently, considerable body of work addressing control part of protocol development is created [22,39]. Control part protocol development is accordingly standard part of university undergraduate curriculum in communication sciences majors. All aspects of control part development received abundant coverage, from the specification of control programs to the range of analysis techniques used on them including various verification techniques like model checking and dynamic testing. The use of more advanced software development techniques including model-driven engineering methods in the context of protocol control was investigated and such techniques entered mainstream practice.

In contrast to this situation, the development of protocol syntax and its interaction with the rest of the protocol development process received relatively little attention. Having well known theoretical base rooted in formal languages and parsing procedures, protocol syntax development is considered a well-understood problem with readily available efficient development techniques applicable in the industrial design organizations settings. Development of Abstract Syntax Notation 1 (ASN.1) [19] and Extended Concrete Notation (ECN) [20] formalisms and related implementation tools delivered to the industry very expressive, versatile out of the box third-party solutions to the protocol syntax development.

However, new challenges in the development of communications software for future systems, on which societal infrastructure will increasingly rely on, are arriving and need to be addressed. Security of developed software, both in terms of security of individual personal data sets, real-time data streams, access, and authorization mechanisms as well in terms of service availability - security of systems from various threats became paramount [33]. Typically, the third-party supplied solutions for protocol syntax development are lacking technical transparency to efficiently back-up forthcoming increased security requirements. Additionally, deployment, integration and variability characteristics of such solutions could be lacking in the support of system-level solutions to the security issues of today communication systems. In plain words, ASN.1 compilers produce source code that must be analyzed to be trusted, including part of delivered protocol encoding/decoding functionality that is requiring binary level verification. ASN.1 third party solutions have poor interaction with the architecture level solution that tries to deal with denial of service type of threats by load balancing and similar techniques. While one can always fall back to the trust on the business-to-business level and ensure a sufficient level of trust by using a combination of legal and business level (jurisdiction selection) measures, more technical and reliable solutions should be possible.

In this paper, we are proposing techniques that deliver more control to the development process of protocol syntax while keeping or improving the presently achieved level of efficiency of the development process and quality of produced software. We are proposing use of model driven engineering (MDE) [8] and domain specific modeling languages (DSML) [26,36] for addressing syntax specification and development of dedicated protocol families or individual protocols.

The structure of this paper is as follows: in Sect. 2 we are reviewing formal and model-based protocol development methods and place our work in this context. Section 3 describes our proposed methodology and describes its variations. Section 4 presents Diameter protocols family for which details of its DSML modeler design is given. Finally, Sect. 5 discuses previous work and conclude the paper.

2   Formal Protocol Development

Over the course of years, two wide families of languages that have the capability of and are used for protocol specification and implementation naturally formed. International Telecommunication Union - Telecommunication sector (ITU-T) [17] standardization body standardized several languages that address most of the problem areas of protocol design. Specification and Description Language (SDL) [21] is an agent-based semantics specification language used as prime specification and elaboration language in the telecommunication industry. While

SDL is more oriented to the architectural and data type descriptions, Message Sequence Chart (MSC) [18], a language from the same family, is used together with SDL for a more computational, executable specification. ASN.1 language [19] is used for the specification of the abstract syntax of various data type entities, with the focus on protocol message specification. Pair language to the ASN.1 is the ECN language [20] that allows for detailed concrete syntax development in tight relation with the ASN.1 specified abstract syntax. Together with other ITU-T languages, they form a complete solution for specification, implementation, and testing of software systems, specifically targeting telecommunication and protocol development domains. When we are referencing the methodology and use of languages from this family in this paper, we are using terms like 'ITU stack' and 'ITU stack languages'. We assume that when we use these two terms when referencing a specific language or concept from this family, it is (from functionality needed to be addressed in that specific context) implicitly clear on what concrete language or concept we mean, or otherwise, it is stated explicitly.

Object Management Group (OMG) [31] organization standardized several languages that are implementing principles of MDE. Focusing ourselves on the general-purpose languages we must mention Unified Modeling Language (UML) [29] as a central MDE language with many standardized extensions. Object Constraint Language (OCL) [27] is a language for query and expression of constraints on UML models with a possibility of application to other languages. These two languages together with UML's extension mechanisms [32] and a number of standardized and user specified profiles [25,30] form a comprehensive general purpose language base. These OMG languages and their variations with different application-specific extensions are used in many present-day development processes and large development organizations. Using specific extensions and customizations they enable embedded systems development as well as the development of communication systems and protocols as its component. Similar to the previous family of languages, when we are referencing the methodology and use of languages from this family in this paper we are using terms like 'OMG stack' and 'OMG stack languages' and assume it is clear from the usage context to which specific language we think is we need to address it.

There were a lot of recent developments in the area of OMG stack languages related to their applicability to the communications systems design [5,25]. Typically, these contributions introduce several extensions to the standard language base to improve its usability and expressiveness in the context of communications systems. Extensions are, usually, done using UML profiles as the most versatile of UML standard extension mechanisms [25,32]. Some of the developments use OMG's standardized design elaboration profiles like MARTE [30] as a base for further developments. Most of these techniques are focused on the control part of protocol design improving on UML's weaknesses, compared to ITU languages.

On the other hand, there is hardly any work that addresses the area of protocol syntax for the OMG stack. ITU language stack, on the other hand, has a much better syntax development support. The existence of ASN.1 and ECN languages with their extensions allow for excellent expressiveness and pragmatics of protocol syntax design. This is one of the advantages of ITU stack over the OMG stack development stack. Such an advantage is retained to the present days despite many extensions for development productivity added to the OMG stack tools over time. One solution to this problem would be to follow the same principle of adding extensions to the OMG languages to make syntax design in them more pragmatic. This approach would be realized by developing UML profiles that extend structural UML specification mechanisms and enable their use for syntax specification. While certainly possible, this kind of an approach would result in languages and related tools that rate very badly in their pragmatic properties. To start with, implementing some formal language for a specification of syntax by use of stereotyped classes would have very unnatural, clumsy concrete syntax.

The present situation of protocol standardization gives little opportunity for use of formal development properties of ITU stack languages both in the area of syntax as well as in the control part. Most protocols, both the legacy and new ones, are specified in an informal way or by some form of fundamental formal language specification formalism. The control parts of protocols are specified in an informal, narrative and descriptive form with no or few exceptions. Formally specified syntax of protocol would be amenable to the automated development processes using ITU languages supporting tools. Still, most of the protocols do not use ITU ASN.1 and ECN as specification languages.

The described situation places both ITU and OMG based development stacks as well as any of their possible combinations in a position that no integrated, formal and automated protocol syntax development can be done. ITU tools must translate most of the protocol specifications into ASN.1 and ECN formalisms to completely take advantage of automatic tools implementing that syntax and to seamlessly interface with the design of control part of the protocol. Such translation is a time-consuming and error-prone process as already mentioned that makes overall benefits of ITU stacks much less attractive.

OMG tools are more and more used for protocol development due to its larger user base as well as because they are typically implemented in the development process of embedded communication systems. Developing control part of protocols in OMG tools are acceptable or even more favorable compared to the ITU stack tools. However, presently, OMG tools have no means to specify syntax efficiently and in a formal way making them amenable to the automated generation of its implementations. The most common solution is such a situation is the use of external custom formalism to specify the syntax of a protocol and possibly use tools related to that formalism that can generate code implementing actual coding and decoding of messages of a specified protocol. This scenario leads to the additional requirements on the development process in the form of keeping track of versions of different artifacts produced. One has protocol specification, externally produced encoding and decoding code corresponding to that specification as well as to them related data types making up interface code to the control part of the code of a protocol. To archive integration of an externally specified protocol syntax and to it related and generated coding and encoding code with the control part of protocol one needs to create custom tools. Another option is to rely on the manual translation of generated data types corresponding to the specified abstract syntax of the protocol specification to the data types corresponding to the implementation of the control part of the protocol.

The described situation is happening in practice, for example, in case of implementation of radio access stratum protocol terminations in radio base stations and controllers of 3G/4G/5G cellular network infrastructure. Protocols such as Radio Resource Control protocol (RRC) [2] and similar protocols of the 3GPP cellular radio access networks are one of a minority of today's relevant and used protocols that formally specify its syntax by use of ASN.1 and ECN languages. Naturally, producing corresponding coding and decoding realization is done by using dedicated ASN.1 compiler tools typically supplied by third parties. However, these tools produce a programming interface consisting of a set of complicated data types corresponding to the protocol specification content and particularities of these external tools. Implementing control part of this protocol needs referencing this interface and its content in the form of data types. So, after specification and generation of protocol syntax, one needs to respecify produced data types in a tool that will specify and implement control part of those protocols. Since this is error-prone process and additional work to be done, even in a relatively favorable situation in which we have formal protocol syntax specification and in OMG stack modeled control part of the protocol, we are in an unfavorable situation. Such a situation requires additional tool development, and integration effort to provide a translation of syntax specification to the interface data types generated - work that depends on third party tool semantics. Otherwise, the designer needs to model abstract syntax generated by external tools in UML and match MDE code generation patterns with one external syntax tool.

Described not so favorable scenarios of protocol development appear after decades of development of procedures, formalisms, and tools that should support seamless communication protocols development. We argue that such a situation gradually developed due to years of development in two or more separate silos with the lack of interworking considerations. Methods and tools in silos of ITU, OMG and other approaches gradually diverged to the point that today interworking among them at least on the syntax development level is rarely considered. In this paper, we present our approach towards the solution of this specific narrow problem of protocol syntax development. Practical industrial experience in the development of telecommunications software leads us to the recognition of the importance of addressing the described situation. Providing methodology and tools that would allow for formal, automated and integrated development of protocols would be of great help for concerned development communities.

Following motivation and problem description, this paper proposes a solution to this situation that enables the integration of formal and informal protocol specifications with modeling tools that can interface with such formal protocol specifications and produce consistent corresponding encoding and decoding code. On the technical implementation level, the proposed solution is based and is in line with principles of model-driven engineering and uses domain-specific modeling languages to provide an effective solution to this problem. Our approach allows both ITU and OMG stacks to seamlessly integrate any new as well as legacy protocols specified in any format with at least some level of formality. Such a solution can coexist with the eventual use of ASN.1 tools for the protocols that have its syntax specified in that format. We automate or partially automate the creation of formal protocol syntax specifications from standards documents creating permissive importing tools that partially recognize informally specified content of that documents. Additionally, we integrate created tools for protocol syntax specification with the modeling languages of OMG and ITU stacks where control part of protocols will be developed as well as with tools that produce coding and encoding functionality corresponding to the protocol syntax specifications.

The described approach allows for a trade-off between the design effort invested in the development of proposed tools and the design-time convenience and efficacy of these tools when they are used for actual protocol development. Using the DSML approach we have the benefits of domain-specific based development paradigm which allows for the above trade-off. One can choose to implement various tool extensions that streamline the development effort for particular fragments of protocol development functionally as well for individual protocols or protocol families. We are mentioning several options to implement different functionality of protocol syntax development as an illustration:

- automatic import of legacy protocol specifications into the format defined by this DSML tool
- formal syntax development that is same or very close to the notation of original protocol specifications
- literate development of new protocols enabling sharing the same document that represents tool specification artifact and original protocol specification document format
- integrated and much more streamlined maintenance and evolution of protocol specifications.

Since we are using technological space that is of MDE nature, all MDE related benefits are readily available to our approach, benefits such as:

- platform-independent model (PIM) and platform-specific models (PSM) separation allowing for multiple target efficiency
- fast and seamless integration with the same technological domain tools as UML modelers
- the same features availability for ITU stack tools provided, they are implemented on the same technical space as MDE tools.

This paper illustrates the overall process of the development of supportive tooling for a particular family of protocols. Such an approach would illustrate how the similar tool support can be created for other protocols or protocol families and at the same time develops and presents tool support for one important protocol family, the family of Diameter application protocols [6].

3 DSML Based Protocol Syntax

Protocol syntax description proposed in this paper is realized using DSML [23] approach. Domain-specific orientation [23] allows for the specification of domain concepts with any chosen level of their detail. The model-based approach aspect gives to our proposal all of the model-based approach advantages. Among other things, such an approach allows for the PIM based specification. For implementation purposes, the proposed framework can add PSM orientation. PSM features are achieved with the addition of separate adornment models to basic semantics content models. Proposed DSMLs enable creating structures consisting of models having mutual relations. This DSML feature is achieved by using the mega modeling approach [7]. The next subsection discusses in more detail the architecture of DSML, it's model-based layers and the pragmatics of its implementation.

3.1 Model Based Protocol Syntax Design

While one could choose any existing model-based technology as a basis for implementation, dominant tools implementation for some of the legacy tools is making choice obvious. Eclipse platform [37] based EMF framework [35] is currently being most frequently used one, especially for OMG stack tools implementations. Its architecture consists of the usual three-four layer modeling setup introducing the notion of models (M), metamodels (MM) and meta-metamodels (MMM). These are corresponding to the usual notation of meta-levels named M1, M2, and M3, in the same order of appearance as in [14]. EMF's meta-metamodel is based on the Ecore language that can be seen as the almost ideal implementation of OMG's CMOF [28] sublanguage. With this choice, we are giving to our proposal genericity since OMG's MOF metamodeling language and its concepts are well known and theoretically founded. From the pragmatic side, the choice of EMF is sound since it makes integration with existing tools easier because many OMG stack tools are made on the same platform. DSML consists of Ecore compliant MM that describes domain language abstract syntax. Since it is a modeling language, it enables for graph-based expressiveness and with the use of OCL or similar constraints, it can provide additional expressiveness properties. MM content will depend on concepts specific to the protocol but due to Ecore expressiveness it can express any type of syntax description. One of the frequently used generic specification formalism is Extended Backus-Naur Form (EBNF) [16] that has a well-known mapping to modeling and graph-based languages [15].

3.2 DSML Content and Domain Modeling

The core of the proposed DSML language should consist of an appropriately chosen concept that corresponds to the important concepts of the domain of concrete and abstract protocol syntax. This means that classes of the DSML MM should correspond to the recognized concepts that represent essential elements of protocol syntax. However, concepts of the domain of protocol syntax can be modeled at a different level of details and with more or less inclusions of specific concepts of the target protocol. The selected level of detail should lead to the metamodel that is more or less general or more specific to the protocol in question. There is a trade-off between the reusability of MM and the level of detail chosen to be provided by MM. When designing new MM for a new DSLM one can roughly choose between following categories of MM:

- specific protocol
- protocol family-specific
- specification formalism specific
- generic protocol syntax.

Specific protocol MM contains classifiers that are least general and model directly syntax concepts of that specific protocol. A more general approach is to develop MM that is protocol family-specific recognizing important concepts of syntax unique and joint to the family of protocols. Using MM that is specification formalism specific means that we recognize specific concepts of a generic specification formalism used in that protocol such as, for example, some custom combination operators that build more complicated expressions from simple ones. Finally, generic protocol syntax MM means that it only contains most general primitives of some theory that has the power to represent syntax at some useful degree of expressiveness. An example of such style of MM used would be MM of EBNF formalism. This division of DSML MMs is not strict and serves the purpose to illustrate possible approaches. Concrete MM for particular DSMLs addressing specific protocol could use a mix of four singled out approaches. Using generic protocol syntax MM would mean that we are reusing universal MMs. For the first time, such MM corresponding to the, for example, EBNF would need to be created but any other its use would mean reuse with made more or less small modifications to the original MM. Moving from that kind of MMs to the specific protocol MMs would mean less and less generic MMs with fewer and fewer possibilities of its reuse.

The type of metamodeling used for DSML would mainly depend on the type of protocol for which we are creating DSML. In this paper, we are presenting the implementation of the DSML modeler and the corresponding tool-set for the family of Diameter-based protocols. We selected this protocol class of DSMLs due to the number of pedagogical reasons. Protocol family-specific type of MM that was used for its implementation is a good example of reuse possible in the approach to the protocol syntax proposed in this paper. Most of the design details and constructs are also applicable to the other classes of syntax DSMLs and hence give a good overview of issues in protocol DSML design for all classes. Diameter protocols are a good example of heavy reuse/modularity, diverse specification formats, and their formal base specification mechanism of EBNF.

The next section, building on this exposition, describes concrete Diameter protocol modeler development details as a show-case example. It is obvious that all solutions, discussions, and issues about this exposition can be applied for any DSML based protocol front end.

4   Diameter Protocol Family

Diameter protocol consists of Diameter Base Protocol (DBP) [6] and Diameter Application protocols (DAP) [1,10]. DBP is a generic protocol layer that is providing basic communication services for all DAPs. Application protocols are application-specific extensions that define specific syntactic and semantics details for application at hand. From a practical point of view, DAPs are concrete user application level protocols. There is one instance of DBP protocol implementation and there can be many DAP instances that all use single DBP instance. From a formal specification point of view, both DAPs and DBP are using the same mechanisms for protocol definition on both semantic and syntactic levels.

The semantics of all the Diameter protocol is specified informally, using narrative, hence with textual descriptions and with little or no automation possibility. In any case, this is a situation that holds for semantics for almost all protocols as well as for most programming languages of today. Hence the manual design of the control part of Diameter is the only option. Usage of the model and formal driven UML/SDL languages and its extensions are a natural choice in this case. Syntax of Diameter is defined with decorated EBNF rules that are for this specification usage specified in [9]. Decorations added to the EBNF are Diameter specific syntax mechanisms allowing specification of specific syntax fragments related to the primitive data types and similar typically highly protocol specific mechanisms. Decorations are not expressed using any of standard formal specification mechanisms but are integrated with documentation format and follow the same formatting rules in all Diameter specification documents. This allows for consistent and formal specification of decorations on the same level as main formal syntax specifications. Uniform specification documents structure, both on subsection level as well as on whole document level and its close relationship with the formal part of syntax specification allow for additional usability gains. All user text parts of specification documents can be stored in corresponding MM that is part of DSML. These models are having content that is preserving specification document structure with links to related formal syntax specifications. In turn, this allows for a literate model-based description of protocol specification allowing for round trip protocol modeling and specification on the documentation/specification side.

In summary, abstract syntax of Diameter DSML consists of three logical parts. Two of them, namely formal EBNF representation and its decorations are closely related and intertwined in one MM. Specification document informal content in a textual form corresponding to the protocol documentation in modeling form is represented by a separate MM. These two MMs has semantic mechanisms that realize linking and relation of documentation and formal syntax specification contained in its models. Figure 1 depicts MM of a Diameter modeler realizing formal EBNF representation and decorations. The next section addresses the detailed design of the concrete syntax of the Diameter modeler.

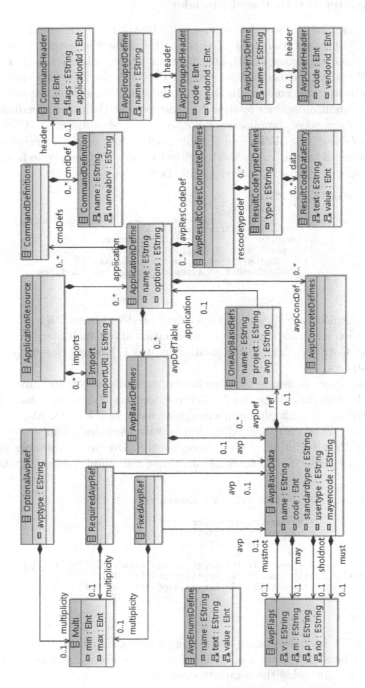

Fig. 1. Metamodel of Diameter protocol family DSML

4.1   Diameter DSML Based Modeler

Concrete syntax of protocol representation of DSML modeler is defined in Xtext [11] as an implementation tool of choice. Based on the design principles of Xtext, concrete syntax of DSML specification induces abstract syntax/MM of that DSML. DSML defined syntax naturally reflects the Diameter specification domain in its abstract content. In the proceeding of this section, we are describing DSML definition and its relation to constructs in Diameter specification.

Diameter protocol (application) consists of the number of Commands, Attribute Value Pairs (AVP) and Result Code definitions. The protocol itself can have many flags and values as the option values. The next code fragment of the Xtext specification code expresses this fact.

```
ApplicationDefine : APPLICATION
                    '<'? name=NAME '>'?
                    '{'
                        options=ApplicationOptions?
                    ( cmdDefs        += CommandDefinitions
                    | avpDefTable    += AvpBasicDefines
                    | avpConcDef     += AvpConcreteDefines
                    | avpResCodeDef  += AvpResultCodesConcreteDefines
                    )*
                    '}' ;
```

All of the elements are spread over-specification document with any order and documentation structure should store information about their place in documentation MM. Corresponding documentation syntax is having reference to each of these constructs.

Commands are messages that are having message unique identification and optional elements inhabiting its header portion. Its content consists of many AVPs with different multiplicity specified with usual EBNF signs. AVP contained in command can be AVP defined in own specification document or one that is referencing AVP definition in other specification. Due to the number of AVPs and its heavy reuse in Diameter applications, this implementation feature is important.

```
CommandDefinition : '<' name+=NAME (',' nameabrv+=NAME)? '>'
                    '::='
                    header=CommandHeader
                    avpS+=( FixedAvpRef
                          | RequiredAvpRef
                          | OptionalAvpRef )+ ;
FixedAvpRef    : multip=(Qual)? '<' avp=[AvpBasicData|NAME] '>' ;
RequiredAvpRef : multip=(Qual)? '{' avp=[AvpBasicData|NAME] '}' ;
OptionalAvpRef : multip=(Qual)? '[' ( avp=[AvpBasicData|NAME]
                                    | avptype=AVP
                                    )
                    ']' ;
```

Command's header data are consisting of application and command identification numbers and number of option flags. They are defined in specification documents locally inside the complete command definition.

```
CommandHeader : '<' ( 'Diameter-Header:' | 'Diameter Header:' )
                    id=INT
                    flags+=CommandFlags*
                    (',' applicationId=INT)?
              '>' ;
CommandFlags : ',' ('REQ' | 'PXY' | 'ERR') ;
```

AVPs are either referenced from other models or defined locally. If defined locally, they have a number of standard flags and typed values. These values are defined locally in one or a few tables for all AVPs defined in the concerned specification. Those that are not defined in the specification are having informal links to other defining documents. These links usually take a form of a document and section references even, in many cases, it can have less formal and precise forms. Due to that link and reference resolving mechanisms for AVPs and its validation, proposal, and completion features are useful features to add to the proposed DSML.

```
AvpBasicDefines   : {AvpBasicDefines}
                    AVPBASIC
                    '{'
                      avpDef+=AvpBasicData*
                    '}' ;
AvpBasicData      :
                    (   ref=AvpBasicRefs
                    | name=NAME
                      code=INT
                      ( INT ('.' INT)* )?
                      ( standardtype=AvpTypes
                      | usertype=NAME )
                      must=AvpFlags
                      may=AvpFlags
                      sholdnot=AvpFlags
                      mustnot=AvpFlags
                      mayencode=( 'Y' | 'Yes' | 'y' | 'yes'
                                | 'N' | 'No' | 'n' | 'no' )?
                    )
                    ;
```

Apart from the flag and typed values, locally defined AVPs must have defined syntax of its content. Its content can be in the form of an ordered collection of other AVP's or one of the primitive values, detailed of which are left out here due to lack of space.

All the DSML modeler concepts are defined with criteria of similarity with original specification document notation. This allows for low entry effort to using DSML modeler for protocol implementers already knowledgeable in protocol domain concepts. At the same time, this approach enables the parallel learning of protocol and DSML language for new users. The similarity of protocol specification format and DSML language syntax is at that level of details to enable direct copying of protocol into the modeler's editor. Adding DSML introduced delimiting symbols one can obtain complete DSML syntax from specification document with minimal effort. Modeler's syntax is designed with full delimiting and typing capabilities enabling complete safety and precise error detection. As any syntax/semantics directed modern editor, it supplies users with content assistance, auto-completion and similar productivity add-ones.

5   Discussion and Related Work

To the best of our knowledge, there is no prior work comparable to the one proposed and implemented in this paper. Protocol syntax has a long history, starting from direct language engineering methods use [3] and culminating with the use of ITU standardized ASN.1 language with a set of predefined encoding and custom CS coding language ECN. In the time after ASN.1 and similar approaches there were several proposals that go in the direction of the use of domain-specific languages (DSL) [26] in syntax protocol design. However, all of them propose either host language-internal DSLs or external DSLs staying in the technical space of classical languages and DSLs. These proposals typically address protocol design covering all its aspects leaving less space to focusing on pragmatic properties of syntax development.

Closest to our work is position paper [3] that directly proposes classic DSL as a means of complete protocol design. They focus more on the behavioral (control) part of protocol development and go into the direction of dependent types to increase the expressiveness of specification. Similar comments can be done for relevant work done in [38]. Recent work [24] that builds on the mentioned position paper focuses more on abstract syntax induced data types and its integration into control part of software development. They extend the action language of the modeling language to seamlessly integrate control part development tools with data types and tools related to the syntax. Being oriented on the BNF type of syntax only and not addressing the pragmatic properties of syntax development this work is more complementing our work than addressing the same problem. Work concerning a more pragmatic side of protocol development in the context of MDE is [34] but it only addresses the aspect of platform dependence and gives solutions in the context of the control part of protocol development. Finally, one should mention a large body of work done it the area of data description languages [12,13] where general DSLs to specify more amorphous data patterns were developed. Such developments support more Big data collection type of problems less focusing on strictly formatted protocols and pragmatics of its formal specification formats.

In this paper, we proposed the use of dedicated DSML developed for individual protocols and protocol families. Contrary to the previous work, we focused on the efficiency of the syntax development process and pragmatics of its integration with tools for the control part of the design. The proposed approach fosters the development of editors that allow for efficient specification of such protocols and familiarizes DSML developers and protocol developers with the protocol syntax details. Reuse of protocols fragments and use of developed importers of informal syntax fragments enable fast formal specification process for supported protocols. The integration of a such modelers with UML tools enables efficient development and integration of control parts of protocols with the syntax part. Creation of dedicated safe coders and encoders for protocol by use of MDE code generation is under development. In the future, we plan to improve present pilot coder and encoder generation tools as well as create support for other protocols and protocol families. We are also considering developing translation tools from developed DSMLs to the ASN.1 code to be able to test and compare crated coders and parser with the ones generated by currently more trusted ASN.1 generated code.

References

1. 3GPP: Evolved Packet System (EPS); Mobility Management Entity (MME) and Serving GPRS Support Node (SGSN) related interfaces based on Diameter protocol (2019). https://portal.3gpp.org/desktopmodules/Specifications/ SpecificationDetails.aspx?specificationId=3197, version 15.8.0
2. 3GPP: NR; Radio Resource Control (RRC); Protocol specification (2019). https://portal.3gpp.org/desktopmodules/Specifications/SpecificationDetails. aspx?specificationId=3197, version 15.5.1
3. Abbott, M.B., Peterson, L.L.: A language-based approach to protocol implementation. IEEE/ACM Trans. Netw. 1(1), 4–19 (1993). https://doi.org/10.1109/90. 222903
4. Aho, A., Lam, M., Ullman, J., Sethi, R.: Compilers: Principles, Techniques, and Tools. Pearson Education, London (2011)
5. Al Dallal, J., Saleh, K.: Synthesizing distributed protocol specifications from a UML state machine modeled service specification. J. Comput. Sci. Technol. 27 (2012). https://doi.org/10.1007/s11390-012-1293-1
6. Arkko, J., Loughney, J., Zorn, G.: RFC6733 Diameter Base Protocol (2012). https://tools.ietf.org/html/rfc6733
7. Bézivin, J., Jouault, F., Valduriez, P.: On the need for megamodels. In: Proceedings of the OOPSLA/GPCE: Best Practices for Model-Driven Software Development Workshop, 19th Annual ACM Conference on Object-Oriented Programming, Systems, Languages, and Applications, October 2004, Vancouver, Canada (2004)
8. Bézivin, J.: Model driven engineering: an emerging technical space. In: Lämmel, R., Saraiva, J., Visser, J. (eds.) GTTSE 2005. LNCS, vol. 4143, pp. 36–64. Springer, Heidelberg (2006). https://doi.org/10.1007/11877028_2
9. Crocker, D., Overell, P.: RFC5234 Augmented BNF for Syntax Specifications: ABNF (2008). https://tools.ietf.org/html/rfc5234
10. Eronen, P., Hiller, T., Zorn, G.: RFC4072 Diameter Extensible Authentication Protocol (EAP) Application (2005). https://tools.ietf.org/html/rfc4072
11. Eysholdt, M., Behrens, H.: Xtext: implement your language faster than the quick and dirty way. In: Proceedings of the ACM International Conference Companion on Object Oriented Programming Systems Languages and Applications Companion, OOPSLA 2010, pp. 307–309. ACM, New York (2010). https://doi.org/10.1145/ 1869542.1869625
12. Fisher, K., Mandelbaum, Y., Walker, D.: The next 700 data description languages. J. ACM 57(2), 10:1–10:51 (2010). https://doi.org/10.1145/1667053.1667059
13. Fisher, K., Walker, D.: The PADS project: an overview. In: Proceedings of the 14th International Conference on Database Theory, ICDT 2011, pp. 11–17. ACM, New York (2011). https://doi.org/10.1145/1938551.1938556
14. Gonzalez-Perez, C., Henderson-Sellers, B.: Metamodelling for Software Engineering. Wiley, Chichester (2008)
15. Hopcroft, J., Motwani, R., Ullman, J.: Introduction to Automata Theory, Languages, and Computation. Addison-Wesley Series in Computer Science. Pearson Education International, London (2003)

16. ISO/IEC JTC 1/SC 22: ISO/IEC 14977:1996 Information Technology - Syntactic Metalanguage - Extended BNF (1996). https://www.iso.org/standard/26153.html
17. ITU: International Telecommunication Union - Telecommunication standardization sector web page (2019). https://www.itu.int/en/ITU-T/Pages/default.aspx. Accessed 18 July 2019
18. ITU-T: Message Sequence Chart (MSC) (2011). https://www.itu.int/rec/T-REC-Z.120/en
19. ITU-T: Abstract Syntax Notation One (ASN.1): Specification of basic notation (2015). https://www.itu.int/itu-t/recommendations/rec.aspx?rec=x.680
20. ITU-T: ASN.1 encoding rules: Specification of Encoding Control Notation (ECN) (2015). https://www.itu.int/itu-t/recommendations/rec.aspx?rec=x.692
21. ITU-T: Specification and Description Language (SDL) (2016). https://www.itu.int/rec/T-REC-Z.100/en
22. Kaliappan, P.S., König, H., Kaliappan, V.K.: Designing and verifying communication protocols using model driven architecture and spin model checker. In: International Conference on Computer Science and Software Engineering, CSSE 2008, Volume 2: Software Engineering, 12–14 December 2008, Wuhan, China, pp. 227–230 (2008). https://doi.org/10.1109/CSSE.2008.976
23. Kelly, S., Tolvanen, J.P.: Domain-Specific Modeling. Wiley-IEEE Computer Society Press, Hoboken-Washington, DC (2007)
24. Kistel, T., Vandenhouten, R.: Extended type systems of action languages for the development of communication protocols. In: 2014 IEEE International Conference on Systems, Man, and Cybernetics (SMC), pp. 3054–3057, October 2014. https://doi.org/10.1109/SMC.2014.6974395
25. Kumar, B., Jasperneite, J.: UML profiles for modeling real-time communication protocols. J. Obj. Technol. 9, 178–198 (2010). https://doi.org/10.5381/jot.2010.9.2.a5
26. Mernik, M., Heering, J., Sloane, A.M.: When and how to develop domain-specific languages. ACM Comput. Surv. 37(4), 316–344 (2005). https://doi.org/10.1145/1118890.1118892
27. OMG: Object Constraint Language (2014). https://www.omg.org/spec/OCL
28. OMG: Meta Object Facility (2016). https://www.omg.org/spec/MOF
29. OMG: Unified Modeling Language (2017). https://www.omg.org/spec/UML
30. OMG: UML Profile for MARTE (2018). https://www.omg.org/spec/MARTE
31. OMG: Object Management Group web page (2019). https://www.omg.org/. Accessed 18 July 2019
32. Pardillo, J.: A systematic review on the definition of UML profiles. In: Petriu, D.C., Rouquette, N., Haugen, Ø. (eds.) MODELS 2010. LNCS, vol. 6394, pp. 407–422. Springer, Heidelberg (2010). https://doi.org/10.1007/978-3-642-16145-2_28
33. Rahimi, H., Zibaeenejad, A., Rajabzadeh, P., Safavi, A.A.: On the security of the 5G-IoT architecture. In: Proceedings of the International Conference on Smart Cities and Internet of Things, SCIOT 2018, pp. 10:1–10:8. ACM, New York (2018). https://doi.org/10.1145/3269961.3269968
34. Simonsen, K.: On the use of pragmatics for model-based development of protocol software. In: Proceedings of the International Workshop on Petri Nets and Software Engineering, 20–21 June 2011, Newcastle upon Tyne, UK, vol. 723, pp. 179–190 (2011)
35. Steinberg, D., Budinsky, F., Merks, E., Paternostro, M.: EMF: Eclipse Modeling Framework. Eclipse Series. Pearson Education, Addison-Wesley Professional, London (2008)

36. Tolvanen, J.P., Kelly, S.: Integrating models with domain-specific modeling languages. In: Proceedings of the 10th Workshop on Domain-Specific Modeling, DSM 2010, pp. 10:1–10:6. ACM, New York (2010). https://doi.org/10.1145/2060329.2060354
37. Vogel, L., Milinkovich, M.: Eclipse Rich Client Platform. Vogella Series. Lars Vogel, Hamburg (2015)
38. Wang, Y., Gaspes, V.: An embedded language for programming protocol stacks in embedded systems. In: Proceedings of the 20th ACM SIGPLAN Workshop on Partial Evaluation and Program Manipulation, PEPM 2011, pp. 63–72. ACM, New York (2011). https://doi.org/10.1145/1929501.1929511
39. Werner, C., Kraatz, S., Hogrefe, D.: A UML profile for communicating systems. In: Gotzhein, R., Reed, R. (eds.) SAM 2006. LNCS, vol. 4320, pp. 1–18. Springer, Heidelberg (2006). https://doi.org/10.1007/11951148_1

Industry 4.0 Applications

Use of a Pivot Diagram in SysML to Support an Automated Implementation of a MBSE Design Methodology in an Industry 4.0 Context

Régis Plateaux$^{(\boxtimes)}$ ⓘ, Olivia Penas ⓘ, and Farid Louni ⓘ

QUARTZ Laboratory, EA7393, SUPMECA, Saint-Ouen, France
{regis.plateaux, olivia.penas, farid.louni}@supmeca.fr

Abstract. In the Industry 4.0 context, the high demand for the integration of new emerging IT technologies into production systems requires their designers to find effective ways to manage the impact of these changes during the design phase, while meeting very tight time constraints. Based on the model transformation concept at the SysML (System Modeling Language) diagrams scale, we propose to define a pivot language, through the sequence diagram, to automatically ensure the consistency between the different diagrams used throughout a MBSE (Model-Based System Engineering) design methodology, and then to guarantee the consistency of the relative design artefacts. The transformation rules have been defined between the underlying elements of SysML and could be modified according to the methodology. Finally, some rules were implemented in the PTC Modeler tool to validate the approach.

Keywords: MBSE · Pivot language · Design consistency · SysML methodology · Engineering change management · Industry 4.0

1 Introduction

1.1 Context and Motivations

Current Industry 4.0 developments are encouraging the deployment of cyber-physical systems (CPS) and in particular cyber-physical production systems (CPPS). Whereas current production systems are designed as autonomous devices, consisting of several machines, modules and components, CPS and CPPS design has to integrate multi-domain systems and increasingly automated equipment with sensors, actuators and a communication network in an interconnected global environment [19, 33]. Such a transformation gives rise to a number of issues to be solved for industries that are looking to take advantage of the numerous performance opportunities offered by such systems. As a result, to support this transition, system design methodologies have to include automated design engineering activities [15, 16, 30].

Some recent studies have shown some commonalities between CPS and mechatronic systems considering a multiscale approach [7, 11, 25], particularly with regard to the design constraints resulting from such systems: heterogeneous and cross-domain systems, high functional, multi-domain and multi-disciplinary integrated systems, and

© Springer Nature Switzerland AG 2019
P. Fonseca i Casas et al. (Eds.): SAM 2019, LNCS 11753, pp. 81–98, 2019.
https://doi.org/10.1007/978-3-030-30690-8_5

managing dynamic physical interactions [27]. As a result, existing mechatronic design methodologies can cope with main CP(P)S design constraints.

Traditional system design cycle (analysis of customer needs, generation of derived requirements, functional analysis leading to the functional architecture, then logical and physical, as well as the concurrent pre-dimensioning activities allowing the evaluation of different architectures for the choice of a solution), reveals many discontinuities when moving from one step to another. The numerous design tools and methodologies for existing multidisciplinary and notably mechatronic systems initially came from different fields [3, 6, 28, 34]. Unfortunately, the integration of these tools for a global validation of the complete system was lacking. Still, models unification can help the different disciplines involved in design activities to optimize the system as a whole [4]. In fact, the integration of various multi-domain models of mechatronic systems can be achieved through two main trends: integration within the same tool [29] or through the interoperability of tools and languages [14, 23]. In parallel, the need to integrate the collaborative aspects required by the multidisciplinary integration has generated the development of design methodologies in the context of system engineering [17] and more particularly of model-based system engineering (MBSE). The integration of these different multidisciplinary perspectives into numerical models helps to increase the consistency of data and models across disciplines by improving traceability with requirements. However, sharing models (or at least common parameters) requires a semantic referential, common to all disciplines [26]. Therefore, for unifying the modeling of a multi-domain, multi-level and multiphysical system, such as a mechatronic or CPS system, one solution is to find a generic language/system representation tool. Actually, many MBSE approaches are based on the semiformal SysML (Systems Modeling Language) language [8, 9, 21, 32]. Indeed, SysML allows system architects to specify, analyze the structure and operations, and to define the system and its subsystems. In addition, it allows to verify and validate the feasibility of a system before its realization while offering a unique model at the system level. In this context, each designer can refer to a single model throughout the design cycle and has unique data that are shared by all other design stakeholders. This language has the advantage of offering a great semantic richness, because it allows to represent different views of the system thanks to its different diagrams and is particularly effective in modeling the requirements, structure, behavior, allocations and constraints of the system [10].

The previously developed methodology [21], named SE-READ (for System Engineering based Requirements Elicitation and Architecture Design) helps the System Architects to define the system architecture from stakeholders' requirements [21]. This design methodology aims at ensuring a consistent and complete modeling of the system, generating the System Model (SM). This model is elaborated through two main phases, each decomposed in several steps representing different specific system viewpoints (Fig. 1). The first phase is a black box analysis based on an external point of view of the system, which aims at providing a comprehensive and consistent set of requirements. The second one is a white box analysis based on an internal point of view of the system, which progressively leads to the internal architecture and behavior of the system, based on the previous set of requirements.

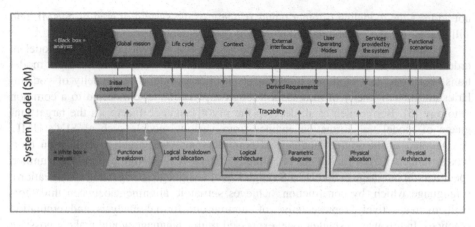

Fig. 1. SE-READ methodology process

However, the consistency of the design artifacts defined in a SysML model is only ensured through the MBSE methodology implementing them. Then, how to formalize the links between the modeling elements, based on a MBSE design methodology and expressed in SysML diagrams, and then automate the consistent design of new systems integrating industry 4.0 innovations?

1.2   State of the Art

Many methods and techniques propose some approaches to automatically verify system requirements based on SysML modeling. They use some profiles or combine their SysML modeling with simulation tools in order to verify that requirements related to the system performances or behavior are fulfilled.

Considering the evaluation of the physical behavior of the system and notably performances requirements verification, research work has focused on the exploitation of the parametric diagram, coupling it with physical simulation tools [22, 24].

Some authors propose to use Petri nets and Linear time Temporal Logic to formalize the specification of the system discrete behavior in SysML and verify the corresponding specifications [20]. Others authors, often from the software community, use UML semantics to automatically generate the algorithm or code to be implemented in software or embedded systems. For example, Apvrille et al. have developed the TURTLE UML profile (for real-time environment) to verify temporal constraints by model transformation in the RT-LOTOS simulation environment [2]. In parallel, Kraemer et al. propose notably to also use the "Petri-like" semantics of activity diagrams to define a set of rules leading to event-driven and bounded specifications that can be automatically implemented by model transformations and efficiently executed using runtime support systems [18].

Even if numerous research development have dealt with the model transformation, based on the UML or SysML semantics (notably of the activity diagram) to simulate and verify the temporal constraints and discrete-event behavior of their system, they do not address the modeling of other points of view of the system offered by SysML and still crucial for the generation of the system requirements specification.

Regarding this issue, some authors propose to use a pivot language or model in order to ensure the interoperability between different formalisms through model transformations. For example, Boukhari et al. address both heterogeneity of vocabularies and heterogeneity of formalism through a pivot model connected to a common ontology [5]. Berthomieu et al. develop the pivot language Fiacre, as the target language of model transformation engines from various models such as SDL, UML, AADL, and as the source language of compilers into the targeted verification toolboxes, namely CADP and Tina [4]. Finally, Aliyu et al. define a high-level unified specification language called HiLLS (High Level Language for Systems specification), a language which, by construction, achieves semantic alignment between three formalisms respectively representative of simulation, formal analysis and emulation practices. In this way, a single model expressed in this language would make it possible to obtain, by semantic correspondence, the artifacts adapted to the analytical methods thus integrated [1]. As a result, pivot models or languages coupled with models transformation appear to be an efficient way to cope with formalisms heterogeneity.

Finally, although SysML, as a semi-formal modeling language, is easy to use to provide a preliminary specification of a complex system including aspects of architecture, behavior and requirements, it does not guarantee that the modeling artifacts generated in the different diagrams of a system model are in line with the MBSE methodology on which they have been developed. Therefore, we propose to develop a pivot "diagram" concept to tackle this issue.

1.3   Case Study Description

Manufacturing industry has significantly improved its competitiveness over the last twenty years thanks to automation. Today, the Industry 4.0 context provides many possibilities for information, control and monitoring of industrial line machines thanks to the presence of numerous sensors and measurement and/or control means integrated into the machines. However, many manufacturing industries still make only limited use of these opportunities. One of the current challenges is to support these industries in adapting their production systems, by notably taking into account the new innovations and constraints of Industry 4.0 in the design or specification of production line machines.

In this context, the EUGENE collaborative project aims, among other objectives, at increasing the industrial productivity of a perfume packaging production line, by using the technologies and approaches developed by Industry 4.0. Thus, one of the challenges of the project is to improve product quality and production line availability by specifying machine adaptations on the production line, in order to: (i) make line maintenance more proactive (more preventive maintenance and less corrective maintenance), (ii) limit the impact of real-time measured deviations in the machines, on the nominal process of the lines, (iii) ensure maximum exploitation of the capacities of the production lines. The redesign of such production machines may, for example, integrate new functionalities, more communication and detection abilities.

The studied perfume packaging production line is described in Fig. 2.

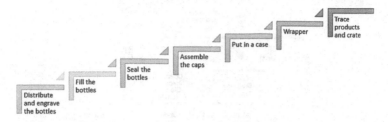

Fig. 2. Packaging production line description

We use the modeling of this case study to illustrate the relevance of our approach. The scenario is used to demonstrate the feasibility of the proposed approach to support the quick design of new innovative CPPS, in accordance with the increasingly shorter time-to-market constraints.

The rest of this paper is structured as follows: in Sect. 2, the dependency links resulting from the chosen illustrative MBSE methodology are described; in Sect. 3, the formalization process is presented through transformation rules and topological analysis; in Sect. 4, some implementation elements are provided, based on the previous case study; in Sect. 5, the approach advantages and limits are discussed; finally, the conclusions and future work directions are indicated in Sect. 6.

2 Methodology-Based Dependency Links

In this paper, the pivot diagram is used to elicit a comprehensive set of Derived Requirements from the constraints induced by each SE-READ sub-view of the black box analysis.

After defining the global mission (or function) of the system, the different lifecycle phases of the system have to be defined, in order to take into account all the constraints related to each phase. In this respect, for each lifecycle phase (LCP), a system context view defines the perimeter of the system and identifies the stakeholders/actors of each LCP and their external interactions between them and the system. Similarly, for each LCP, the "user operating modes" view outlines the operating modes of the system during that phase with respect to the system usage from the external point of view (by external actors). For each main operating mode, the services/functionalities provided by the system to the external actors (previously identified in the context view) have to be defined. In this view, the potential dependence relationships between these functionalities can be expressed. Finally, each functionality can be described through some functional scenarios, which represent the temporal sequences of the communications occurring between the system and the external actors that contribute to the considered functionality.

The logical process of the structural dependencies between these different views is given in Fig. 3.

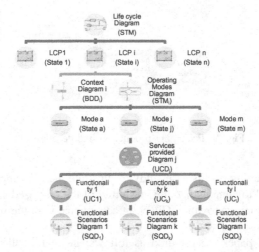

Fig. 3. Black box analysis views structure based on the SE-READ methodology.

3 Formalization

SysML is a composite language with more or less high levels of formalization, with respectively use case and state machine diagrams. Another weakness of SysML is that the relationships between these 9 diagrams are not completely defined and some added rules are necessary to ensure the consistency of the model in accordance with the methodology applied.

3.1 Approach Principles

Our proposal is based on the following idea: using the sequence diagram (SQD), as pivot "language" to capture all the dependency links (implicit and explicit) between the different artefacts generated in the various views required by the SE-READ MBSE design methodology. The idea is to complete SysML links as allocation link partially does and to capture the dynamic of the creation of the model of the system, in addition to describe the dynamic of the system. The principles of the approach are described in Fig. 4.

Two phases are necessary to guarantee the efficiency of this approach: the automation of the creation of new artefacts (Ci), links and diagrams based on the methodology rules and the verification phase, where each generated component has to be checked and updated if necessary. As the elicitation of the requirements is the result of the analysis of all structural and behavioral diagrams, obtained by the means of SE-READ methodology, requirements are dynamically generated as the methodology progresses.

Figure 5 presents the black box down phase allowing an increasing system model refinement to achieve the SQD operations, before the transition to the white box analysis.

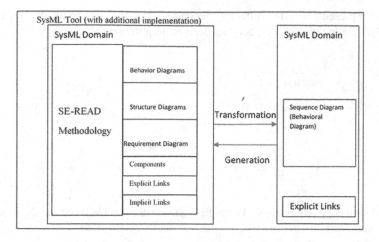

Fig. 4. Scheme describing the internal pivot

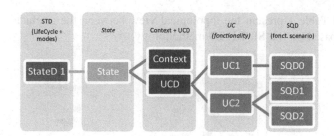

Fig. 5. Black Box down phase and its model refinement process.

During the different phases of the SE-READ methodology black box analysis, new diagrams and new components have to be created, either due to the refinement approach or to the elicitation treatments. Then all the interactions associated to the links between model artefacts will generate a new requirement to manage. Simultaneously, a traceability link is defined between the artefact/link and the new requirement. The hierarchical structure of the diagrams managed by the implementation of the SE-READ methodology in SysML induces then a derived requirements hierarchy (Fig. 6).

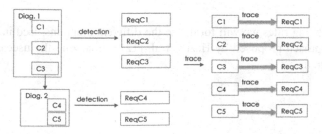

Fig. 6. Generic elicitation phase of requirements obtained by analyzing each diagram and sub-diagram of each view.

Figure 7 presents how the different (dependent) artefacts hierarchically transformed in the SQD are hierarchically traced as derived requirements.

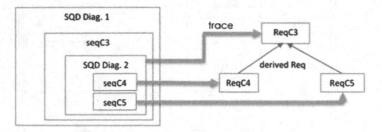

Fig. 7. Methodology process viewed with the sequence diagram hierarchy and the requirement hierarchy associated.

3.2 Transformation Rules and Topological Analysis

Figure 8 and Table 1 present the topological view between the artefacts and the diagrams used based on the SE-READ methodology.

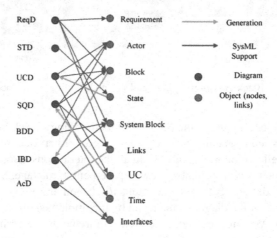

Fig. 8. Partial SysML diagrams/artefacts bipartite graph

Before defining rules we will formalize the different diagrams used in SysML. We extend the approach proposed by Hazra et al. [12] formalizing the usecase, sequence and time diagrams.

Table 1. Associated and generated artefacts in each diagram

Diagrams \ Components	Req	Actor	Block	State	System Block	Traceability/ Allocation	Association	UC	Time	Interfaces
RQD	■				■		■			
STD			■							
UCD		■	■	■			■			
SQD		■	■		■		■		■	
BDD		■	■		■					
IBD			■		■					
ACD		■				■				■

Definition 1. A SE-READ model is defined as a set of SysML diagrams.

M = {RQD, BDD, IBD, UCD, SQD, ACD, PARD) where each type of diagram D is a set of diagrams Di of type D. We use respectively these acronyms to requirement, block definition, internal block, use case (UC), sequence, activity and parametric diagrams.

In this paper, we mainly focus on the UCD and SQD.

Actors were imported from the BDD context into the UCDs. Each actor has to be used at least once in the set of UCDs associated to this context.

One UCD will be created from one State.

One SuperState will generate one UCD. Their sub-states will be linked to UCs of the UCD(SuperState) by the means of traceability links.

Definition 2. UCD is a set of {UC, A, R} as respectively finite sets of use cases, actors and relationships. These relationships could be the association between one actor and one UC, include or extend between two UCs and the generalization of an actor or a UC. As the need is mainly to represent interactions between artefacts and not to package them, the definition of the system boundary is not formalized here.

Definition 3. A $SQD_{(XY)}$ is a SQD generated from the XY diagram. $SQD_{(UCi)}$ is defined as a finite set of sequence diagrams SQD_j linked to a UC_i noted $SQD_{(UCi)}{}^j$.

$$SQD_{UCi} = \{SQD_{UCi}{}^j \mid UCi \in UC\}$$

Definition 4. $SQD_{(UCi)}{}^j$ is tuple {Ps, V, L, E, O, S} respectively Ps the set of lifelines for each participant, V the set of edges linked between two Psi, L the labeling function assigning each message to vi, E a set of events, O the mapping function ei/vi, S a finite set of states to which participant goes.

The SE-READ methodology guarantees a part of consistency defined as rules and automated modelling by following these rules (the developed scripts help the designer to define and to choose the suitable rule):

- A UCD (Use Case Diagram) is composed of a set of UCs (Use Case).
    Rule 1: $\forall UCi, \exists SQDj\ with\ j \in \mathbb{N}^*$
- For each UC, a SQD (sequence diagram) is produced.
    Rule 2: $\forall association, \exists Aj \backslash Psi = Aj$
- All diagrams have been considered as digraphs.
- Each UC is considered as a node in a digraph (directed graph).
- The weight of nodes (wnd) is evaluated thanks to the following rules:
    wnd = N_outer_include + N_inner_extend
  where
    - N_outer_include is the sum of all « include » links outcoming from the node, 1 in the incidence matrix,
    - N_inner_extend is the sum of all extend links incoming into the node, -1 in the incidence matrix.
- All specializations are unweighted.
- The topology of the UCs allows to define root_UCs. These root_UCs are found using the weight of each UC. Root_UCs will be the most weighted nodes.
- A root_SQD$_{(root\_UC)}$ will integrate all references (InteractionUse) to the SQD$_{(UC)}$ weighting on this root UC.
- Extension point condition in root diagram will be translated into the root SQD$_{(root\_UC)}$ as an « if » (Alternative) structure.

Every other structure will be possible when using these InteractionUse and Alternative ones.

- All actors needed in the UCD have to be used in the SQD$_{(UCD)}$.

Then, from the previous topological graph, we have to add specialization links and define actor leaf nodes and their links with other UC nodes. The root_SQD$_{(root\_UC)}$ will capture all the actors defined in the previous diagram (UCD). Actors of other SQD$_{(UC)}$

will be filtered from this diagram cancelling their link to the root_UC. Each UC whose links have been suppressed becomes the root of a subgraph. The following step is to apply a label filter to it, e.g. searching actors coming from an extension link, etc.

Our purposes are to validate and verify the whole model from black box to white box, to increase the ergonomics and to improve traceability. All these additional features are possible thanks to the automatic diagram generation.

Regarding the transition between the blackbox and whitebox parts, when an operation goes through the boundary between external actors and the system, at least one port and one associated artefact, either a receiver or an emitter will be generated on the activity diagram.

Regarding the validation of the transformation rules, the SysML properties are preserved due to the internal pivot language choice but the semantical point of view has to be verified. SysML as a nine diagrams composite language requires the same approach as models transformation to unify them.

It is clear that specific objects of modelling have still to be developed such as history operator needs a specific development to reproduce the behavior of state machine.

4 Implementation and Case Study

In this section, we describe the different software developments, in the PTC integrity modeler tool, which have been made based on previous algorithms, and following the steps included in Fig. 3.

The first script generates the context (BDD) and user modes (STM) diagrams from the life cycle (STM) diagram.

Using the case study of the perfume production line (PPL), we start with an existing STM diagram representing the lifecycle of the PPL (Fig. 9).

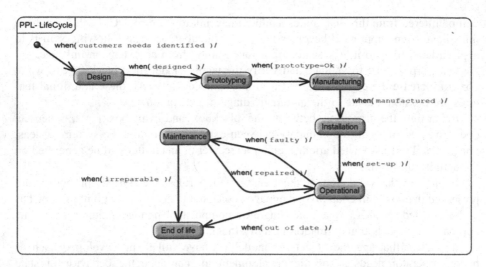

Fig. 9. Starting point: the case study (PPL) lifecycle diagram (STM).

Then the algorithm is described in SysML (through a STM diagram) in Fig. 10 and the developed Visual Basic script (VBS) (Fig. 11).

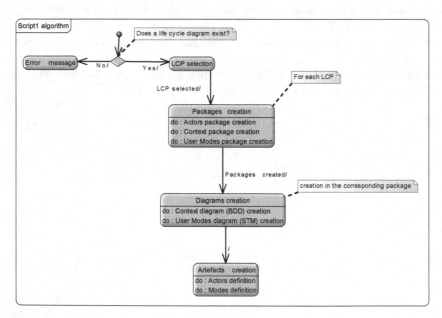

Fig. 10. Algorithm of the first developed Visual Basic script, generating for each lifecycle diagram state, diagrams of context and user mode.

```
Function RunToolUI()
    Set oStateMachineCycle = Dictionary.Item("State Machine","LifeCycle")
if oStateMachineCycle is Nothing Then
    MsgBox("No LifeCycle state machine")
    Exit Function
End if
Set oPackageTest1=Dictionary.Item("Package","Contexts")
if Not oPackageTest1 is Nothing Then
    MsgBox("Already launched")
    Exit Function
End if
creation = MsgBox("Do you want to create a context diagram and a user mode diagram? ",vbYesNo)
if reponse = vbYes Then
    RunToolUI = True
Else
        Exit Function
End if
End Function


Function CommitTool()
    CommitTool=False
' creation of packages
    Set oPackageContexts = Dictionary.Add("Package","Contexts")
    Set oPackageActors = Dictionary.Add("Package","Actors")
    Set oPackageModes = Dictionary.Add("Package","UserMode")
' number and name of actors
    actor_number = InputBox("How many actors do you need?","Number of actors",1)
    For i = 1 to actor_number
        Set oActor = oPackageActors.Add("Actor")
        actor_name = InputBox("What is the name","Name of the Actor"&i, "Actor" & i)
        oActor("Name")=actor_name
    Next
    Set oStateMachineCycle = Dictionary.Item("State Machine","LifeCycle")
    Set oPhases = oStateMachineCycle.Items("State")
    Set oPackageClonage = Dictionary.Item("Package","Clonage SysML")
    Set oBDDToClone = oPackageClonage.Item("Class Diagram", "BDD")
For each oPhase in oPhases
    if oPhase("Name") <> "Initial" and oPhase("Name") <> "Final" Then
        Set oBDD = oPackageContexts.CreateClone(oBDDToClone)
        oBDD("Name")="Context: " & oPhase("Name")
        Set oStateMachine = oPackageModes.Add("State Machine")
            oStateMachine("Name") = "User Mode: " & oPhase("Name")
        Set oStateDiagram = oStateMachine.Add("State Diagram")
            oStateDiagram("Name") = "User Mode: " & oPhase("Name")
    End if
Next
    CommitTool=True
End Function
```

Fig. 11. Basic VBS code necessary to implement the creation of context diagrams and user mode into PTC Modeler

The script asks, to the user, the number of actors and modes to be created and then generates the different modeling parts.

The resulting modeling elements applied on the case study model are presented in Fig. 12. The name have been defined by default but the user can also introduced.

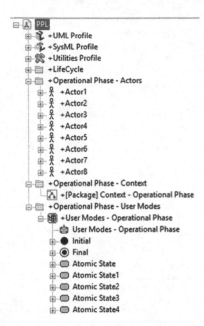

Fig. 12. Results of the first script run on the case study model

Then, the user customizes the generic elements generated in the package (e.g. actors' names) and defines the missing artefacts (system block, associations, transitions, etc.) on the generated diagrams.

Once the context and user modes diagrams completed (Fig. 13), the user can launch the second script, which creates a use case diagram (UCD) for each state/mode included in the user modes diagram. In the same manner as script 1, script 2 queries the selection of the User modes diagram to address, then it creates the Use Cases package, and generates as many UCDs as the modes contained in the User modes diagram, before asking for each UCD, the (primary and secondary) actors concerned and the number of functionalities (UCs) to be created.

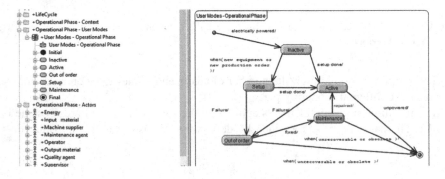

Fig. 13. Case study model manually customized by the user.

The resulting diagrams thus generated (Fig. 14) can then be completed by the user who adds the associations between the UCs and the actors, the name of the UCs, the possible relations between UCs (generalization, include, extend, etc.).

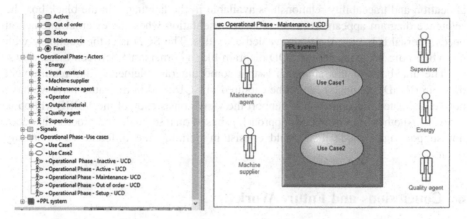

Fig. 14. Use Cases diagram generation applied to the PPL system.

Finally, the third script queries to select the Use cases package and then creates from a functional scenario (sequence diagram) for each UC contained in each UCD and another for the macro functional scenario for each UCD of a given LCP (Fig. 15).

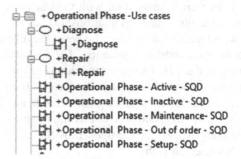

Fig. 15. Resulting model after having run the third script

5   Discussions

The use of external existing pivot languages like FIACRE requires some specific tools to compile the transformation [13]. Therefore to ensure the consistency between the different views and related SysML diagrams used during the blackbox analysis of a MBSE design methodology, we have chosen the sequence diagram as pivot language.

Even if usually, SysML structural diagrams and behavioral ones are natively linked by the means of common components to which they relate, the sequence diagram (SQD), as it offers the most refinement, allows to structurally integrate the depending modeling elements from various SysML diagrams and so to go beyond the simple allocation and traceability relationships available in the language. In the black box the sequence diagram appears as the level of representation where an external interaction needs internal behavior, the first revealed activities. The SQD is at the boundary with the white box. We consider the SQD diagram like a cornerstone between these views.

The drawback of this approach is that some diagram elements (like requirement diagram (ReqD) elements) cannot be captured in SQD, and in the same way, we have not yet validated this approach to support the view consistency of the MBSE whitebox analysis. Another limit is that this approach is based on a serial design process that does not support agile mode that would consist in defining the different views in any sequence.

6   Conclusions and Future Work

The purpose of our paper is to achieve a continuous structure of heterogeneous SysML diagrams using a pivot language. The unification of these diagrams has been done using SQD as pivot diagram. Each of them, excepted requirement diagram, has been transformed into a specific SQD.

We have presented in this paper a pivot language approach using the Sequence Diagram (SQD), as pivot diagram to capture, from the multiple views offered by different SysML diagrams, the dependent modeling elements of the black box analysis of a MBSE design methodology. The dependency links of the SE-READ methodology have been described. Then their formalization with the transformation rules capturing the SE-READ process and implicit diagram relationships has been done. The obtained SQD diagram brings out a topological structure between the different diagrams used in the methodology and all the modeling elements of the system model. Finally, the software implementation in the PTC integrity modeler to support the automation of a consistent design has been illustrated through an industry 4.0 case study. The current shortcomings of this approach, linked to its sequential mode and its restriction to only one part of the design methodology, could be overcome by using the formalism of the categories applied to ontologies, i.e. ologs, proposed by Spivak [31]. Work is currently underway to explore this research path.

References

1. Aliyu, H.O., Maïga, O., Traoré, M.K.: Un langage graphique pour la modélisation et l'analyse des systèmes réactifs. In: 11ème Colloque sur la Modélisation des Systèmes Réactif (MSR 2017), Marseille, France, 20 p. (2017)
2. Apvrille, L., Courtiat, J.-P., Lohr, C., de Saqui-Sannes, P.: TURTLE: a real-time UML profile supported by a formal validation toolkit. IEEE Trans. Softw. Eng. **30**, 473–487 (2004). https://doi.org/10.1109/TSE.2004.34

3. Bernardi, M., Bley, H., Schmidt, B.: New approaches for developing mechatronical products in multidisciplinary teamwork. In: 35th CIRP International Seminar on Manufacturing Systems, Seoul, Korea (2002)
4. Berthomieu, B., et al.: Fiacre: an Intermediate Language for Model Verification in the Topcased Environment (2008)
5. Boukhari, I., Bellatreche, L., Jean, S.: An ontological pivot model to interoperate heterogeneous user requirements. In: Margaria, T., Steffen, B. (eds.) ISoLA 2012. LNCS, vol. 7610, pp. 344–358. Springer, Heidelberg (2012). https://doi.org/10.1007/978-3-642-34032-1_35
6. Choley, J.-Y.: Mécatronique : une nouvelle démarche de conception des systèmes complexes. Technologies et Formations, pp. 29–35 (2006)
7. Choley, J.-Y., Mhenni, F., Nguyen, N., Baklouti, A.: Topology-based safety analysis for safety critical CPS. Procedia Comput. Sci. **95**, 32–39 (2016). https://doi.org/10.1016/j.procs.2016.09.290
8. Estefan, J.A.: Survey of model-based systems engineering (MBSE) methodologies. Incose MBSE Focus Group **25**, 1–12 (2007)
9. Friedenthal, S., Moore, A., Steiner, R.: A Practical Guide to SysML - the Systems Modeling Language. Elsevier/Morgan Kaufmann, Amsterdam; Boston (2008)
10. Friedenthal, S., Moore, A., Steiner, R.: OMG systems modeling language (OMG SysMLTM) tutorial. In: INCOSE International Symposium, vol. 18, pp. 1731–1862 (2008). https://doi.org/10.1002/j.2334-5837.2008.tb00914.x
11. Guérineau, B., Bricogne, M., Durupt, A., Rivest, L.: Mechatronics vs. cyber physical systems: towards a conceptual framework for a suitable design methodology. In: 2016 11th France-Japan 9th Europe-Asia Congress on Mechatronics (MECATRONICS)/17th International Conference on Research and Education in Mechatronics (REM), pp. 314–320 (2016)
12. Hazra, R., Dey, S.: Consistency between use case, sequence and timing diagram for real time software systems. Int. J. Comput. Appl. **85**, 17–23 (2014). https://doi.org/10.5120/14924-3444
13. Heng, S.: Transformation de modèles UML vers des programmes Fiacre. LABSTICC/ENSTA Bretagne (2012)
14. Iraqi-Houssaini, M., Kleiner, M., Roucoules, L.: Vers une ingénierie produit collaborative et interopérable basée sur les modèles. Un cadre général pour l'acquisition des données métier. Revue des Sciences et Technol. de l'Inf. - Série ISI: Ingénierie des Systèmes d'Inf. **17**, 79–94 (2012)
15. Jarratt, T.A.W., Eckert, C.M., Caldwell, N.H.M., Clarkson, P.J.: Engineering change: an overview and perspective on the literature. Res. Eng. Des. **22**, 103–124 (2011). https://doi.org/10.1007/s00163-010-0097-y
16. Kidd, M.W., Thompson, G.: Engineering design change management. Integr. Manuf. Syst. **11**, 74–77 (2000)
17. Kossiakoff, A., Sweet, W.N., Seymour, S.J., Biemer, S.M.: Systems Engineering Principles and Practice. Wiley, Hoboken (2011)
18. Kraemer, F.A., Herrmann, P.: Reactive semantics for distributed UML activities. Formal Tech. Distrib. Syst. 17–31 (2010). https://doi.org/10.1007/978-3-642-13464-7_3
19. Lee, E.A.: Cyber physical systems: design challenges. In: 2008 11th IEEE International Symposium on Object and Component-Oriented Real-Time Distributed Computing (ISORC), pp 363–369 (2008)
20. Linhares, M.V., de Oliveira, R.S., Farines, J., Vernadat, F.: Introducing the modeling and verification process in SysML. In: 2007 IEEE Conference on Emerging Technologies and Factory Automation (EFTA 2007), pp. 344–351 (2007)

21. Mhenni, F., Choley, J.-Y., Penas, O., Plateaux, R., Hammadi, M.: A SysML-based methodology for mechatronic systems architectural design. Adv. Eng. Inform. **28**, 218–231 (2014)
22. Morkevicius, A., Jankevicius, N.: An approach: SysML-based automated requirements verification. In: 2015 IEEE International Symposium on Systems Engineering (ISSE), pp. 92–97 (2015)
23. Paviot, T.: Méthodologie de résolution des problèmes d'interopérabilité dans le domaine du Product Lifecycle Management. Ph.D. thesis, École Centrale Paris (2010)
24. Peak, R.S., Burkhart, R.M., Friedenthal, S.A., Wilson, M.W., Bajaj, M., Kim, I.: 9.3.2 simulation-based design using SysML part 1: a parametrics primer. In: INCOSE International Symposium, vol. 17, pp. 1516–1535 (2007). https://doi.org/10.1002/j.2334-5837.2007.tb02964.x
25. Penas, O., Plateaux, R., Patalano, S., Hammadi, M.: Multi-scale approach from mechatronic to Cyber-Physical Systems for the design of manufacturing systems. Comput. Ind. **86**, 52–69 (2017)
26. Plateaux, R., Penas, O., Bricogne, M., Guerineau, J., Rowson, H., Maquin, K.: A semantic dictionary to support multidisciplinary design collaboration in an extended enterprise context. In: 20th International Conference on Research and Education in Mechatronics (REM 2019)/IEEE. Wels, Austria (2019)
27. Plateaux, R., Penas, O., Choley, J., Mhenni, F., Hammadi, M., Louni, F.: Evolution from mechatronics to cyber physical systems: an educational point of view. In: 2016 11th France-Japan 9th Europe-Asia Congress on Mechatronics (MECATRONICS)/17th International Conference on Research and Education in Mechatronics (REM), pp. 360–366 (2016)
28. Sell, R., Tamre, M.: Integration of V-model and SysML for advanced mechatronics system design. In: The 6th International Workshop on Research and Education in Mechatronics REM, pp. 276–280 (2005)
29. Sharpe, J.E.: Computer tools for integrated conceptual design. Des. Stud. **16**, 471–488 (1995)
30. Siddharth, L., Sarkar, P.: A methodology for predicting the effect of engineering design changes. Procedia CIRP **60**, 452–457 (2017). https://doi.org/10.1016/j.procir.2017.03.071
31. Spivak, D.I., Kent, R.E.: Ologs: a categorical framework for knowledge representation. PLoS ONE **7**, e24274 (2012). https://doi.org/10.1371/journal.pone.0024274
32. Thramboulidis, K.: The 3 + 1 SysML view-model in model integrated mechatronics. J. Softw. Eng. Appl. **03**, 109–118 (2010). https://doi.org/10.4236/jsea.2010.32014
33. Wang, L., Törngren, M., Onori, M.: Current status and advancement of cyber-physical systems in manufacturing. J. Manuf. Syst. **37**, 517–527 (2015). https://doi.org/10.1016/j.jmsy.2015.04.008
34. Yan, H.-S.: A methodology for creative mechanism design. Mech. Mach. Theory **27**, 235–242 (1992)

Modeling and Code Generation Framework for IoT

Mohammad Sharaf[1]($\boxtimes$), Mai Abusair[1], Rami Eleiwi[2], Yara Shana'a[2], Ithar Saleh[2], and Henry Muccini[3]

[1] Computer Science Department, An-Najah National University, Nablus, Palestine
massharaf@yahoo.com, mai.abusair@gmail.com
[2] Networks and Security Department, An-Najah National University, Nablus, Palestine
rami.ilaiwi1997@gmail.com, yaraadnan177@gmail.com, net.itharsaleh@gmail.com
[3] DISIM Department, University of L'Aquila, L'Aquila, Italy
henry.muccini@univaq.it

Abstract. In the Internet of Things (IoT) every physical device has an embedded technology that interacts with internal and external states. The heterogeneity of devices and networks complicates the mission of implementing and integrating the objects in IoT systems. In this paper, we present our model driven code generation framework, called CAPSml. The framework enables IoT designers and architects who are using CAPS environment to transform CAPS software model into ThingML model. CAPS is an architecture-driven modeling framework for the development of IoT Systems. ThingML includes modeling language and framework designed for IoT systems to support code generation for multi-platform targets.

1 Introduction

Nowadays most systems are relying in their development and evolution on reusing and customizing open-source components, services and frameworks. Model-Driven Engineering (MDE) has been widely used in system development. MDE can enable analysis process, promote communications between system stakeholders, simplify design process and facilitate software production [1].

IoT technologies aim at integrating objects into a communicating environment. A significant challenge in IoT system development is to produce a code that reflects concerns of IoT system specification and design. Accordingly, many issues in IoT systems life cycle are targeted by researchers. The CAPS has been realized to model and analyze IoT architectures [2]. ThingML framework adopted the idea of facilitating code generation for IoT systems [3]. Our approach aims at covering a full chain of modeling and analyzing using CAPS, and then implementing using the power of ThingML code generation.

This paper proposes CAPSml code generation framework built of top of CAPS modeling framework [4,5]. The framework follows MDE approach to

© Springer Nature Switzerland AG 2019
P. Fonseca i Casas et al. (Eds.): SAM 2019, LNCS 11753, pp. 99–115, 2019.
https://doi.org/10.1007/978-3-030-30690-8_6

transform SAML-CAPS model into ThingML model. SAML model represents the software architecture structural and behavioral view in CAPS framework [6]. ThingML model represents software components and configurations that describe their interconnection in ThingML framework [3]. The transformation from SAML to ThingML is performed using CAPSml code generation framework. The aim of CAPSml is to allow IoT developers to mitigate their worries of learning programming languages that implement their IoT systems. In addition, the paper suggests a methodology for modeling, transforming and generating code for IoT systems. It aims to facilitate IoT systems development.

This paper is organized as follows: Sect. 2 presents a brief description for CAPS. Section 3 presents a brief description for ThingML. Then, Sect. 4 introduces the CAPSml code generation framework. Afterward, Sect. 5 provides the modeling and code generation methodology. Section 6 shows a case study example. Finally, Sect. 7 concludes the work.

2   The CAPS Background

CAPS is a modeling framework that was formerly initiated at The University of L'Aquila [4,6]. It has a tool for Architecting Cyber-Physical Systems (CPS) [2,7,8]. The terms CPS and IoT are used interchangeably. They both refer to the integration of digital capabilities, including systems of physical devices and network connectivity [9].

CAPS offers a rich modeling framework that performs a separation of concerns among different modeling views. It is designed and implemented taking into account three architectural views: the software architecture structural and behavioral view (SAML), see Figs. 1 and 2, respectively, the hardware view (HWML), and the physical space view (SPML) [6]. Moreover, CAPS tool provides a graphical user interface for modeling the three views. Accordingly, CAPS provides abstractions for low-level details of the different views, enhances reuse, and supports the ability to model the time and space. Moreover, CAPS allows stakeholders to perform analysis for architectural design decisions at earlier stages of the CPS development life cycle.

In this paper, we focus on SAML view for the sake of performing code generation. SAML modeling allows designers to define a software architecture that is basically constructed of a collection of software Components and Connections: (i) The Component: It is a unit of computation with internal state and defined interface. Each Component can contain several modes that specify its state. The behavior in each Component's mode is denoted by a set of events, actions and conditions. The Components can exchange data by passing messages through message ports. (ii) The Connection: It defines the communication between Components. It sets the source and target Components for the communication channel between two message ports of two different Components. For more information about SAML, refer to the full work in [6].

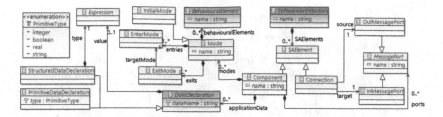

Fig. 1. SAML metamodel: structural concepts [6]

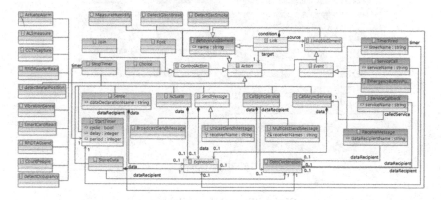

Fig. 2. SAML metamodel: behavioral concepts [6]

3   The ThingML Background

ThingML includes a modeling language combines software modeling constructs for designing and implementing IoT systems [3]. It has an open-source tool designed for supporting code generation and a highly customizable multi-platform code generation framework. ThingML tool targets heterogeneous platforms and has a set of compilers able to transform a ThingML model into fully operational code, in various languages (e.g. C, Java, Javascript), ready to build and run.

The ThingML language is based on two fundamental structures [3], see Fig. 3: (i) Thing: It represents software component. It is an implementation unit, also referred to as process or component. A Thing can assign properties, functions, messages and ports. Moreover, it can contain a set of state machines conforming to the UML state charts. The properties represent the variables that are defined locally inside the Thing. The functions can be treated as local functions inside the Thing and can not be accessed from the outside world. The ports are the only public interface in the ThingML language and they are used to send and receive messages that are defined within a Thing. Further, the internal behavior of a Thing is demonstrated using orchestration of composite states that are expressed using Event-Condition-Action (ECA) fashion. (ii) Configuration: It

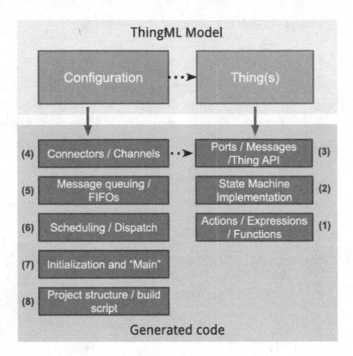

Fig. 3. ThingML model [3]

describes the Things interconnection. It has a set of instances of the pre-defined Things, and a set of connectors between instances ports.

ThingML was developed based on MDE principles. It is used to develop IoT systems ranging from research case studies to product development in industry projects. For more information about ThingML, refer to [3].

4   CAPSml Code Generation Framework

In this section, we will introduce our CAPSml framework that aims to transform SAML model in CAPS into ThingML language. The transformation process in CAPSml starts from the ecore and xmi files of SAML. Then, through several model to text transformations, performed in Acceleo[1], the contents of SAML model is mapped to contents in ThingML model. Finally, a complete ThingML language is generated automatically and is able to be imported directly in ThingML framework.

The fundamental part in the code generation framework is the process of mapping SAML to ThingML. The mapping benefits from the similarities in concepts between the SAML and ThingML models. Basically, the Component in SAML meets the Thing in ThingML; both of them declare a computational unit

---

[1] https://www.eclipse.org/acceleo/.

which includes a set of behavioral elements like actions, events and conditions. Further, the Connection between the Components in SAML is mapped to the connector in the Configurations part of the ThingML language.

The CAPSml code generation framework passes through four phases to perform model transformation. The preparation, component conversion and connection conversion phases, Sects. 4.1, 4.2 and 4.3, respectively, aim to build the Acceleo code file. The fourth phase, Sect. 4.4, aims to launch the CAPSml framework to be ready for converting CAPS-SAML model xmi file into ThingML file. These phases are described in the following sections.

4.1   Preparation Phase

In this phase, we set the URI of the SAML meta model, see Line 2 Fig. 4. Then, we set the starting point of the conversion at the top class in SAML, which is the SoftwareArchitecture class shown in Line 4 Fig. 4. From this main class we can move gradually to all the software elements indicated in SAML meta model. Further, we set the target name of the file that will have the conversion results (CAPS.thingml), see Line 7 Fig. 4. Finally, we import a special library in ThingML language that will be needed for the data types definitions, see Line 8 Fig. 4.

```
1  [comment encoding = UTF-8 /]
2  [module main('http://ualberta.ssrg.components')/]
3
4  [template public main(element : SoftwareArchitecture)]
5   [comment @main /]
6
7  [file ('CAPS.thingml', false, 'UTF-8')]
8  import "datatypes.thingml" from stl
9
```

Fig. 4. Code generation preparation

4.2   Component Conversion Phase

In this phase, we map the Component with its elements in SAML to the Thing and their correspondences in ThingML. The conversion starts from mapping the Component into Thing, see Fig. 6. Basically, any Component in SAML has primitive data declarations, ports and modes. These are transformed as follows:

1. Primitive data declarations: They are variables defined and used locally during the processes performed inside the Component. Every data declaration is mapped into property in ThingML language, see Fig. 7. Each property represents a local variable to be used inside the Thing. It is important to mention that the real data type in CAPS is converted into float data type in ThingML

```
10  thing fragment Messages {
11    [for (messComp : Component | Components)]
12      [for (dataDec : PrimitiveDataDeclaration | applicationData->
            filter(PrimitiveDataDeclaration)->asSequence())]
13        [if (dataDec.type.toString().equalsIgnoreCase('real'))]
14    message [dataDec.dataName/] (value : Float)
15        [else]
16    message [dataDec.dataName/] (value : [dataDec.type.toString()
                                        .toUpperFirst()/])
17      [/if]
18    [/for]
19    [/for]
20  }
```

Fig. 5. Messages variables transformation

```
22  [for (comp : Component | Components)][comment building Things /]
23  thing [comp.name/] includes Messages {
24
```

Fig. 6. Component transformation

```
25  // ***** Variables *****
26    [for (var : PrimitiveDataDeclaration | applicationData->
          filter(PrimitiveDataDeclaration)->asSequence())]
27    property [var.dataName/] : [if (var.type.toString()
            .equalsIgnoreCase('real'))]Float[else]
            [var.type.toString().toUpperFirst()/][/if]
28    [/for]
29
```

Fig. 7. Data declarations variables transformation

that does not define real data type. In addition, variables that are used in exchanging messages between Components in SAML are mapped to messages in ThingML. We created a special kind for the Thing, named fragment, used to define all the variables to be used in components messages exchanging. Thus, every Component has a message to be sent or received will include the fragment to be able to use the messages values. Transformation of messages variables is shown in Fig. 5.

2. Ports: They are used as an interface for the Component. Each Component in SAML has zero or more message ports. These message ports might be InMessagePort or OutMessagePort. A Connection links the OutMessagePort as a source to InMessagePort as a target. These ports might receive four different types of messages; UnicastSendMessage, BroadcastSendMessage, MulticastSendMessage or a ReceiveMessage. The InMessagePort in SAML is mapped to 'required port' in ThingML, and the OutMessagePort is mapped to 'provided port' in ThingML. The type of message to be sent through the ports in ThingML can be determined using 'sends' and 'receives' elements. In case of broadcast message, we determine only the data to be sent from the 'provided port' in 'sends' and it will reach all connected ports. Otherwise, in unicast

```
41   // ***** Ports *****
42   [for (modePorts : Mode | modes)]
43    [for (it : BehaviouralElement | behaviouralElements)]
44     [if (oclIsKindOf(UnicastSendMessage))]
45      [for (mess : MessagePort | it->
             filter(UnicastSendMessage).toMessagePorts)]
46   provided port [mess.name/] {
47    sends [it->filter(UnicastSendMessage).dataRecipient.dataName/]
48    receives [it->filter(UnicastSendMessage).receiverName/]
49   }
50      [/for]
51     [elseif (oclIsKindOf(BroadcastSendMessage))]
52      [for (mess : MessagePort | it->
             filter(BroadcastSendMessage).toMessagePorts)]
53   provided port [mess.name/] {
54    sends [it->filter(BroadcastSendMessage).dataRecipient.dataName/]
55   }
56      [/for]
57     [elseif (oclIsKindOf(MulticastSendMessage))]
58      [for (mess : MessagePort | it->
             filter(MulticastSendMessage).toMessagePorts)]
59   provided port [mess.name/] {
60    sends [it->filter(MulticastSendMessage).dataRecipient.dataName/]
61      [for (receivers : String | it->
               filter(MulticastSendMessage).receiverNames->asSequence())]
62    receives [receivers/]
63      [/for]
64   }
65      [/for]
66     [elseif (oclIsKindOf(ReceiveMessage))]
67      [for (mess : MessagePort | it->
             filter(ReceiveMessage).fromMessagePorts)]
68   required port [mess.name/] {
69    receives [it->filter(ReceiveMessage).dataRecipient.dataName/]
70   }
71      [/for]
72     [/if]
73    [/for]
74   [/for]
```

Fig. 8. Ports transformation

message, we determine the data to be sent in 'sends' and the receiver of the data in 'receives'. Moreover, in multicast message, we determine the data to be sent in 'sends' and the group of selected receivers (filtered out from SAML MultiCastMessage) in 'receives'. Finally, if the port receives a message, then we set the port name in the 'required port' and we determine the data to be received in 'receives'. Figure 8 shows the ports transformations that take in consideration the different message types.

3. Modes: It represents the behavioral part of the Component. The Component can have several modes in which the initial mode is determined and the orchestration of the entrance and exit for the rest of modes is specified. ThingML has a corresponding similar concept to modes called states. ThingML has a statechart that includes one or more states which illustrate the behavioral execution of the Thing. Each statechart indicates the initial mode in CAPS-SAML as initial state (statechart init) and other modes as states. Typically,

each state has an entry source that can be determined through 'on entry' in ThingML. Mode transformation to state is shown in Fig. 10. Every mode has behavioral elements that describe the concept of the mode's execution. The behavioral elements can mainly be events, conditions and actions, and can also be the links that specify the source and target behavioral elements. Every link between behavioral elements must consider the event that causes the transition from a behavioral element to another, the condition to be checked in a choice and the action to be taken. The action might be nested choice, send message or behavioral functionality. Every concept in these behavioral elements has almost its correspondence in ThingML. Accordingly, every event in CAPS-SAML is mapped to event in ThingML, condition is mapped to guard, link is mapped to transition, and action in CAPS-SAML can be translated to action in ThingML (in case the action is send message or choice), see Fig. 11, or otherwise to function in ThingML. The function can be responsible of several actions like sensing data, store data, actuating, etc. See Fig. 12 to see behavioral element in the mode turned into function. See Fig. 9 that summarizes the mapping between Component and Thing elements.

4.3　Connection Conversion Phase

In this phase, we map the Connection concept in SAML to the Configuration concept in ThingML. The Connection specifies the communication link between Components ports in SAML. Thus, in the configuration part in ThingML, we specify for every Component in SAML an instance in ThingML. The Connection between the target and source ports in SAML is mapped to Connector in ThingML with the required port name => provided port name. See Fig. 13 for Connection transformation. By the end of this phase, we will have "CAPSml.mtl" file that contains the Acceleo code required for ThingML code generation.

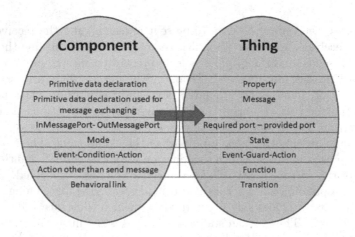

Fig. 9. Mapping between Component elements in SAML and Thing elements in ThingML

```
76   // ***** States *****
77   [for (mode : Mode | modes)][comment display states /]
78   [if (mode.oclIsTypeOf(InitialMode))]statechart init [mode.name/] {[/if]
79    state [mode.name/] {
80     on entry do
81     [for (onEntry : BehaviouralElement | behaviouralElements)]
82      [if (onEntry.eClass().eSuperTypes->last().name.equalsIgnoreCase('Action'))]
83       [if (onEntry->filter(Action).incoming.source.oclIsKindOf(Choice)
             ->asSequence()->first().toString().equalsIgnoreCase('true')._not())]
84       [onEntry.name/]([if (onEntry.oclIsKindOf(StartTimer))]
                            [onEntry->filter(StartTimer).period/]
                          [else][onEntry.eCrossReferences()->
                              filter(PrimitiveDataDeclaration).value/][/if])
85       [/if]
86      [/if]
87     [/for]
88    end
```

Fig. 10. Modes transformation

```
90    [for (behaveChoice : BehaviouralElement | behaviouralElements)]
91     [if (oclIsKindOf(Choice))]
92      [for (linkChoice : Link | behaveChoice->
             filter(Choice).outgoing->asSequence())]
93       [if (linkChoice.target.oclIsKindOf(SendMessage))]
94        [if (linkChoice.target.oclIsKindOf(UnicastSendMessage))]
95       transition -> [mode.name/] event e: [linkChoice.target->
             filter(UnicastSendMessage).toMessagePorts.name/]?[linkChoice.target->
             filter(UnicastSendMessage).receiverName/] guard [linkChoice.condition/]
             action [linkChoice.target->filter(UnicastSendMessage).toMessagePorts.name/]!
             [linkChoice.target->filter(UnicastSendMessage).dataRecipient.dataName/]
             ([linkChoice.target->filter(UnicastSendMessage).dataRecipient.dataName/])
96         [elseif (linkChoice.target.oclIsKindOf(MulticastSendMessage))]
97          [for (receivers : String | linkChoice.target->
                filter(MulticastSendMessage).receiverNames->asSequence())]
98       transition -> [mode.name/] event e: [linkChoice.target->
             filter(MulticastSendMessage).toMessagePorts.name/]?[receivers/] action
             [linkChoice.target->filter(MulticastSendMessage).toMessagePorts.name/]!
             [linkChoice.target->filter(MulticastSendMessage).dataRecipient.dataName/]([linkChoice
             .target->filter(MulticastSendMessage).dataRecipient.dataName/])
99          [/for]
100        [elseif (linkChoice.target.oclIsKindOf(BroadcastSendMessage))]
101      transition -> [mode.name/] guard [linkChoice.target->
             filter(BroadcastSendMessage).dataRecipient.dataName/] action
             [linkChoice.target->filter(BroadcastSendMessage).toMessagePorts.name/]!
             [linkChoice.target->filter(BroadcastSendMessage).dataRecipient.dataName/]
             ([linkChoice.target->filter(BroadcastSendMessage).dataRecipient.dataName/])
102        [/if]
103       [/if]
104      [/for]
105     [/if]
106     [if (oclIsKindOf(Choice))]
107      [for (linkChoice : Link | behaveChoice->filter(Choice).outgoing->asSequence())]
108       [if (linkChoice.target.oclIsKindOf(SendMessage)._not()._and(linkChoice.target
               .oclIsKindOf(ReceiveMessage)._not()))]
109      internal guard [linkChoice.condition/] action [linkChoice.target.name/]
             ([if (behaveChoice.oclIsKindOf(StartTimer))][behaveChoice->
                  filter(StartTimer).period/][else]
                [behaveChoice.eCrossReferences()->
                    filter(PrimitiveDataDeclaration).value/][/if])
110       [/if]
111      [/for]
112     [/if]
113    [/for]
```

Fig. 11. Choice and messages transformation

4.4   Launching Code Generator Phase

In this phase, we run the Acceleo file that resulted from the first three phases. Therefore, we build a Java launcher project that import the MTCLauncher

```
30    // ***** Behavioural Elements (Functions) *****
31    [for (modeFunc : Mode | modes)]
      [comment display Behavioural Elements in each mode as functions /]
32     [for (behaveFunc : BehaviouralElement | behaviouralElements)]
33      [if (oclIsKindOf(Link)._not()
           ._and(oclIsKindOf(UnicastSendMessage)._not())
           ._and(oclIsKindOf(MulticastSendMessage)._not())
           ._and(oclIsKindOf(BroadcastSendMessage)._not())
           ._and(oclIsKindOf(ReceiveMessage)._not())
           ._and(oclIsKindOf(Choice)._not())
           ._and(oclIsKindOf(TimerFired)._not()))]
34      function [behaveFunc.name/]([if (behaveFunc.oclIsKindOf(StartTimer))]
             val : Float[elseif (behaveFunc.eCrossReferences()->
             filter(PrimitiveDataDeclaration).type->notEmpty())]
             [if (behaveFunc.eCrossReferences()->
             filter(PrimitiveDataDeclaration).type->first()
               .toString().equalsIgnoreCase('real')) ]val : Float
             [else]val : [behaveFunc.eCrossReferences()->
               filter(PrimitiveDataDeclaration).type.toString()
                 .toUpperFirst()/][/if][/if]) do
35      // Do something
36      end
37       [/if][comment end if testing /]
38      [/for][comment end Behavioural Elements /]
39    [/for][comment end Modes 1 /]
```

Fig. 12. Behavioral elements transformation

```
135   [/for][comment end Component /]
136   // ***** Configurations *****
137   configuration result {
138   [for (compConf : Component | Components)]
139     instance [compConf.name/]: [compConf.name/]
140   [/for]
141
142   [for (conn : Connection | element.SAElements->filter(Connection))]
143     connector
           [conn.target.eContainer(Component).name/].[conn.target.name/]
           => [conn.source.eContainer(Component).name/].[conn.source.name/]
144   [/for]
145   }
146   [/file]
147
148   [/template]
149
```

Fig. 13. Connection transformation

library [10]. The MTCLauncher is a library developed by a researcher, called Victor Guana, at the University of Alberta [10]. The library allows running ATL model-to-model transformations, and Acceleo model-to-text transformations in an isolated fashion and can be executed in a command line outside Eclipse. It helps in avoiding errors in running Acceleo code in Java environment. In the launcher project, the SAML metamodel ecore file is included under metamodel folder, the CAPSml.mtl file is included under the AcceleoTransformations folder. To start the conversion for any SAML model, we need to open the launcher project and include the SAML model xmi file under models folder in the launcher project. Then, we run the project to get the ThingML output file (CAPS.thingml) created under the gen folder. The thingml file will contain the ThingML language transformed from SAML model.

The CAPSml framework is able to produce a complete thingml file. It acts as a link between CAPS-SAML and ThingML frameworks. Thus, it enables IoT designers, who are using SAML-CAPS to model and analyze their IoT systems, to benefit from the power of ThingML in code generation. The generated thingml file can be imported in ThingML framework to allow designers to select among several compilers the one that targets their desirable platform.

5   Modeling and Code Generation Methodology

The modeling and code generation methodology can be used during IoT systems life cycle. It benefits from CAPS, CAPSml, and ThingML frameworks. It encompasses three phases illustrated in Fig. 14:

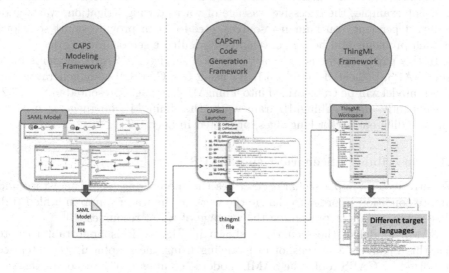

Fig. 14. Modeling and code generation methodology

1. Modeling using CAPS framework: In this phase, the designers architect their IoT systems. They will benefit from the power of CAPS in modeling and analyzing IoT systems [11]. Moreover, they will benefit from the graphical user interface supported by CAPS framework for modeling. The necessary output from this modeling phase is the SAML model xmi file.
2. Running CAPSml framework: In this phase, the designers run CAPSml framework to transform CAPS-SAML model into ThingML model. The transformation process automatically starts from the xmi and ecore files of SAML. Then, the contents of SAML model is mapped to contents in ThingML model. Finally, a complete ThingML language is generated automatically in a thingml file.

3. Running ThingML framework: In this phase, the designers use the thingml file that resulted from phase two for running the ThingML framework. ThingML framework allows the designers to select among several compilers the one that targets their desirable platform.

Following this methodology helps developers to model, analyze and produce IoT systems. It mitigates the developers problems in learning ThingML language and thus the programming languages that can be generated using ThingML framework. In the following section, we show the phases of our methodology on smart irrigation case study example.

6   Smart Irrigation Case Study

The agriculture is one of the most vital resources of nation's economy and food's production. There are many concerns related to traditional methods of agriculture. For example, the excessive wastage of water during irrigation, wastage of money, dependency on human resources, etc. IoT can provide smart solutions for such problems and help in developing agriculture sector in countries.

In this paper, we focus on smart irrigation services. A SAML model is built using CAPS, presented in Sect. 6.1. By using our CAPSml code generator, the SAML model will be transformed into ThingML language, presented in Sect. 6.2. Consequently, using ThingML framework, the ThingML language is used to generate different target languages, presented in Sect. 6.2.

6.1   Describing a Scenario Using CAPS

We introduce a simple scenario describes the monitoring of soil moisture and climate condition in order to change the work of the water pump in a filed [12]. This scenario aims at preventing the wastage of water resources [13].

SAML model of the scenario is shown in Fig. 15. It is important to note that this Figure is a screenshot of modeling using the graphical user interface supported by CAPS tool. The SAML model is composed of four components:

1. The SenseMoisture component: It is responsible for sensing the soil moisture value. It includes two modes:

– Normal mode: In this mode, the moisture sensor senses the moisture value from the soil every 100 s. Then, it saves the value in Moisture primitive variable. After all, it uses the unicast message to send the values to the Controller component. If the moisture value is more than 3, the SenseMoisture component enters the Critical mode.
– Critical mode: In this mode, the sensor senses the moisture value every one second. It saves the value in Moisture primitive variable. Then, it uses the unicast message to send the value to the Controller component. If the moisture value is less than 3, the SenseMoisture component enters the Normal mode.

2. The SenseRainfall component: It is responsible for sensing the rainfall. It includes one mode that is RainFall.

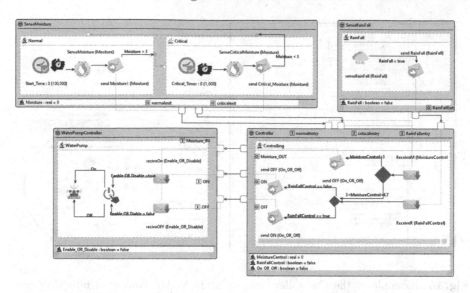

Fig. 15. Software architecture of simple scenario in smart irrigation case study

– Rainfall Mode: In this mode, there is an interrupt sensor that senses if there is a rainfall or not. The value taken from this sensor is kept in a primitive variable. It uses a unicast message to send the value to the Controller component.

3. The Controller component: It is responsible for making decisions to turn the water pump on or off. It includes one mode that is Controlling.

– Controlling mode: In this mode, the values received from the Moisture and Rainfall messages are stored in primitive variables. These values are used for making decisions depending on the current condition. If the Moisture is more than 3 and less than 4.7 and the weather does not rain, the Controller sends a message to the water pump to turn it on. While, if the Moisture is more than 3 and less than 4.7 and the weather is Rainfall, the Controller sends a message to the water pump to turn it off. Moreover, if the Moisture is less than 3 the Controller sends a message to the water pump to keep it off.

4. The WaterPumpController component: It is responsible for turning the pump on or off depending on the decision from the Controller. It includes one mode that is WaterPump.

– WaterPump mode: It receives a message from the Controller component and stores it in a primitive variable. The value stored in the primitive variable specifies if the pump is turned on or off. This value is sent to an actuator. If the sent value is true, the actuator turns the pump on. If the sent value is false, the actuator turns the pump off.

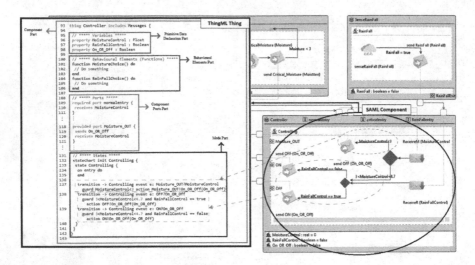

Fig. 16. Example of the Controller component in SAML converted into Controller Thing in ThingML language

6.2 Code Generation Using CAPSml

In this section, we describe the results of running SAML model on the CAPSml framework. Then, we show the code generated using ThingML code generation framework.

```
180  // ***** Configurations *****
181⊝ configuration result {
182      instance SenseMoisture: SenseMoisture
183      instance SenseRainFall: SenseRainFall
184      instance Controller: Controller
185      instance WaterPumpController: WaterPumpController
186
187      connector Controller.RainFallentry => SenseRainFall.RainFallExit
188      connector Controller.normalentry => SenseMoisture.criticalexit
189      connector Controller.criticalentry => SenseMoisture.normalexit
190      connector WaterPumpController.ON => Controller.ON
191      connector WaterPumpController.OFF => Controller.OFF
192      connector WaterPumpController.Moisture_IN => Controller.Moisture_OUT
193  }
```

Fig. 17. Part of the generated ThingML Configuration

Before running CAPSml framework, we need to specify the model, described in Fig. 15, in xmi format and the meta model of SAML in ecore format. Then, to run CAPSml framework launcher project, we need to find the xmi file for the model generated using CAPS-SAML. After running CAPSml launcher, we will automatically have a thingml file that has a complete ThingML language in the gen folder of the launcher project. Figure 16 shows part of converting

```
3⊖thing fragment Messages {
4       message Moisture (value : Float)
5       message RainFall (value : Boolean)
6       message MoistureControl (value : Float)
7       message RainFallControl (value : Boolean)
8       message On_OR_Off (value : Boolean)
9       message Enable_OR_Disable (value : Boolean)
10 }
```

Fig. 18. Part of the generated Thing fragment

```
49 // On Exit Actions:
50 void Controller_OnExit(int state, struct Controller_Instance *_instance) {
51 switch(state) {
52 case CONTROLLER_STATE:{
53 Controller_OnExit(_instance->Controller_State, _instance);
54 break;}
55 case CONTROLLER_NULL_CONTROLLING_STATE:{
56 break;}
57 default: break;
58 }
59 }
60
61 // Event Handlers for incoming messages:
62 void Controller_handle_OFF_On_OR_Off(struct Controller_Instance *_instance, bool value) {
63 if(!(_instance->active)) return;
64 //Region null
65 uint8_t Controller_State_event_consumed = 0;
66 if (_instance->Controller_State == CONTROLLER_NULL_CONTROLLING_STATE) {
67 if (Controller_State_event_consumed == 0 && 3 < _instance->Controller_MoistureControl_var < 4.7
     && _instance->Controller_RainFallControl_var == 1) {
68 Controller_OnExit(CONTROLLER_NULL_CONTROLLING_STATE, _instance);
69 _instance->Controller_State = CONTROLLER_NULL_CONTROLLING_STATE;
70 Controller_send_OFF_On_OR_Off(_instance, _instance->Controller_On_OR_Off_var);
71 Controller_OnEntry(CONTROLLER_NULL_CONTROLLING_STATE, _instance);
72 Controller_State_event_consumed = 1;
73 }
74 }
```

Fig. 19. Part of C++ code generated for Controller Thing/Component

Controller component in SAML into Controller Thing in ThingML language. Figure 17 shows part of the generated Configuration for the Things in ThingML language. Figure 18 shows part of the generated Thing fragment that contains the messages to be exchanged between components.

Consequently, the ThingML language, that resulted from running CAPSml, was used to run ThingML code generator framework for producing several target languages. We experimented the code generation using different compilers supported by ThingML framework. The results show successful transformations to different targeted languages and platforms. For the sake of space, we present a snippet for the results of only running Posix compiler in the ThingML framework. Posix Generates C/C++ code for Linux or other Posix runtime environments. Figure 19 shows part of the C++ code generated for the Controller Component/Thing.

7   Conclusions

In this paper, we presented CAPSml, a code generation framework built on top of CAPS modeling framework and targets ThingML framework. CAPS framework offers a graphical user interface that facilitates the production of IoT systems architecture. While, ThingML offers a code generation framework that brings MDE to the late design and implementation stages.

CAPSml transforms CAPS model into ThingML language. Thus, CAPS users can generate code for their models using ThingML framework. Moreover, CAPS users do not need to learn ThingML modeling language. To show the utilization of our tool, we ran an example on smart irrigation case study and clarified how our code generation approach can take place in IoT systems life cycle.

References

1. Ciccozzi, F., Spalazzese, R.: MDE4IoT: supporting the internet of things with model-driven engineering. Intelligent Distributed Computing X. SCI, vol. 678, pp. 67–76. Springer, Cham (2017). https://doi.org/10.1007/978-3-319-48829-5_7
2. Muccini, H., Sharaf, M.: Caps: a tool for architecting situational-aware cyber-physical systems. In: 2017 IEEE International Conference on Software Architecture Workshops (ICSAW), pp. 286–289. IEEE (2017)
3. Harrand, N., Fleurey, F., Morin, B., Husa, K.E.: ThingML: a language and code generation framework for heterogeneous targets. In: Proceedings of the ACM/IEEE 19th International Conference on Model Driven Engineering Languages and Systems, pp. 125–135. ACM (2016)
4. Sharaf, M., Abughazala, M., Muccini, H., Abusair, M.: An architecture framework for modelling and simulation of situational-aware cyber-physical systems. In: Lopes, A., de Lemos, R. (eds.) ECSA 2017. LNCS, vol. 10475, pp. 95–111. Springer, Cham (2017). https://doi.org/10.1007/978-3-319-65831-5_7
5. Sharaf, M., Muccini, H., Abughazala, M.: ArIA: arduino code generation based on the caps. In: Proceedings of the 12th European Conference on Software Architecture: Companion Proceedings, p. 4. ACM (2018)
6. Muccini, H., Sharaf, M.: Caps: architecture description of situational aware cyber physical systems. In: 2017 IEEE International Conference on Software Architecture (ICSA), pp. 211–220. IEEE (2017)
7. Sharaf, M., Abughazala, M., Muccini, H., Abusair, M.: CAPSim: simulation and code generation based on the CAPS. In: Proceedings of the 11th European Conference on Software Architecture: Companion Proceedings, pp. 56–60. ACM (2017)
8. Sharaf, M., Abughazala, M., Muccini, H., Abusair, M.: Simulating architectures of situational-aware cyber-physical space. In: Proceedings of the 11th European Conference on Software Architecture: Companion Proceedings, pp. 66–67. ACM (2017)
9. Yan, Z., Zhang, P., Vasilakos, A.V.: A survey on trust management for internet of things. J. Netw. Comput. Appl. **42**, 120–134 (2014)
10. Guana, V.: Running Acceleo and ATL Transformations Programmatically. University of Alberta (2016). http://victorguana.blogspot.com/2016/05/running-acceleo-and-atl-transformations.html

11. Sharaf, M., Abughazala, M., Muccini, H.: Arduino realization of CAPS IoT architecture descriptions. In: Proceedings of the 12th European Conference on Software Architecture: Companion Proceedings, p. 6. ACM (2018)
12. Sharaf, M., Abusair, M., Eleiwi, R., Yara, S., Ithar, S., Muccini, H.: Architecture description language for climate smart agriculture systems. In: Proceedings of the 13th European Conference on Software Architecture: Companion Proceedings. ACM (2019)
13. Gondchawar, N., Kawitkar, R.: IOT based smart agriculture. Int. J. Adv. Res. Comput. Commun. Eng. 5(6), 838–842 (2016)

Process Enactment with Traceability Support for NFV Systems

Omar Hassane[1], Sadaf Mustafiz[1], Ferhat Khendek[1($\boxtimes$)],
and Maria Toeroe[2]

[1] ECE, Concordia University, Montreal, Canada
o_assane@encs.concordia.ca, {sadaf.mustafiz,
ferhat.khendek}@concordia.ca
[2] Ericsson Inc., Montreal, Canada
maria.toeroe@ericsson.com

Abstract. The Network Functions Virtualization (NFV) paradigm is heading towards an evolution with the recent zero-touch automation initiative. In particular, automating the orchestration and management of network services (NS) could progress rapidly with the help of model-driven engineering methods and tools. We have earlier proposed an integrated process modelling and enactment environment, MAPLE, for NS management. In our approach, enactment is enabled by transformation chaining and megamodelling. In this paper, we present our extension, MAPLE-T, which incorporates traceability information generation and analysis support in MAPLE. MAPLE-T allows the generation of both local and global traceability information during the enactment of a process model (PM), all of which is retained in the megamodel. The megamodel enables end-to-end navigation of the source and target artifacts in the PM and thus allows advanced traceability analysis to be carried out. We applied MAPLE-T on a NS design process to demonstrate the application of the change impact analysis feature.

Keywords: Process enactment · Megamodelling · Traceability ·
Network Functions Virtualization (NFV)

1 Introduction

With the advent of 5G, the telecommunications industry is faced with opportunities and challenges which require rapid innovations. Traditional networks have a high dependence on proprietary hardware. Telecoms are moving from such networks to virtualized networks. Telecoms are leveraging the Network Functions Virtualization (NFV) paradigm which is a key enabler for 5G. NFV builds on cloud computing and virtualization technologies which enable the automation of the orchestration and the management of network services [10, 24].

We believe model-driven engineering (MDE) methods and tools can help with the automation. As a first step, we have earlier proposed an approach for explicitly modelling and enacting NFV processes and have applied our work to the NS design and management process [25–27]. Our NS Management Process Model is compliant with the NFV reference framework. MAPLE (MAGIC Process Modelling and Enactment Environment) provides an integrated environment for creating and enacting process models (PM) with the use of model transformation chains. Transformation chaining is the preferred technique for modelling the composition of different model transformations and orchestrating them. MAPLE supports the enactment of heterogeneous (cross-technology) transformation chains based on megamodels used for supporting model management, and on composition of transformations. Megamodels provide complex structures to link all relevant artifacts (models, transformations, and other metadata) forming a map for model management [15, 16]. We have built MAPLE in the Eclipse Papyrus environment [12], which is the modeling environment of choice of the European Telecommunications Standards Institute (ETSI) NFV [13].

Advanced support for discoverability and traceability have been identified as essential features in virtualizing network services [7]. Traceability support enables information recovery, origin tracking (for instance, backtracking from design to requirements artifacts), change impact analysis, change propagation, dependency visualization, and even defect detection and prediction [9, 33]. Traceability management can be effectively carried out with MDE methods and tools [29]. While NFV would greatly benefit from end-to-end traceability support, there has been very little done in this regard in this domain.

In this paper, we extend MAPLE with traceability support for NFV systems. We integrate means for local (transformation-level) and global (process model-level) traceability information generation and also provide the groundwork for change impact analysis. We apply our work in the NFV domain to the traceability analysis of the network service design process in order to assess the impact of changes in the source models. The vendor-provided virtualized network function (VNF) form the core of a network service, and any changes in the VNF descriptors (VNFD) can affect the target artifacts and the process itself. It would be highly beneficial in NFV systems to be able to assess the impact of a change and to provide feedback.

The rest of this paper is structured as follows: Sect. 2 gives a brief background on traceability in MDE. Section 3 proposes a model-driven process enactment approach with traceability support and presents our MAPLE-T environment. Section 4 describes an application of MAPLE-T in the NFV domain. Section 5 discusses related work and Sect. 6 concludes with some future work.

2 Background

Traceability is defined as *the degree to which a relationship can be established between two or more products of the development process, especially products having a predecessor-successor or master-subordinate relationship to one another [2].*

Traceability information in MDE can be classified as *generic* (no semantics retained with trace links) or *specific* (domain-dependent with semantically rich links) [4]. Traceability information can be represented as models conforming to an external metamodel (extra-model traceability), or as part of the traced models (intra-model traceability) thus requiring the metamodels of the traced models to be extended and polluted with trace information [32].

Traceability metamodelling can follow a *pure metamodel* approach or a *tag-based* approach [32]. In the first approach, all the required trace types along with their usage semantics are specified at the metamodel level making the traceability metamodel rigid to change and therefore hard to reuse in other projects. The trace tagging approach uses a general traceability metamodel which can be annotated with specific tags. This allows for more flexible traces that can be used in any project, but with weak usage semantics specified in the metamodel.

When referring to traceability at the model transformation level, the trace links are between the elements of the source and target artifacts associated with the transformation. A trace model is created for each transformation. This is referred to as *local traceability* or *traceability in the small*. However, the link between the different trace models across multiple model transformations (or a model transformation chain) needs to be created to produce *global traceability* (or *traceability in the large*) information. This enables end-to-end navigation throughout a chain of intermediately created trace models [6].

In our work, megamodels are used to build traceability support. Megamodelling is generally used for model management, to provide structures for handling and interrelating models [15, 16]. A megamodel may contain heterogeneous models, relations between them (e.g., transformations) and any other relevant metadata. It can be used to capture conformance links and also to enable compatibility checks.

3   MAPLE-T Approach

We have earlier proposed an integrated process modelling and enactment approach, MAPLE [25]. MAPLE supports process modelling with UML Activity Diagrams. The MAPLE enactment approach is based on model transformation chaining and megamodelling. We have used megamodels (MgM) to manage all the resources needed for the enactment. We begin with a process model (PM) and the repository of resources (metamodels, profiles, model instances, model transformations, programs). In MAPLE, the MgM was used as a resource repository that aggregates and links all these resources as well as their metadata. This was quite useful for gathering and managing the relevant information regarding the transformations that need to be enacted.

An initial megamodel (MgM) is automatically derived based on the resources registered. When the PM is registered in the MgM, it leads to the creation of a *weave model*. This *weave model* binds the PM and the MgM together. The PM is then mapped to a model transformation chain, with the help of the MgM and the *weave model*, and it can be executed using token-based semantics. The MgM is dynamically updated with the generated models during enactment. MAPLE is built on top of Eclipse Papyrus. For further details, the reader can refer to [25]. We propose an extension to our process enactment approach providing traceability support. Our goal is to go further and use the MgM for advanced traceability of model transformation chains. The MAPLE-T approach is shown in Fig. 1. Following the derivation of the megamodel (MgM) and the construction of the model transformation (MT) chain, the chain execution results in the generation of artifacts. During this execution, trace models will also be output (*traceability in the small* context) and will be retained in the MgM in order to build a global traceability map (*traceability in the large* context). The global traceability map can then be used for traceability analysis. As an add-on, the map can also be used as a basis for traceability visualization.

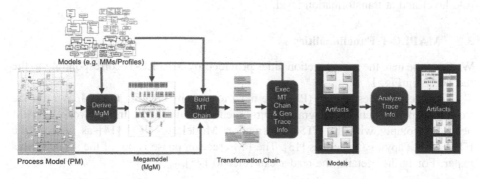

Fig. 1. MAPLE-T approach (Color figure online)

3.1   Traceability Support in MAPLE-T

Traceability support for process enactment can be incrementally built in three stages: (1) traceability information generation, (2) traceability analysis, and (3) traceability visualization. While traceability information generation is required to proceed with any analysis or visualization, the latter two stages can be carried out in parallel. This paper discusses the first two phases: the generation and analysis.

Traceability Generation. The first phase of the project involves building support for the generation of traceability information and global model management in MAPLE. Each of the transformations in the MT chain is first augmented such that trace models are generated as extra artifacts with the execution of each transformation. We refer to these local trace models as LTrace models.

During enactment, this augmented MT chain is executed, hence generating the output as defined in each transformation along with the LTrace model for every transformation. The generated artifacts, including the trace models, are dynamically added to the MgM during enactment. Each LTrace model in the MgM is connected to the relevant input and output models. In addition to the links between input and output models via the LTrace model, the links between the trace models are also saved in the MgM. The links retained are at the model-level as well as at the model-element level. This leads to the creation of the global traceability map within the MgM, which we refer to as the GTrace.

Traceability Analysis. Once we have a repository of traceability information and the global traceability map, the next step is to discover any *useful* trace information that can be analyzed for a given purpose. Whether a piece of trace information is *useful* is typically application-dependent. Discovering such trace links is possible when using the trace tagging method [32]. In the MgM, each LTrace model is associated with a corresponding *tag* representing the context of the traced transformation. The purpose behind this *tag* is to specialize our trace models with application-specific semantics. In MAPLE-T, the notion of *tags* has been incorporated at two levels: at transformation rule level and at transformation level.

3.2   MAPLE-T Functionalities

We describe here the main functionalities provided by MAPLE-T, corresponding to the red boxes in Fig. 1.

To enact a process model (PM), we need to start by creating the PM. We use the Eclipse Papyrus Activity Diagram environment to build PMs. In our work, the PM needs to comply with the ETSI Information Model for NFV [14] as well as the ETSI NFV Papyrus Guidelines [13]. The PM creation phase is out of the scope of this paper. For further details, the reader can refer to [25].

Deriving the MgM. In MAPLE, the actions in the PM are implemented with model transformations. A transformation involves several input and output models, possibly conforming to different metamodels that can be expressed using heterogeneous technologies. Moreover, a PM can be implemented with a heterogeneous set of languages (for instance, ATL, Epsilon, Java, or C), and hence MAPLE supports execution of cross-technology model transformation chains. Due to this, deploying model management techniques is essential in MAPLE. As described in [25], we use megamodels for this purpose. While megamodels have been very useful in MAPLE for managing resources and for enacting the PM, we wanted to go further and use the MgM for advanced traceability support. In MAPLE-T, we have introduced new traceability-related features in the MgM as well as new extensions with respect to the implementation of these features. To enable traceability at both levels (local and global), our MgM now supports storing the same resources with different versions over time, i.e. whenever they are being used or changed. The MgM also retains model instances per enactment. In addition to that, each transformation resource is now linked with a trace model - representing local traceability (LTrace models). This LTrace model contains the trace links for each input and output of the transformation execution and conforms to an LTrace metamodel which represents local traceability information elements both at the model element-level and at the attribute-level. The main elements in the LTrace are mentioned below and also shown in Fig. 2.

- TraceLinkSet: This represents the set of all the traced rules of a transformation execution as well as all the trace links linking input and output elements of the traced models.
- TracedRule: This represents the rule responsible for creating/transforming the traced output model element(s) from the corresponding traced input model element(s).
- TraceLink: This represents the set of input elements and their corresponding output elements within a rule.

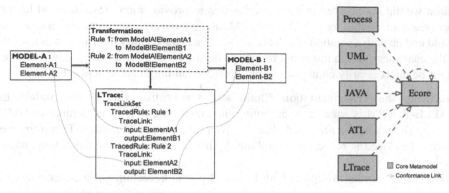

Fig. 2. LTrace structure   **Fig. 3.** Base MgM

The MgM is derived after registering the resources and the PM. First, a base MgM is loaded as part of MAPLE-T environment and consists of the metamodels of the built-in loaders (needed to load resources) and the pre-loaded meta-metamodels (e.g., Ecore) and their conformance links. This MgM is incrementally updated by registering the different resources which are part of the project (metamodels/profiles). This is carried out automatically by going through the project workspace (referred to as *workspace discovery*), and as a result an initial MgM is derived at this stage. A base LTrace metamodel conforming to the Ecore metamodel is also registered in the MgM (see Fig. 3). Each trace model generated as a byproduct of a transformation execution conforms to this metamodel.

As the next step, the MgM is refined by carrying out a *PM discovery*. This involves updating the MgM with new resources: the PM and the associated transformations. Since we wanted the MgM to be PM-agnostic, a *weave model* is automatically created behind the scenes whenever a PM is registered. The *weave model* binds all the necessary elements of the PM to their equivalent resources in the MgM.

At this point, the MgM holds all the essential resources which are required for enactment. During enactment, the LTrace models generated are added to the MgM which makes it possible to construct the GTrace (part of the MgM).

Building the Transformation Chain. The PM is given translational semantics by mapping it to a transformation chain. The chain is in essence a schedule with the required details (sequence of actions, transformations used, inputs and outputs of the transformations). This allows us to build a generic enacter, instead of having an enacter for each kind of PM. Having a generic enacter also leaves scope for integrating other formalisms for modelling the PM.

The translation from a PM to an MT chain is implemented using an ATL transformation which takes relevant inputs (including the MgM and the PM) and produces the target transformation chain.

This phase of the process has no traceability-related extensions. It would be possible to augment the transformation chain to build a chain with traceability support. The reason we did not proceed in that direction was to provide more flexibility and let the user enable or disable traceability within MAPLE-T during enactment. Otherwise, we would end up with a solution which always generates traceability information as a result of the enactment, which might not be always desirable, as generating trace information might be unnecessarily cumbersome and time-consuming in some applications.

Executing the Transformation Chain and Generating the Trace Models. In MAPLE-T, a PM is enacted by executing the underlying MT chain. Similar to UML Activity Diagrams, the generated chain is given token-based semantics. Therefore, the enacter developed is based on controlling the tokens and activating the actions when needed.

However, in order to support both local and global traceability, it was necessary to integrate means to generate local traces of the transformations chain execution. Additionally, these trace models are linked in the MgM to construct the global traceability map. The MgM also needs to be updated with these new model instances and their relationships.

Generating Trace Models. One of the issues we had to address when building a traceability solution with MAPLE-T was how to actually generate traceability information during enactment. One might consider a naive approach in which each model transformation implementing an action in the PM is refined manually with new traceability-related rule bindings or blocks of code. In such a case, each transformation will need to be manually modified to generate new target models for the trace information. This approach is clearly not ideal, as extensively refining every transformation manually results in a very cumbersome process that is in total opposition of our main vision, which is full automation. For this reason, we adopted an approach that augments the transformation chain automatically with traceability information (see Fig. 4). Similar to [22] we used the well-known concept of higher order transformation (HOT), and we defined an HOT to systematically enrich our transformations with traceability notions. The HOT takes the transformations parts of the chain and augments them, resulting in a new chain which has the same flow but with traceability-augmented transformations. Each transformation ends up having in addition to its original input/output parameters, a new target parameter representing the trace model to be generated - the LTrace model.

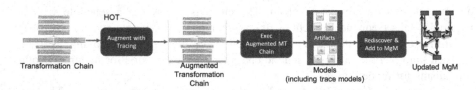

Fig. 4. MAPLE-T traceability generation approach

While MAPLE provides enactment support for a heterogeneous set of transformation languages (e.g., ATL, Java), MAPLE-T only supports implementations with ATL transformations at the moment. The HOT implementation augments transformation models conforming to the ATL metamodel. Also, the LTrace metamodel is built to represent trace models produced from the execution of the augmented ATL transformations.

Updating the MgM. During enactment, the MgM is updated on the fly with the augmented transformation executions and their corresponding input/output instances including the LTrace models. Once the enactment is done, the MgM is completely updated with all the newly generated artifacts. At this point, the MgM also provides a global traceability map, the GTrace. The set of global links as well as the local traces generated for each transformation form the basis for carrying out traceability analysis in MAPLE-T.

Analyzing Traceability Information. Following the generation of traceability information, traceability analysis can be carried out on the basis of the GTrace. For this purpose, we have incorporated means to analyze trace information within MAPLE-T which can be easily extended and adapted to the targeted application domain. We have built a core traceability analysis solution that exposes common traceability analysis features (via an API). The exposed features allow the generated LTrace models and GTrace links to be parsed and manipulated, typically with the use of the rule-level and transformation-level tags that provide richer semantics for the analysis.

We have incorporated traceability analysis support, specifically to carry out *change impact analysis* in MAPLE-T, which relies on the proposed traceability generation means. The change impact analysis is triggered by a request specifying the element or the model for which the change impact is to be analyzed. The purpose is to determine how impactful a model or an element is on the whole process (i.e., how impactful it is on the other involved models, model elements, and transformations) at both the metamodel and the model levels. The process starts first by filtering all the relevant information from the GTrace and LTrace models based on what was provided as input at the metamodel level. Based on this, we can conclude whether the input is impactful or impactless at the metamodel level. In case it is *impactless at the metamodel level*, then it is inferred to be *impactless at the model level* as well. In this case, it is concluded that the input model or model element is *impactless at both levels* and no further analysis is required. On the other hand, if the input model or model element turns out to be impactful at the metamodel level, then the decision is not as straightforward as in the previous case. MAPLE-T then continues to analyze the gathered traceability information (LTrace models and GTrace links) at the model level as well. As a result, the impact decision is further categorized into two outcomes.

- The input is *impactful at the model level*: This means that the provided input has been used in the enacted process and changing it requires re-enactment. Additionally, the solution collects the set of all the impacted resources (models, model elements, and transformations) and provides them as outputs of the change impact analysis along with the impact decision.

– The input is *impactless at the model level*: This means that although the type of the input model/element has an impact on the enacted process, the actual input model/element instance has never been used and has no impact on that specific enactment.

4   NFV Application

In this section, we use MAPLE-T to enact an NS design process and to carry out traceability analysis, in particular, a change impact analysis. The process is a subset of the NS Design and Deployment PM proposed earlier in [27].

A network service is a composition of network function(s) (NF) and/or other nested NSs to provide a desired functionality/behaviour (e.g. VoIP). An NF is a functional block identified by well-defined functional behaviour and external interfaces. NFs within an NS can be a physical NF (PNF) (e.g. a traditional firewall device) or a virtual network function (VNF) (e.g. a virtual firewall) decoupled from the infrastructure and implemented as software that can be deployed on a virtualized infrastructure. The different NFs/nested NSs within an NS are interconnected with one or more forwarding graphs (FG) that define the traffic flows between them.

The main goal behind the NS design process (proposed in [26]) is to automatically design an NS and generate an NS Descriptor (NSD) which is a template used for the deployment and management of the NS. The process starts by specifying the functional and non-functional characteristics of the NS as the NS requirements (NSReq). The functionalities in the NSReq are then decomposed with the help of an NF ontology (NFOntology) which represents a knowledge-base capturing known NF decompositions and their architectures. After decomposition to a certain level, VNFs are selected from a catalog (VNFCatalog) by matching the decomposed functionalities. The traffic flows in the NS are then defined with the design of the VNF FGs (VNFFGs) and the NS dimensioned according to the non-functional requirements. The NFOntology may be updated with new information from NSReq after a successful design, with the onboarding of new VNFs, and manually by an expert. A VNF is described by a VNFD which captures all its deployment characteristics. One main element within the VNF is a VNF component (VNFC) which represents an internal component of the VNF that provides part of the VNF functionality. A Virtual Deployment Unit (VDU) is the deployment template or descriptor of the VNFC and it is an element contained within the VNFD. The generated NSD is compliant to ETSI NFV definition and refers to the NS constituent descriptors including VNFDs and VNFFG descriptors (VNFFGDs). For a detailed description of the NS Design process, the reader can refer to [26]. Figure 5 presents the NS design PM.

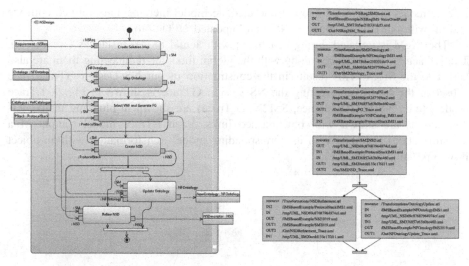

Fig. 5. NS design PM [25]   **Fig. 6.** Augmented MT chain

4.1 Enactment and Traceability Generation with MAPLE-T

In order to enact the NS Design PM, we need to register all the needed resources/profiles (NSReq, NSD profiles, etc.). As a result, the base MgM (Fig. 3) is updated with all the registered UML profiles as well as conformance links. Figure 7 shows the initial MgM with UML profiles. Next, we need to register the PM which automatically registers all the underlying model transformations implementing the actions in the PM. Consequently, the MgM is updated (see Fig. 8) with the following: (1) a new resource representing the NS Design PM as a UML activity diagram conforming to the UML metamodel (shown in gray), (2) the ATL transformations conforming to the ATL metamodel (shown in brown), and also (3) the weave model containing the MgM and PM mappings (shown in gray). With this MgM, MAPLE-T has all the necessary resources to enact the PM, and therefore enable NS Design traceability generation and analysis.

Once all the model instances are specified, an initial transformation chain is built based on the NS design PM. This transformation chain is then augmented so that each transformation is able to generate LTrace model instances in addition to its original output model instance(s) (see Fig. 6).

The execution of this MT chain includes six augmented transformation executions. The first transformation starts by taking the NSReq model as input and generates an initial intermediate model as well as the LTrace model corresponding to that transformation execution. In the same way, the execution process continues according to the order defined in the MT chain. For each subsequent transformation execution, the

LTrace model is generated and the intermediate model incrementally refined until we end up with our desired models: NSD and updated NFOntology.

The MgM is updated during enactment with actual model instances (see Fig. 8). The LTrace model instances along with the global links interconnecting them are also added to the MgM. This results in the construction of our NS Design GTrace. The subset of the MgM representing the NS Design GTrace is shown in Fig. 9. LTrace models (e.g., NSReq2SM Trace, SM2NSD Trace) are shown in blue and their interconnections are shown with blue dashed links. Each LTrace model (output of a transformation) is linked with its corresponding model transformation with an object flow link (solid black line).

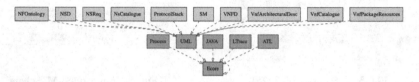

Fig. 7. Initial NS design MgM

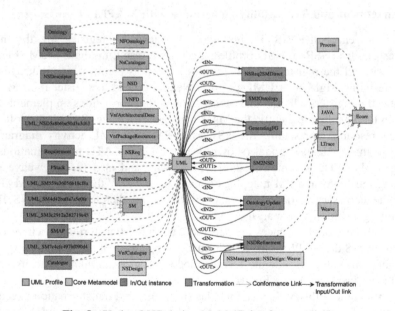

Fig. 8. Updated NS design MgM (Color figure online)

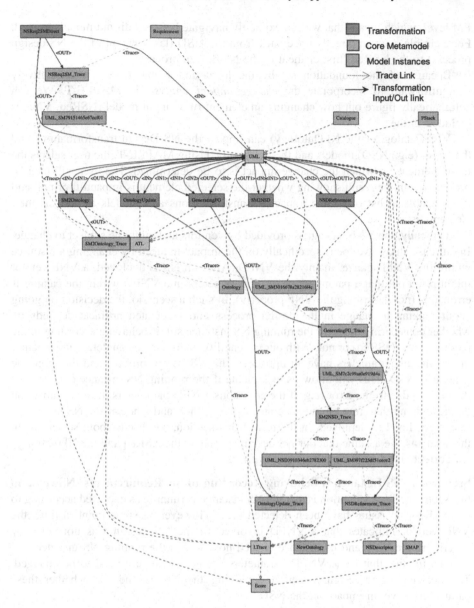

Fig. 9. NS design GTrace (Color figure online)

4.2 Traceability Analysis with MAPLE-T

Now that all the NS Design models are interlinked via LTrace models and GTrace links, we can automatically trace back and forth between all the involved source and target resources i.e.; NSReq, Ontology, the VNFCatalog and its constituent VNFDs as well as the resulting NSD and the updated Ontology. Each LTrace model enables navigation at the element level of adjacent models. Additionally, the GTrace enables navigation at the

PM level, which means that we can explicitly navigate between distant models as well. For example, we can directly trace back from the NSD (last element of the NS design process) to the NSReq (first element of the NS design process).

Because of the foundation set by the local and global traces, it is relatively straightforward to incorporate the *change impact analysis* in MAPLE-T. We can automatically figure out how changing an element of an input model (NSReq, VNFDs included in the

VNFCatalog, or the NFOntology) can impact the NS Design transformations and the target (e.g., NSD) models and their elements. Using MAPLE-T, the user selects the input element for which the change impact is to be determined. The user will then be provided with the result showing whether the selected element is impactful or not, and if applicable, a list of all the impacted transformations and models as well as their elements is provided.

Typically, the VNFPackage is provided by vendors and might be subject to change. In our case study, we focus specifically on the impact induced by changing a resource within the VNFPackage, mainly the VNFD. After an NS is deployed, a VNF vendor might point out that a parameter or set of parameters in a VNFD within the catalog is erroneous (not describing the VNF properly). In such a scenario, the decision on going about making a change in the design process and associated artifacts depends on whether considering the error the running NS instance still is behaving according to the requirements (NSReq) or not. With our traceability analysis, we can determine whether the erroneous parameters have an impact on the NS design process and therefore the generated NSD. This will allow us to evaluate if the running NS instance cannot meet the NSReq due to the error (e.g. if the erroneous VNFD parameters have an impact on the design and therefore on the generated NSD) or not, and whether the NS should be re-designed and re-deployed. In the rest of this section, we discuss both scenarios. In this analysis, we assume that our NS design approach, the NSReq and the NFOntology are correct and cannot be the source of errors.

Scenario 1: NS Instance is Behaving According to the Requirements (NSReq). In this scenario, the assumption is that the NS instance is running as expected according to the NSReq, no issues have been detected (yet). However, at some point in time, the VNF vendor indicates that a VNFD involved in the NS design was not correctly describing the VNF and its instance is used now within the running NS instance.

This implies that some VNFD parameters are erroneous and need to be changed. The decision of re-designing and re-deploying the NS depends on whether these parameters have an impact on the NSD.

Parameters are Impactless at the Metamodel Level: In this case, since the erroneous parameters have no impact on the design and the NS instance is behaving as expected according to the NSReq, there is no action to take. For instance, the vendor might point out that the software image descriptor (SwImageDesc) used in the VNFD is erroneous. After analyzing the change impact of the SwImageDesc element on the NS Design process, it turns out that it is impactless as shown in Fig. 10(d) since it is never considered in the design process. Changing this element will never impact the generated NSD, and therefore there is no need to re-design or re-deploy the NS.

Parameters are Impactful at the Metamodel Level: In this case, the impact at the model level should be considered.

– Parameters are *impactful at the model level*: As opposed to the previous case, we need to consider re-designing the NS even though it is running as expected according to NSReq. In this case, the erroneous parameters were used to design the NS and therefore they are impactful. For example, the vendor might report that an Instantiation Level element (which specifies the number of instances of each VNFC within the VNF) within the VNFD is erroneous and needs to be corrected. The change impact analysis of this element finds it impactful (e.g., as shown in Fig. 10 (c)). This means that, while the NS instance shows no problem (yet), this does not preclude the possibility that the provisioning of VNFC instances is not done inefficiently (e.g. VNFC instances may be over-provisioned) and/or incorrectly (e.g. the parameter value may not have been used yet), and therefore the re-design of the NS needs to be considered in this case.
– Parameters are *impactless at the model level*: In this case, since the parameters are impactful at the metamodel level but not at the model level, it is not straightforward to conclude whether the re-enactment of the NS Design is needed or not. A new parameter value might make a previously impactless parameter impactful after the change. Using the generated traces to analyze the impact of such parameters might provide a *false negative* result, in the sense that the impact analysis will suggest that changing the parameter would be impactless, even though it is not the case. For instance, the vendor might indicate that the name of a Vdu element referenced in the VNFD is erroneous. As shown in Fig. 10(b), the analysis of the change impact of the Vdu name parameter on the NS Design process suggests that it is impactless. However, the reason may be that the Vdu with the incorrect name was not selected because it did not meet the requirements. On the other hand, the correct Vdu name might point to a VDU, which meets the requirements making the parameter impactful at the model level as well. In this case if we re-run the NS design enactment with the changed parameter value and generate new traces, our change impact analysis will suggest that this element is impactful. Thus, at this point, no conclusion can be made in this case from the analysis and it is better to re-enact the NS Design with the changed parameters.

Scenario 2: NS is Not Meeting the Requirements (NSReq). In this scenario the NS instance is not behaving as expected according to the NSReq. Similar to the previous scenario, the VNF vendor indicates that a provided VNFD is erroneous and requires changes. Using MAPLE-T, we can try to determine if the erroneous behaviour of the NS instance is due to the erroneous VNFD or not.

Parameters are Impactless at the Metamodel Level: Since the erroneous parameters of the VNFD are impactless (case shown in Fig. 10(d)), we can conclude that the erroneous behaviour of the NS instance is not due to the erroneous VNFD.

```
Element : "Vdu:vdu-VC"
Impact at Metamodel level: "Impactful"
Impact at model level: "Impactful"
Impacted Transformations: "GeneratingFG, SM2NSD, OntologyUpdate, NSDRefinement"
Impacted Models: "UML_SM7c2c99aa0e919d4a, UML_SM397f225df51cece2,
UML_NSD3910346eb2782300, SMAP, NSDescriptor, NewOntology"
Impacted Model Elements:  "UML_SM7c2c99aa0e919d4a!Functionality[VoiceCall],
                 UML_SM397f225df51cece2!Functionality[VoiceCall],
                 UML_SM397f225df51cece2!ArchBlock[AS],
UML_SM397f225df51cece2!NonFunctionalRequirement[NFR3(MCS:8),
NFR1(T:400)], SMAP!ArchDep(AS-S, AS-HSS, AS-IMSLoc),
SMAP!InterfaceInfo(AS-ISC, AS-HSS, AS-SH),NSD!VNFD(AS),
NSDescriptor!VNFFGD[VNFFGD CONTROL PLANE]
,NSDescriptor!NFPD[NFP-VoiceCall1],NSDescriptor!NsDf[NsDf-NsDf - NSD: VoIP (From :
PreVNFFG 1-AFG 8-FFG 1 )-001],NSDescriptor!VNFProfile(AS), NSDescriptor!VnfDf(VnfDf1),
NSDescriptor!InsLvl(InsLvL2) "
```

```
Element : "Vdu:vdu-Mess"
Impact at Metamodel level:
"Impactful"
Impact at model level: "Impactless"
Impacted Transformations: "Null"
Impacted Models: "Null"
Impacted Model Elements:  "Null"
```

(a) Impactful Vdu Element   (b) Impactless Vdu Element

```
Element : "InstantiationLevel:InsLvl1 (from VNFD)"
Impact at Metamodel level: "Impactful"
Impact at model level: "Impactful"
Impacted Transformations: "GeneratingFG, SM2NSD, OntologyUpdate, NSDRefinement"
Impacted Models: "UML_SM7c2c99aa0e919d4a, UML_SM397f225df51cece2,
UML_NSD3910346eb2782300, SMAP, NSDescriptor, NewOntology"
Impacted Model Elements:  "UML_SM7c2c99aa0e919d4a!Functionality[VoiceCall],
                 UML_SM397f225df51cece2!Functionality[VoiceCall],
                 UML_SM397f225df51cece2!ArchBlock[AS],
UML_SM397f225df51cece2!NonFunctionalRequirement[NFR3(MCS:8),
NFR1(T:400)], NSDescriptor!VNFFGD[VNFFGD CONTROL PLANE]
,NSDescriptor!NFPD[NFP-VoiceCall1],NSDescriptor!NsDf[NsDf-NsDf - NSD: VoIP (From :
PreVNFFG 1-AFG 8-FFG 1 )-001],NSDescriptor!VNFProfile(AS), NSDescriptor!VnfDf(VnfDf1),
NSDescriptor!InsLvl(InsLvL2) "
```

```
Element : "SwImageDesc"
Impact at Metamodel level:
"Impactless"
Impact at model level: "Impactless"
Impacted Transformations: "Null"
Impacted Models: "Null"
Impacted Model Elements:  "Null"
```

(c) Impactful InstantiationLevel Element   (d) Impactless SwImageDesc Element

Fig. 10. VNFD change impact results in MAPLE-T

It might be due to other NS management activities (instantiation, configuration, etc.), but the error did not originate from the VNFD parameters used in the design.

Parameters are Impactful at the Metamodel Level: Similar to the first scenario, we also consider the impact at the model level.

– Parameters are *impactful at the model level* (shown by the example in Fig. 10(c)): This means that the generated NSD is erroneous. Thus, we can infer that the misbehaviour is possibly due to the incorrectly-designed NS, which was due to input errors (in the VNFDs). One needs to re-design the NS and re-deploy it.
– Parameters are *impactless at the model level*: As discussed in the first scenario, this case is inconclusive. Even if the change impact analysis suggests that the parameters are impactless, we cannot know if this result is accurate or if it is a *false negative*. The only way we can determine this is to re-enact and generate new traces (but that is what we are trying to avoid in the first place).

A summary of the two scenarios, their different cases, and analysis results is shown in Table 1.

Table 1. Summary of VNFD change impact analysis results

Impact decision	Running NS instance	
	No problem has been detected	Problems have been detected
Impactless at both metamodel and model levels	No re-design is required	NS instance misbehaviour does not originate from the parameter error, no re-design is required
Impactful at both metamodel and model levels	NS needs to be re-designed (e.g., over-provisioning)	NS instance misbehaviour may originate from the parameter error. NS needs to be re-designed
Impactful at metamodel level and impactless at model level	Inconclusive, NS re-design needs to be considered	Inconclusive, NS re-design needs to be considered

In this section we considered only one NS and analyzed the impact of erroneous VNFDs on its design and the behavior of its instances. The same analysis applies similarly to all NSs in which the erroneous VNFDs are involved. Moreover, one may undertake the huge task of analyzing all designed NSs including NSs where the VNFDs are not involved as this could be the result of exclusion due to the erroneous VNFDs. This is along the same lines as reconsidering the design of any NS once a new VNF is made available, but this might be unrealistic.

5 Related Work

We have covered the state of the art on model-driven enactment support for NFV systems in [25]. Although there exists some work on model-based approaches in the NFV literature, to the best of our knowledge there is currently no published work on model-based traceability generation or/and change impact analysis for NFV systems.

In this section, we discuss some MDE approaches and projects related to process enactment, transformation chaining and model management with traceability generation and change impact analysis support.

5.1 Traceability Generation Support

There has been a lot of work done on traceability in MDE, and these are discussed and summarized in [1, 4, 19, 30, 33]. We only discuss here approaches that specifically address traceability generation and/or analysis in the context of model management, process enactment and model transformation chains.

Fritzsche et al. [16, 17] and Jouault et al. [23] have proposed approaches similar to ours in terms of using model transformation chaining and/or model management via megamodelling to enable traceability. The former combines both techniques and proposes automatic generation of trace models as byproducts of the execution of augmented ATL transformations. However, the generated trace models lack in details, since both the higher-order transformation and the corresponding traceability metamodel used are very basic and do not cover more granular trace information. While the latter work constructs model element-level traces (referred to as LTraces in our work) and model-level traces (links within the GTrace in our case) within the megamodel, no explicit support is provided with regards to process enactment nor automatic augmentation of transformation chains with traceability information.

von Pilgrim et al. [28] extend UNiTI [31] (an Eclipse-based tool to construct, reuse and execute transformation chains) with traceability generation support. Although they assume that the transformations explicitly generate trace models as target models, they do not mention anything about how the transformations are augmented (manually by the developer or automatically using a HOT).

In the MegaM@Rt2 ECSEL project [3], they attempt to use a traceability management approach with megamodels in order to handle and link runtime artifacts with their corresponding design artifacts. The generated trace models conform to a traceability metamodel which is much more generic than our LTrace metamodel in terms of the generated trace links. In our case, trace links are contained within model transformation rules (TracedRules). This gives us a more detailed view not only of what source and target elements are linked but also in which rule at the implementation level this trace link has been constructed. Moreover, to the best of our knowledge, no support for transformation chaining nor process enactment was proposed as part of their documents.

Beyhl et al. [8] presents a framework for retaining and maintaining traceability links between the artifacts within a hierarchical megamodel. However, no support for linking distant artifacts using global traceability links has been mentioned in their approach.

Other work exist which focuses solely on generating local traces as a result of transformation executions [5, 11, 21, 22, 34] and are not elaborated here.

5.2   Traceability Analysis Support

There has been extensive work carried out on change impact analysis in the requirements engineering community [20, 30, 33]. However, these approaches do not support process enactment and megamodelling techniques.

van Amstel et al. [5] propose TraceVis, a tool which uses traces to visualize the relationships between traced models. Using their generated traceability visualization, change impact analysis can be implicitly (manually) inferred from the visualization results, but no method or approach has been proposed to automatically analyze the change impact using the generated traces.

Fung et al. [18] presents MMINT-A, a tool built on top of a model management framework (MMINT) using megamodels, which identifies the impact of software system changes on their assurance cases. However, it is not clear whether their megamodel has traceability extensions enabling navigation between artifacts at the global and local levels.

6 Conclusion

In this paper, we presented MAPLE-T, a model-driven traceability information generation and analysis environment built on top of MAPLE [25], an extensible environment which enables model-driven process enactment by interleaving transformation chaining and model management means. MAPLE-T provides support for automatic generation of local and global traceability information during process enactment. Our approach starts with a PM and a set of resources (metamodels, profiles), which are all registered in an MgM. The PM is then mapped to a transformation chain with the help of the MgM. When process enactment begins, the transformation chain is augmented with traceability support on the fly. During enactment of the PM, MAPLE-T executes the underlying transformations and generates the target models as well as the trace models (transformation traces). Trace links are generated both at the model-level and at the model element-level. The generated artifacts are retained in the MgM. The global trace map (provides traceability information at the PM-level) is also part of the MgM.

We have applied our approach on an NFV case study, namely on the NS design, to carry out change impact analysis. The goal was to assess whether changes in the building blocks of a network service, the VNFs, have any impact on the process and the generated deployment templates. As future work, we intend to use MAPLE-T for traceability analysis of the NS design, deployment, and management process.

Acknowledgement. The authors would like to thank Navid Nazarzadeoghaz for the discussions on the NFV application. This work is partly funded by the Natural Sciences and Engineering Research Council (NSERC) of Canada and Ericsson.

References

1. D4.1: Foundations for model management and traceability. Technical report, MegaM@Rt2, September 2017
2. ISO/IEC/IEEE International Standard - Systems and Software Engineering – Vocabulary. ISO/IEC/IEEE 24765:2017(E), pp. 1–541, August 2017
3. D4.3: Model and Traceability Management (MTM) Tool Set – Intermediate version. Technical report, MegaM@Rt2, November 2018
4. Aizenbud-Reshef, N., Nolan, B.T., Rubin, J., Shaham-Gafni, Y.: Model traceability. IBM Syst. J. **45**(3), 515–526 (2006)
5. van Amstel, M.F., van den Brand, M.G.J., Serebrenik, A.: Traceability visualization in model transformations with TraceVis. In: Hu, Z., de Lara, J. (eds.) ICMT 2012. LNCS, vol. 7307, pp. 152–159. Springer, Heidelberg (2012). https://doi.org/10.1007/978-3-642-30476-7_10
6. Baelen, S.V., Vanhoof, B.: MARTES: Traceability management toolset D2.3. Technical report, EUREKA - ITEA 04006, September 2007
7. Basilier, H., Darula, M., Wilke, J.: Virtualizing network services - the telecom cloud. Ericsson Technol. Rev. **91**, 1–9 (2014). https://www.ericsson.com/en/ericsson-technology-review/archive/2014/virtualizing-network-services—the-telecom-cloud
8. Beyhl, T., Hebig, R., Giese, H.: A model management framework for maintaining traceability links. In: Software Engineering 2013 – Workshopband, pp. 453–457 (2013)

9. Borg, M., Runeson, P., Ardö, A.: Recovering from a decade: a systematic mapping of information retrieval approaches to software traceability. Empir. Softw. Eng. **19**(6), 1565–1616 (2014)
10. Chen, Y., Qin, Y., Lambe, M., Chu, W.: Realizing network function virtualization management and orchestration with model-based open architecture. In: 11th International Conference on Network and Service Management (CNSM 2015), pp. 410–418. IEEE (2015)
11. Eclipse: ATL EMF Transformation Virtual Machine (ATL EMFTVM). https://wiki.eclipse.org/ATL/EMFTVM
12. Eclipse: Papyrus. https://eclipse.org/papyrus/
13. ETSI: Network Functions Virtualisation (NFV) Release 2; Information Modeling; Papyrus Guidelines: ETSI GR NFV-IFA 016 V2.1.1, March 2017
14. ETSI: Network Functions Virtualisation (NFV) Release 2; Management and Orchestration; Report on NFV Information Model: ETSI GR NFV-IFA 015 V2.1.1, January 2017
15. Favre, J.M., Nguyen, T.: Towards a megamodel to model software evolution through transformations. Electron. Notes Theor. Comput. Sci. **127**(3), 59–74 (2005)
16. Fritzsche, M., Brunelière, H., Vanhooff, B., Berbers, Y., Jouault, F., Gilani, W.: Applying megamodelling to model driven performance engineering. In: 16th IEEE, ECBS 2009, pp. 244–253, April 2009
17. Fritzsche, M., Johannes, J., Zschaler, S., Zherebtsov, A., Terekhov, A.: Application of tracing techniques in model-driven performance engineering. In: 4th ECMDA Traceability Workshop, pp. 1–10 (2008)
18. Fung, N.L.S., Kokaly, S., Di Sandro, A., Salay, R., Chechik, M.: MMINT-A: a tool for automated change impact assessment on assurance cases. In: Gallina, B., Skavhaug, A., Schoitsch, E., Bitsch, F. (eds.) SAFECOMP 2018. LNCS, vol. 11094, pp. 60–70. Springer, Cham (2018). https://doi.org/10.1007/978-3-319-99229-7_7
19. Galvao, I., Goknil, A.: Survey of traceability approaches in model-driven engineering. In: IEEE EDOC 2007, p. 313, October 2007
20. Göknil, A., Ivanov, I., van den Berg, K.: Change impact analysis based on formalization of trace relations for requirements. In: ECMDA Traceability Workshop (ECMDA-TW), pp. 59–75. No. 274, SINTEF Report, June 2008
21. Guana, V., Stroulia, E.: ChainTracker, a model-transformation trace analysis tool for code-generation environments. In: Di Ruscio, D., Varró, D. (eds.) ICMT 2014. LNCS, vol. 8568, pp. 146–153. Springer, Cham (2014). https://doi.org/10.1007/978-3-319-08789-4_11
22. Jouault, F.: Loosely coupled traceability for ATL. In: ECMDA Workshop on Traceability, pp. 29–37 (2005)
23. Jouault, F., Vanhooff, B., Bruneliere, H., Doux, G., Berbers, Y., Bézivin, J.: Inter-DSL coordination support by combining megamodeling and model weaving. In: ACM 25th SAC 2010, pp. 2011–2018, March 2010
24. Mijumbi, R., Serrat, J., Gorricho, J.L., Latre, S., Charalambides, M., Lopez, D.: Management and orchestration challenges in network functions virtualization. IEEE Commun. Mag. **54**(1), 98–105 (2016)
25. Mustafiz, S., Dupont, G., Khendek, F., Toeroe, M.: MAPLE: An integrated environment for process modelling and enactment for NFV systems. In: Pierantonio, A., Trujillo, S. (eds.) ECMFA 2018. LNCS, vol. 10890, pp. 164–178. Springer, Cham (2018). https://doi.org/10.1007/978-3-319-92997-2_11
26. Mustafiz, S., Nazarzadeoghaz, N., Dupont, G., Khendek, F., Toeroe, M.: A model-driven process enactment approach for network service design. In: Csöndes, T., Kovács, G., Réthy, G. (eds.) SDL 2017. LNCS, vol. 10567, pp. 99–118. Springer, Cham (2017). https://doi.org/10.1007/978-3-319-68015-6_7

27. Mustafiz, S., Palma, F., Toeroe, M., Khendek, F.: A network service design and deployment process for NFV systems. In: 15th IEEE NCA 2016, pp. 131–139. IEEE Computer Society (2016)
28. von Pilgrim, J., Vanhooff, B., Schulz-Gerlach, I., Berbers, Y.: Constructing and visualizing transformation chains. In: Schieferdecker, I., Hartman, A. (eds.) ECMDA-FA 2008. LNCS, vol. 5095, pp. 17–32. Springer, Heidelberg (2008). https://doi.org/10.1007/978-3-540-69100-6_2
29. Santiago, I., Jiménez, A., Vara, J.M., De Castro, V., Bollati, V.A., Marcos, E.: Model-driven engineering as a new landscape for traceability management: A systematic literature review. Inf. Softw. Technol. 54(12), 1340–1356 (2012)
30. Santiago, I., Vara, J.M., de Castro, M.V., Marcos, E.: Towards the effective use of traceability in model-driven engineering projects. In: Ng, W., Storey, V.C., Trujillo, J.C. (eds.) ER 2013. LNCS, vol. 8217, pp. 429–437. Springer, Heidelberg (2013). https://doi.org/10.1007/978-3-642-41924-9_35
31. Vanhooff, B., Ayed, D., Van Baelen, S., Joosen, W., Berbers, Y.: UniTI: A unified transformation infrastructure. In: Engels, G., Opdyke, B., Schmidt, D.C., Weil, F. (eds.) MODELS 2007. LNCS, vol. 4735, pp. 31–45. Springer, Heidelberg (2007). https://doi.org/10.1007/978-3-540-75209-7_3
32. Vanhooff, B., Van Baelen, S., Joosen, W., Berbers, Y.: Traceability as input for model transformations. In: ECMDA Traceability Workshop (ECMDA-TW), pp. 37–46. SINTEF (2007)
33. Winkler, S., Pilgrim, J.: A survey of traceability in requirements engineering and model-driven development. Softw. Syst. Model. 9(4), 529–565 (2010)
34. Yie, A., Wagelaar, D.: Advanced traceability for ATL. In: 1st International Workshop on Model Transformation with ATL (MtATL 2009) (2009)

Modeling in Environmental Social and Industrial Systems

On the Structure of Avionics Systems Architecture

Visar Januzaj[1,2]([⊠])[iD] and Stefan Kugele[3][iD]

[1] RheinMain University of Applied Sciences, Wiesbaden Rüsselsheim, Germany
visar.januzaj@hs-rm.de
[2] Technische Universität Darmstadt, Darmstadt, Germany
[3] Technical University of Munich, Garching, Germany
stefan.kugele@tum.de

Abstract. Integrated Modular Avionics (IMA) systems, contrary to classical avionics systems, enable the execution of multiple aircraft functions on the same hardware modules. This leads to reductions, e. g. in cost and weight, but it becomes also challenging for the design space exploration, in particular due to many system deployment choices. The system management concept of IMA systems allows the expert in advance to manually partition the system into a hierarchical structure, consisting of groups (or clusters) of closely related system components. To automatically partition the software architecture of such IMA systems, we introduce an approach based on data mining methods, such as hierarchical clustering. To determine the closeness between software components, thus, to cluster components with dense intercommunication, the execution time interval (period) and the amount of data transmitted during such intercommunications are used. Leading to favourable effects w.r.t. network load at the deployment level. Furthermore, we propose a method to define cut points on the resultant clustering, in order to determine the final number of clusters, thus, the partitioning of the system.

Keywords: Software architecture · Clustering · Avionics systems · System modelling

1 Introduction

While *federated avionics systems* follow a decentralised approach requiring unique hardware for aircraft functions, such as flight management or autopilot, to be bound to, in *Integrated Modular Avionics* (IMA) [3,13] systems the hardware, so-called *cabinet of processors*, is shared by multiple aircraft functions. While reductions, e. g. cost, power consumption, and weight, are thereby achieved, the IMA concept, due to the continuously increased system complexity, is faced with new challenges, such as safety and resource requirements [2,4]. Januzaj and Kugele [7] presented methods for the modelling and the calculations of system (re-)configurations for IMA systems. There, the software architecture is hierarchically (cf. Sect. 2.1) partitioned in such a way that closely related

© Springer Nature Switzerland AG 2019
P. Fonseca i Casas et al. (Eds.): SAM 2019, LNCS 11753, pp. 139–149, 2019.
https://doi.org/10.1007/978-3-030-30690-8_8

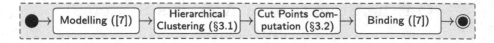

Fig. 1. Data mining-based automated architecture partitioning.

applications are grouped to preferably be bound to the same hardware module. A domain expert manually performs this step. Automated results are, however, invaluable for the design space exploration, as they can provide an insight into various, or even improved, solutions which the domain expert might not have considered [2,4,8].

In this work in progress paper, we introduce an approach to automatically calculate the partitioning of the software architecture, by replacing the manual partitioning [7], as depicted in Fig. 1. For this purpose we apply a data mining method [5,15], *hierarchical clustering* (cf. Sect. 2.2), which represents the partitioning as a binary tree, a so-called *dendrogram*. Each branch of the tree, depending on the *cut point*, represents a closely related group (or *cluster*) of applications. The introduced method is an extension of previous work [6], where the closeness of applications is based on their degree of intercommunication [14], given by the execution time interval (*period*) of their subcomponents (processes and threads). Therefore, applications with a dense intercommunication are put into the same cluster, in order to reduce the overall communication between hardware modules and, thus, the network load/utilisation [4]. This work provides the following contributions (cf. Sect. 3.2):

(a) *Data exchange.* Aiming to further minimise the network load, we extend the former method [6] by considering the amount of transmitted data during intercommunications between applications.
(b) *Cut points.* The formerly introduced method [6] does not define any means for the creation of final clusters, once the hierarchical clustering is performed. Therefore we propose cut points w.r.t. the execution times of processes/threads residing in applications, to support the selection of the final architecture.

2   Preliminaries

In this section, we roughly describe the type of considered IMA systems and the applied clustering technique.

2.1   Integrated Modular Avionics (IMA)

In this paper, we consider IMA systems based on the NATO Standardization Agreement (STANAG 4626) and European Standard 4660 that originated from the ASAAC (Allied Standard Avionics Architecture Council) programme. We refer to such systems throughout the paper as *IMA/ASAAC systems*.

The *system management* hierarchy, consisting of aircraft (AC), integration area (IA), and resource element (RE) levels, is one of the major concepts introduced by the aforementioned standards. An example of such a hierarchy is shown in Fig. 2. While AC represents the top level that manages the whole underlying

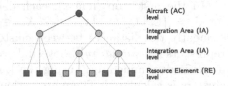

Fig. 2. ASAAC hierarchy [7].

system and RE the lowest level (hardware components), the IA level can consist of further nested and hierarchically arranged IA levels. Each IA level represents and manages subsystems of closely related software components (applications), and is assigned to particular hardware components in the RE level. Software components of IAs at a higher level in the hierarchy can be bound to the hardware components (RE level) assigned to the underlying IAs as well. They may, or may not, have additional hardware components assigned to. The whole system hierarchy is modelled by a number of blueprints [7], using AADL (Architecture Analysis and Design Language), a common modelling language in the avionics domain. The software architecture is modelled in the so-called *application blueprint*, where the corresponding requirements (memory, execution period, (worst-case) execution time, etc.) and communication connectivity between applications are given. Each application consists of processes/threads that communicate through *in*- and *out*-ports.

2.2   Hierarchical Clustering

Data mining aims at identifying understandable patterns in data and extracting knowledge from it [5]. One of the data mining techniques is *clustering*, which partitions a given dataset X into disjoint groups, so-called *clusters*. We assume that $X = \{x_1, \ldots, x_n\}$ consists of $n = |X|$ elements. Such a partitioning/grouping

---

Algorithm 1. Hierarchical Clustering

1: **function** HiClu(X, k)
2:     $\mathcal{C} = \texttt{initialise}(X)$;
3:     D = $\texttt{calculateSimilarity}(\mathcal{C})$;
4:     **while** $|\mathcal{C}| \geq k$ **do**
5:         $(\mathsf{C}_i, \mathsf{C}_j) = \texttt{getClosest}(D)$;
6:         $\mathcal{C} = \mathcal{C} \setminus \{\mathsf{C}_i, \mathsf{C}_j\} \cup \{\mathsf{C}_i \cup \mathsf{C}_j\}$;
7:         D = $\texttt{calculateSimilarity}(\mathcal{C})$;

---

is called *clustering*, denoted $\mathcal{C}$. Each cluster $\mathsf{C}_i \in \mathcal{C}$ contains a set of data $\mathsf{C}_i \subseteq X$. The aim is that the data within a cluster is very similar, whereas the data across clusters is as dissimilar as possible. Data that is not included in a cluster is considered as *noise* (or *outlier*). Unsupervised data mining techniques, such as *clustering*, do not require any prior knowledge about the structure of the data, nor do they need to know what the result should be. One of many existing clustering methods is *hierarchical clustering* [15], which represents the clustering by means of a binary tree, a so-called *dendrogram* (cf. Fig. 3, right). Due to its nature, hierarchical clustering does not consider data as noise, as each data item in its own is a cluster, i.e., a cluster C_i can consist of only one single data item. An algorithm for hierarchical clustering is given in Algorithm 1 (cf. [15]).

In the first step (line 2), each data item in X is put into its own cluster $\mathcal{C} = \{C_i \mid C_i = \{x_i\}, x_i \in X, i \in \{1, \ldots, |X|\}\}$, thus, initialising $\mathcal{C}$. Subsequently the distances between clusters are calculated (line 3). The distance represents the *similarity*[1] between data items. Once the similarity between data items is determined, e.g. using the Euclidean distance, the similarity between clusters is calculated. There are various methods, such as single link, complete link, group average, mean distance, Ward's method, or own methods that can be applied [15]. The rest of the algorithm (from line 4) performs the following steps: (i) two most similar clusters are determined (line 5), (ii) these clusters are merged into a new cluster $C_{ij} = C_i \cup C_j$ and added to the clustering $\mathcal{C}$ (line 6), and (iii) the similarities w.r.t. the new cluster are calculated (line 7).

The size of $\mathcal{C}$ is decreased in each step, until a sought particular number k of clusters is reached, i.e., $|\mathcal{C}| = k$ (line 4). For a given value $k = 1$ the algorithm stops only after all clusters are merged into one single cluster.

3   Approach

In this section, we describe the former clustering method [6] and introduce the extension w.r.t. data transmission and cut points.

3.1   Frequency-Based Clustering

As outlined in Sect. 2.1, in an *application blueprint* the software architecture of an IMA/ASAAC system is modelled. The similarity between applications is based on their degree of intercommunication [6], given by the execution *period* of their underlying processes.

Since applications consist of processes, which communicate with each other and/or processes of other applications, two applications, e.g. a and b in Fig. 3, can have multiple ways of communication (source $\rightarrow$ target). If we consider these communications and their execution period as a *weighted directed graph*, then each application would represent a *vertex*, each communication (through its associated in- and out-ports) an *edge* and the *weight* of each edge would be the corresponding period. Let A represent the set of all applications of the modelled system. The set of all edges adjacent to an application $a \in A$ is described as $E_a = \{(s, t) \mid s = a \lor t = a\}$. Let $E_{i,j} = \{E_i \cap E_j \mid i \neq j\}$ denote the set of all edges adjacent to only two applications $i, j \in A$. The execution period of a communication (edge) from the source application s to a target application t is described by the weight function $w(e)$, with $e = (s, t) \in E_{s,t}$. Let the *set of periods* between two applications i and j be defined as: $\Pi_{i,j} = \{w(e) \mid e \in E_{i,j}\}$. The similarity between two applications i and j is defined as:

$$\sigma(i, j) = \sum_{\pi \in \Pi_{i,j}} \frac{1}{\pi}, \quad i \neq j \land i, j \in A. \tag{1}$$

---

[1] Note that we use throughout the paper the term similarity instead of distance to describe the closeness between clusters.

The higher the intercommunication degree between two applications, the higher their similarity. An example is shown in Fig. 3,
where the applications a and b have
a higher similarity (σ (a, b) = 1/1 +

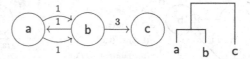

Fig. 3. Example dendrogram

$1/1 + 1/1 = 3$) than b and c (σ (b, c) = 1/3) and, thus, they are merged first.
The clustering is shown by the dendrogram on the right. The weights on edges
denote the corresponding periods.

As mentioned in Sect. 2.2, besides defining means to calculate the similarity
between data items, in our case applications, it is also required to define the
similarity between two clusters $C_i, C_j \in \mathcal{C}$, which is shown below:

$$\sigma (C_i, C_j) = \sum_{x \in C_i} \sum_{y \in C_j} \sigma (x, y) . \tag{2}$$

Now that the similarity is defined, it is possible to apply Algorithm 1 to
cluster the software architecture of IMA/ASAAC system models. However, the
newly defined similarity in (2) is used instead in lines 3 and 7, and X is replaced
by A, the set of all applications of the system. We have to add here, that the
method, and the corresponding extensions introduced in the following section,
can be applied to any architecture model, provided that the required data (about
the connectivity and period) is given. Depending on the chosen value for k, the
clustering is performed as described in Algorithm 1 until k clusters are formed.
An example is depicted in Fig. 4(a), where the clustering process of applications
a, b, c, and d is shown step-by-step.

3.2 Extension

The intercommunication frequency, used in the previous section for similarity
calculation [6], gives indeed a good overview of the structure of the communication intensity between software components [14]. However, the amount of
data transmitted during such intercommunications is essential to minimise the
network load [4].

Let us again consider the example in Fig. 3, assuming that it represents a
small subset of a larger system. As can be seen, the applications a and b interact
with each other very frequently (every 1 time unit), thus, are connected first
and put into the same cluster. They may, however, only send small data chunks,
e. g. 1 data unit. Application c does not interact with b as frequently (every 3
time units) as a, but the amount of data transferred may be considerably higher,
for instance, 15 data units. From the network load point of view, it would make
more sense to put b and c into the same cluster first. Application a may end up
at some point, though, in the same cluster as b and c, depending on the size of
the system.

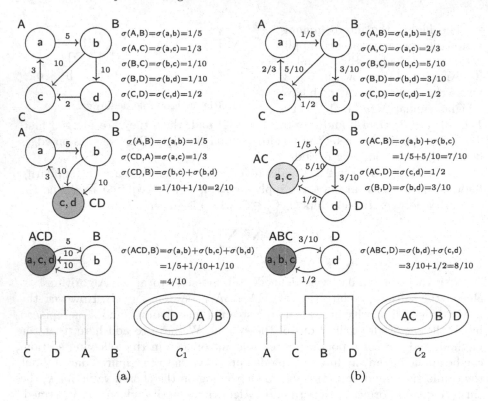

Fig. 4. Comparison: (a) only period, (b) data included.

Similarity. In order to incorporate the data transmission between applications into the clustering process, we need to:

(a) redefine, as shown in (3), the similarity between applications defined in (1) in the previous section and

(b) modify the weight function (cf. Sect. 3.1), i. e., $w(e) = \frac{d}{\pi}$, with d representing the data and π the execution period.

The similarity between clusters, as defined in (2), remains unaffected. Thus, the new similarity is defined as:

$$\sigma(i,j) = \sum_{\frac{d}{\pi} \in \Pi_{i,j}} \frac{d}{\pi}, \quad i \neq j \wedge i, j \in A. \tag{3}$$

In Fig. 4(b) the same graph (system model) as in Fig. 4(a) has been extended with corresponding amount of transferred data pro period. It can easily be seen, that now (in the first step) the two most similar applications are, contrary to Fig. 4(a), a and c. Thus, they are merged first. We see that the final clustering C_2 differs from the clustering C_1 in Fig. 4(a) as well.

To compare both cluster methods w.r.t. the data exchange, we calculate the data transferred in an interval $[0, H]$, and compare the amount of transferred data between clusters created by both methods, (1) and (3). The hyper-period H is usually used in schedulability analyses of system configurations [7], since within the interval $[0, H]$ all tasks/processes are executed; thus, all their deadlines are met. We define H as the *least common multiple* (lcm) of all periods of the periodic processes. For our example in Fig. 4, we get $H = 30$, with $H = \text{lcm}(2, 3, 5, 10)$ for the periods 2 (between d and c), 3 (between c and a), 5 (between a and b), and 10 (between b and c and between b and d, respectively).

In Fig. 4(a) and (b) the same system is modelled with different levels of granularity. While both models include the period in which the applications communicate with each other, the former model lacks the information about the data transmitted during such communications. For the purpose of comparison, we use the same data transmission values (cf. Fig. 4(b)) on the final clustering of both methods. For instance, applications a and b transfer pro period 1 data unit, b and d 3 data units, and b and c 5 data units.

Since the frequency-based method, applying similarity in (1), does not consider data transmission in its clustering process, we apply the similarity in (3) to calculate the data transferred within the interval $[0, H]$, i.e., $\sigma(i, j) \cdot H$.

The result of the comparison is given in Table 1. Note that cluster C is omitted, as it is connected first in both clusterings. Nonetheless, if we compare the amount of data transferred between clusters C and D from $\mathcal{C}_1$, i.e., $\sigma(\text{c}, \text{d}) \cdot H = \frac{1}{2} \cdot 30 = 15$, and that between clusters A and C from $\mathcal{C}_2$, i.e., $\sigma(\text{a}, \text{c}) \cdot H = \frac{2}{3} \cdot 30 = 20$, it is easy to notice that the cluster AC (cal-

Table 1. Comparing clustering based on (1) and (3).

Clusters	CD	ACD	AC	ABC
A	20	–	–	–
B	24	30	21	–
D	–	–	15	24

culated with (3)) has a higher data exchange than the cluster CD (calculated with (1)). And this is exactly what we want to achieve, in order to reduce the network load between hardware modules. The same applies to the other clusters of clustering $\mathcal{C}_1$, calculated using the frequency-based method [6] defined in (1). Hence, clustering $\mathcal{C}_1$ will have a higher network load (if those clusters are not mapped on the same hardware module) than clustering $\mathcal{C}_2$. Therefore, the proposed similarity method (3) yields better clustering w.r.t. network load.

Cut Points. In previous work [6], no means are given to determine the final number of clusters, i.e., the final partitioning of the software architecture, in order to create the IAs. One can indeed specify a k-value, which is required to be known in advance, to determine the expected number of clusters. This, however, depends on the case study, the modelled system, and the domain the method is applied to, e.g. when the number of bird species is known in advance, and the dataset describing birds shall be clustered accordingly. Usually, the number of clusters is not defined a priori; therefore, the final number of clusters is calculated afterwards, e.g. by defining *cut points* in the dendrogram. The branches that are created due to the cutting on the specified points, each define a cluster, thus, creating the final clustering. Regarding the underlying hardware architecture, where the software finally will be bound to and executed on, and especially when dealing with IMA/ASAAC systems, we propose a metric to specify cut points based on requirements, such as period and worst-case execution time, defined on the software model. As described in Sect. 2.1, each IA consists of a number of applications that in turn consist of a number of processes, and to each IA a group of hardware components, specified in the RE level, is assigned to. Using the processor utilisation[2] formula, cf. [10], we propose the following metric to determine the cut points:

$$V(\mathsf{C}_i) = \sum_{a \in \mathsf{C}_i} \sum_{p \in a} \frac{wcet_p}{\pi_p}, \tag{4}$$

where $V(\mathsf{C}_i)$ describes the processor utilisation of the whole cluster C_i, $wcet_p$ the worst-case execution time of a process p residing in application a and π_p the period of p. The cut points are calculated in a depth-first search manner, by cutting the dendrogram at points where $V(\mathsf{C}_i) \leq m$ is first reached. The resulting branch is cut and marked as a cluster. The search then continues on the other uncut branches until no further cuts can be performed. The value m gives roughly the number of required processors that might be used to execute the applications of a cluster. Depending on the scheduling algorithm finally chosen and final binding, this number can vary. Taking into account the execution time requirements for the cut points, we expect better clustering than by defining $k > 1$. The latter may lead to unbalanced clusters w.r.t. the hardware requirements, making the proposed metric more suitable for IMA/ASAAC systems and potentially applicable in a hardware/software co-design process. We have to stress, however, that the proposed metric is not mature enough and it needs to be further investigated and thoroughly evaluated by comparing it with other methods, e. g. graph clustering methods, such as normalised cut [15].

An example, of how the proposed cut points method can be applied, is illustrated in Fig. 5. For this purpose, we use the same model and its clustering as in Fig. 4(b). The required data, which is generally included in the application blueprint [7], about the worst-case execution time of the processes of our system can be found on the top right in Fig. 5. This data is partially based on the data of a flight control system case study [9]. For the sake of clarity, we assume that the applications in our model consist only of the processes that are used to communicate with other applications. A detailed calculation (applying (4)) of utilisations of the clusters A, B, C, and D is given on top of the dendrograms. The utilisation is similarly calculated for clusters AC and ABC, thus, a detailed description of the corresponding calculation is omitted. The dotted (red) lines represent the cut points for the given clustering. There are shown three cut points scenarios, based on different values for m. In the first scenario ($m = 1$), according to the utilisation value $V(\mathsf{C}_i) \leq m$, we get the clusters AC, B, and D. These resulting clusters can be each interpreted as a separate IA. To reduce network load, applications in the cluster/IA AC are to be executed on/bound to the same hardware module, defined in the RE level. Depending on the chosen

---

[2] The utilisation $U(z)$ is usually used to check the schedulability of tasks bound to a processor z, e. g. for $U(z) \leq 1$ means that the binding is schedulable for EDF.

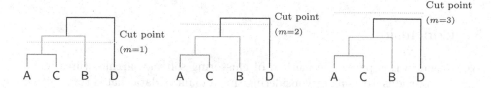

$$V(A) = \frac{wcet_{p_1}}{\pi_{p_1}} = \frac{2.5}{5} = \frac{1}{2}, \; V(B) = \frac{wcet_{p_2}}{\pi_{p_2}} + \frac{wcet_{p_3}}{\pi_{p_3}} = \frac{5}{10} + \frac{5}{10} = 1,$$

$$V(C) = \frac{wcet_{p_4}}{\pi_{p_4}} = \frac{1}{2}, \; V(D) = \frac{wcet_{p_5}}{\pi_{p_5}} = \frac{1.5}{3} = \frac{1}{2},$$

$$V(AC) = \frac{1}{2} + \frac{1}{2} = 1, \; V(ABC) = \frac{1}{2} + 1 + \frac{1}{2} = 2$$

Fig. 5. Example: cut points calculation. (Color figure online)

hierarchy, the application residing in B can form its own IA with its own assigned hardware module(s). It can, however, if placed a level higher in the hierarchy, be assigned to the same hardware module(s) as the applications of the cluster AC. The same applies to the application residing in D. Once the cut points are calculated, it is at the discretion of the experienced domain expert to decides which hierarchy will be finally chosen. For $m = 2$ we get clusters ABC and D. Similarly, applications residing in ABC are to be bound to the assigned hardware module(s) in the RE level. For the application in D applies the same as above. In the last scenario, for $m = 3$, all applications are on the same cluster, i.e., they form together an IA and are assigned to the same hardware module(s) in the RE level.

4   Related Work

Apart from *data mining*, when considered as an integral part of the process chain [7], our approach overlaps with the research area of *design space exploration* as well. Due to the broad research spectrum conducted in both areas and due to space restrictions, we will name just a few. A substantial overview on design space exploration and optimisation methods is given in [1,11]. Network bandwidth and processor utilisation of avionics systems are minimised using heuristic bin-packing and metaheuristic algorithms [4]. The optimisation problem for IMA systems, given as a binary program, is solved by applying branch-an-cut methods [2]. A combination of methods based on *Satisfiability Modulo Theory, Integer Linear Programming*, and multi-objective evolutionary algorithms can be used to optimise the system deployment [9]. For the estimation of the performance of system configurations, machine learning techniques, such as neural networks and linear regression, are applied [12]. The applicability of data mining methods to cluster space mission architectures is successfully shown in [8]. Hierarchical clustering is used to cluster software components based on their interaction [14], which is closest to the spirit of our work, besides the work that we extend [6]. Contrary to our work, however, their degree of interaction is based on the coupling type (inheritance and data) and not on the amount of transmitted data and the execution period. Furthermore, no means w.r.t. cut points are given. Besides that none of the above-mentioned methods deals with IMA/ASAAC systems, none of them tackles the system deployment at an early stage of modelling, e. g. in the absence of the hardware architecture.

5   Conclusion

We extend in this paper the method of clustering software architectures introduced in previous work [6], by considering the amount of data that is transmitted between software components. The aim is to automatically partition the software architecture of IMA/ASAAC systems, which is manually performed [7], and group applications with high data exchange in order to reduce the network load at system deployment. The viability of our extension is shown by a simple example (cf. Fig. 4 and Table 1). Furthermore, we propose a method to define cut points in order to determine the final number of clusters. The proposed clustering approach can be separately applied on other domains as well, such as automotive, where similar scenarios exist. This work is a work in progress and as such still needs further investigation and evaluation, e. g. by applying clustering validation techniques, such as normalised cut measure [15], to assess the clustering quality of our proposed method. At this point, we do not consider requirements regarding software safety levels, dislocality, and redundancy, which might be addressed in future work.

References

1. Aleti, A., Buhnova, B., Grunske, L., Koziolek, A., Meedeniya, I.: Software architecture optimization methods: a systematic literature review. IEEE Trans. Softw. Eng. **39**(5), 658–683 (2013). https://doi.org/10.1109/TSE.2012.64
2. Annighöfer, B., Thielecke, F.: A systems architecting framework for optimal distributed integrated modular avionics architectures. CEAS Aeronaut. J. **6**(3), 485–496 (2015). https://doi.org/10.1007/s13272-015-0156-1
3. ARINC 653-1: Avionics application software standard interface, October 2003
4. Dougherty, B., Schmidt, D.C., White, J., Kegley, R., Preston, J.: Deployment optimization for embedded flight avionics systems. In: CrossTalk, p. 31 (2011)

5. Han, J., Kamber, M.: Data Mining: Concepts and Techniques. Morgan Kaufmann Publishers Inc., San Francisco (2000)
6. Januzaj, V.: Data mining meets system modelling. In: Proceedings of the 21st ACM/IEEE International Conference on Model Driven Engineering Languages and Systems MODELS 2018: Companion Proceedings, MODELS 2018, pp. 55–56. ACM, New York (2018). https://doi.org/10.1145/3270112.3270133
7. Januzaj, V., Kugele, S., Biechele, F., Mauersberger, R.: A configuration approach for IMA systems. In: Eleftherakis, G., Hinchey, M., Holcombe, M. (eds.) SEFM 2012. LNCS, vol. 7504, pp. 203–217. Springer, Heidelberg (2012). https://doi.org/10.1007/978-3-642-33826-7_14
8. Kinneer, C., Herzig, S.J.I.: Dissimilarity measures for clustering space mission architectures. In: Proceedings of the 21st ACM/IEEE International Conference on Model Driven Engineering Languages and Systems ACM/IEEE MODELS 2018, pp. 392–402. ACM, New York (2018). https://doi.org/10.1145/3239372.3239390
9. Kugele, S., Pucea, G., Popa, R., Dieudonné, L., Eckardt, H.: On the deployment problem of embedded systems. In: ACM/IEEE International Conference on Formal Methods and Models for Codesign, MEMOCODE 2015, Austin, TX, USA, 21–23 September 2015, pp. 158–167. IEEE (2015). https://doi.org/10.1109/MEMCOD.2015.7340482
10. Liu, C.L., Layland, J.W.: Scheduling algorithms for multiprogramming in a hard-real-time environment. J. ACM **20**(1), 46–61 (1973). https://doi.org/10.1145/321738.321743
11. Mehiaoui, A., Wozniak, E., Babau, J.P., Tucci-Piergiovanni, S., Mraidha, C.: Optimizing the deployment of tree-shaped functional graphs of real-time system on distributed architectures. Autom. Softw. Eng. **26**(1), 1–57 (2019). https://doi.org/10.1007/s10515-018-0244-7
12. Özisikyilmaz, B., Memik, G., Choudhary, A.: Efficient system design space exploration using machine learning techniques. In: 2008 45th ACM/IEEE Design Automation Conference, pp. 966–969. IEEE (2008). https://doi.org/10.1145/1391469.1391712
13. RTCA DO-297: Integrated Modular Avionics (IMA) Development Guidance and Certification Considerations, August 2005
14. Yu, L., Ramaswamy, S.: Verifying design modularity, hierarchy, and interaction locality using data clustering techniques. In: Proceedings of the 45th Annual Southeast Regional Conference, ACM-SE 45, pp. 419–424. ACM, New York (2007). https://doi.org/10.1145/1233341.1233417
15. Zaki, M.J., Wagner Meira, J.: Data Mining and Analysis: Fundamental Concepts and Algorithms. Cambridge University Press, Cambridge (2014)

Generating Executable Code
from High-Level Social
or Socio-Ecological Model Descriptions

Themis Dimitra Xanthopoulou[1]([mail]) (iD), Andreas Prinz[1] (iD),
and F. LeRon Shults[2] (iD)

[1] Department of Information and Communication Technology, University of Agder,
Jon Lilletuns vei 9, 4879 Grimstad, Norway
{themis.d.xanthopoulou,andreas.prinz}@uia.no
https://www.uia.no/en/kk/profil/themisdx
[2] Institute for Global Development and Social Planning, University of Agder,
Universitetsveien 19, 4630 Kristiansand, Norway
leron.shults@uia.no

Abstract. Agent-Based Modelling has been used for social simulation because of the several benefits it entails. Social models are often constructed by inter-disciplinary teams that include subject-matter experts with no programming skills. These experts are typically involved in the creation of the conceptual model, but not the verification or validation of the simulation model. The Overview, Design concepts, and Details (ODD) protocol has emerged as a way of presenting a model at a high level of abstraction and as an effort towards improving the reproducibility of Agent-Based Models (ABMs) but it is typically written after a model has been completed. This paper reverses the process and provides non-programming experts with a user-friendly and extensible tool called ODD2ABM for creating and altering models on their own. This is done by formalizing ODD using concepts abstracted from the NetLogo language, enabling users to generate NetLogo code from an ODD description automatically. We verified the ODD2ABM tool with three existing NetLogo models.

Keywords: Social model · Metamodel · Code generation · Abstraction · Formality · Reproducibility · Verification

1 Introduction

In recent years there has been a rapid rise in the use of the Agent-Based Modelling [1]. ABMs offer unique capabilities and are widely used by a growing number of scientists and policy professionals [3,6,7,13] with social simulations as a prominent application.

Hassan et al. [7] have identified four roles typically involved in the development of an ABM: the thematician, the modeller, the computer scientist and

© Springer Nature Switzerland AG 2019
P. Fonseca i Casas et al. (Eds.): SAM 2019, LNCS 11753, pp. 150–162, 2019.
https://doi.org/10.1007/978-3-030-30690-8_9

the programmer. The roles fit well the conceptual model of the model development process presented by Sargent in [14]. According to Sargent, a model is the representation of a real-life system. The *thematician*, who is the expert in the problem entity, uses her experience to create the high-level informal model description or conceptual model of the system, see Fig. 1. The description of the entities of the system in the conceptual model is formal, and their attributes and interactions informal. The *modeller* transforms the description of the conceptual model into a detailed informal model, the simulation model specification [14], with formalised attributes and informal procedures. The *computer scientist* finds an executable approximation or a high-level formal model description. In this stage, the informal procedures of the previous step become formal. Finally, the *programmer* implements the simulation model using a suitable programming language and platform and providing a detailed formal model.

Rarely can one researcher alone fill all these roles. Moreover, complex models usually require perspectives from different disciplines and therefore more than one thematician. These are the reasons why ABMs are typically constructed by multidisciplinary teams. These teams face several challenges. First of all, communication of the model among such diverse researchers can be difficult [7,13]. Since the product of each development step depends on each individual's conceptual understanding, different teams may come up with dissimilar simulation models even if they are working with the same "thematician". This dissimilarity hinders reproducibility of results, which is one of the pillars of the scientific method [5].

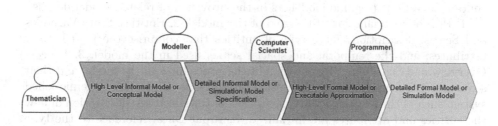

Fig. 1. Modelling and simulation: roles and stages

One of the ways to ensure reproducibility is to perform verification from one step to another. Sargent [14] specifies two types of verification: the *specification verification* that takes place between the conceptual model and the simulation model specification and the *implementation verification* that takes place between the simulation model specification and the simulation model. The complicating issue is that subject-matter experts, who build the conceptual model of the system, are not usually skilled in modelling and computer programming and cannot perform the verifications. They typically find the executable code obscure [2]. The definition of the model becomes 'hidden' in the code and cannot be perceived, validated or changed by the experts [2-4,7,13].

Consequently, we want to solve the following problem with this paper: How can we make ABMs more accessible to subject-matter experts to ensure verification and to enable validation of the simulation models? One proposed approach favours building blocks that could enable non-programming experts to develop and modify their ABMs [6]. Continuing with this thought, we want to create a domain-specific language (DSL) and an associated tool allowing subject-matter experts to create and change simulations models.

The remainder of this paper is structured as follows: Sect. 2 introduces ODD, NetLogo, and DSLs and provides an overview of related work. Section 3 describes the process we developed to build each metamodel component, and Sect. 4 discusses the quality of the outcome. Finally, Sect. 5 summarizes the paper. Throughout the paper, we illustrate the steps of the methodology with the Wolf Sheep Simple 5 model [15].

2   Background and Related Work

2.1   ODD

Many scholars in the Agent-Based Modelling community have adopted the Overview, Design concepts, and Details (ODD) protocol. ODD emerged as an effort to boost "Communication of Results, Replication, Model Comparison, and Interdisciplinary Dialogue" [5]. The ODD description process is an artefact of the conceptual and the simulation model specification stage as shown in Fig. 1.

The protocol has the following seven thematic sections [5], where each section contains questions to guide modellers in the provision of related model details.

1. Purpose: explanation of the goal of the model. 2. Entities, State Variables and Scales: description of the type of entities that comprise the model, their attributes, and the temporal and spatial scales used in the model. 3. Process Overview and Scheduling: clarification of the procedures in the model and their sequence. 4. Design Concepts: discussion of more specific topics of the modelled system such as the learning ability of entities. 5. Initialization: description of how the entities and attributes are initialized. 6. Input Data: reference to the type and specifics of the external data used by the model. 7. Sub-models: explanation of the sub-processes in the model.

Figure 2 shows the questions for the "Entities, State Variables and Scales" element of an ODD, retrieved from [5], and provides an example of a specification. The modeller must provide the model definition by answering all of the questions in each of the thematic sections. The emerging document with the ODD specifications can be quite large, depending on the model it describes. The answers appear informally, and one can portray the protocol as a group of informal entities. The questions attempt to cover different perspectives of the conceptual model to promote a unified impression of what the model entails. Nowadays, many journals consider the ODD protocol as a prerequisite for the publication of an ABM model. Although this is a big step towards verification, validation and reproducibility of simulation models, the informal character of the answers allows ambiguities in the model description. Platforms such as

ODD Element	Questions	Specification
Entity, State Variables, and Scales	What kind of entities are in the model? Do they represent managers, voters, landowners, firms or something else? By what state variables or attributes are these entities characterised? What are the temporal and spatial resolutions and extents of the model?	The agents represent sheep and wolves, and the environment is grassland that they inhabit. Both wolves and sheep have energy that they use to move around. On the other hand, the grass contains energy. The space represents a grassland and the time is not defined by the modeller, but, given the model dynamics, it should be within the lifetime of a sheep.

Fig. 2. Informal ODD: questions and specification

the "ComSES Network OpenABM" mentioned in [8] enable the uploading and sharing of ABMs in terms of executable code, ODD and other descriptions to promote model transparency and reuse and to move further towards a scientific handling of ABMs.

2.2 DSLs and MPS

Domain-specific languages (DSLs) facilitate the efficient development of models and the production of artefacts. However, it is not enough to define a DSL; one also needs an appropriate tool to work with the DSL. This is normally accomplished with a meta-tool that creates a DSL tool out of a DSL description. Such a meta-tool is called a language workbench.

To build our tool, which we call ODD2ABM, we selected the Meta Programming System (MPS), a free platform for the creation of DSLs [9], mainly because of its user-friendliness. It is also important that MPS provides tabular and diagrammatic notations in addition to plain text. MPS structures a DSL description in the aspects of *structure*, which is the abstract syntax, *editor*, which is the concrete syntax, *constraints*, which is the static semantics, and *generator*, which are the dynamic semantics and the definition of the transformation.

2.3 Related Work

Domain-specific languages together with Model Driven Development (MDD) [2] have often been used to solve problems similar to ours. DSLs aspire to provide the model definition in a high-level language so that experts can understand and modify the domain-specific model. MDD aims to automate the processes from the high-level informal description to the detailed formal description shown in Fig. 1. The developer defines the transformations from one stage to the other. The end user inputs specifications in the high-level format and the DSL tool automatically generates the next stage artefact or the simulation model.

Some researchers have worked on the formalisation of certain aspects of ABMs, such as interactions [11]. Others have built metamodels that specialise within specific domains. The MAIA metamodel (Modelling Agent systems based on Institutional Analysis) covers Social Simulations with Institutional Analysis and semi-automatic code generation [4]. MDA4ABMS merges both DSL and MDD methodologies, but the user needs some modelling experience to handle the high-level language, and the tool does not automatically provide the low-level language artefact [2]. Also, the inclusion of UML (Unified Modelling Language), which is applied in the methodology, has often been discarded by other researchers due to its lack of expressiveness [13]. Similarly, the easyABMS methodology includes UML and does not provide automatic code generation but takes into account all the modelling and simulation phases and can be used for general processes [3]. The metamodel introduced by Santos et al. [13] automatically generates code, and has been evaluated as very efficient; however, it only applies to the adaptive traffic signal control domain. Finally, adaptations of Multi-Agent methodologies to Agent-Based methodologies have been able to establish a common high-level formal language, but these do not include automatic code generation [7].

3   Methodology

The central idea is that a user can input the model description in the DSL and the tool will automatically generate the simulation model in executable code. Apart from advantages related to the creation or modification time of conceptual and simulation models, this approach provides built-in verification of the model. The main reason is that there is a deterministic relationship between input (formally described conceptual model) and output (executable code or simulation model). In essence, we automate the transitions from stage one to stage four shown in Fig. 1. To do that we bring formality to the model description in a way that the thematician can still handle it and define the model in the DSL.

The goal is to start from simple models, so that we obtain a proof of concept for our idea, and then extend the work to more complex ABMs. The tool should be easy to use, extensible, and allow automatic code generation from the model definitions produced by subject-matter experts. Our methodology integrates aspects of MDD and DSL. The DSL ensures user-friendliness and accommodates diverse models, while the MDD is used to provide the detailed formal model in an executable form. Using MPS for the DSL development enables to shift the focus on the language description. MPS will automatically generate a neat and efficient DSL tool directly from the language description.

As ODD already is a DSL for social models, a tool that transforms an ODD to NetLogo would solve our problem. However, ODD is not formal enough for a direct transformation. Still, we argue that instead of creating our DSL from scratch, using the methodologies proposed by [3,7,13], we can take advantage of the accumulated experience of researchers that the ODD incorporates and make the descriptions more formal already in ODD. Some of the advantages of using the protocol as a starting point include its existing structure [10] and its inclusion of Agent-Based Modelling domain concerns that cover the need for the DSL's broadness and extensibility enabling us to skip the domain analysis. Although Santos et al. [13] used the ODD protocol to refine the collection of concepts for the domain analysis of their case study, researchers have not yet taken full advantage of it to render ABMs more accessible.

There are more than 80 platforms that accommodate ABMs based on different programming languages [1]. Unsurprisingly, all of them display shortcomings. Our choice for a low-level language and simulation platform is NetLogo [16]. Uri Wilensky created NetLogo to facilitate the development of Agent-Based Modelling and Simulation. The platform has been widely used in the modelling community. Not only does NetLogo make it easier for non-programmers to develop a model [1,6], but it also provides an interface that facilitates simulations and reduces the amount of time needed to design them. In essence, a person with no modelling experience can explore a NetLogo model on the platform. Finally, NetLogo is an open source software with full documentation in [1]. We argue that NetLogo provides a good starting point as the simulation language of our tool since it accommodates a variety of models (but not large scale ones) [1].

Using this method, the two remaining challenges are: (1) a formalisation of the sections of ODD with important information for the simulation, and (2) a description of the transformation from ODD to NetLogo. The formalisation of ODD is closely related to the user-friendliness of ODD2ABM. We want to make our DSL so accessible that it could be used by experts without any programming experience. This ease of use is intended to encourage and enable such users to construct and adapt ABMs without overly relying on computer scientists and coders. Finally, we want to make our DSL capable of incorporating a broad thematic range of models to ensure robustness.

The two main challenges in the creation of a formal ODD are repetition of information, and missing information. Missing information is information that is available in the NetLogo code, but that is not present in the ODD. To include such information we have to find out whether it can be generated from other existing information, or whether it must be included into the ODD. Repeated information could be handled by just ignoring the duplicated parts. However, it is important that the formal parts of an ODD are reliable and if there is duplicated information, it has to be synchronized. In MPS, dealing with this problem involves determining the placement of the information and referring to it every time the information appears.

One aspect of the tool's friendliness is its capacity to automatically generate executable code, a task which has previously required programming skills. Using MPS, it is straightforward for non-programming experts to run their simulations. Although we have chosen NetLogo as a target language for the code generation, there is still a lot of variability in the actual code to be produced. This again might influence the choice of concepts in the DSL, as we prefer concepts that are easily implemented.

3.1   Metamodel Elements

To create ODD2ABM in MPS, we needed to define the structure, constraints, editor, and generation rules of the DSL. ODD itself comes with an editor as shown in Fig. 2. ODD2ABM uses a similar editor reusing existing elements and adding new ones when necessary. It was not clear from the start which formal elements would be needed for ODD. To determine them, we used the systematic procedure described below. Finally, we created generation rules for automatic code generation.

3.2   Procedure for Defining the Metamodel Structure

Collection of the ODD Elements and Questions. We selected the ODD version from Grimm et al. [5]. From this version we gathered the questions related to each element and registered them.

Selection of NetLogo Models for Concrete Model Instances and Code. The concrete model instances aim at verifying our procedure. Since this is the first version of ODD2ABM, we chose to start with simple models from the Net-Logo library. For each of the models, we had an ODD description and NetLogo code. In parallel, we consulted the NetLogo dictionary [12] and a chapter focusing on Agent-Based modelling concepts for NetLogo [17]. The dictionary and the ABM concept overview ensured that the simplicity of the first test models will not compromise the extensibility and expressivity of our metamodel.

Matching of Each Element with the Corresponding Code. For each element in the code of the selected models, we attempted to find matching information in the ODD description. For example, the answers for the element "Entities, State variables, and Scales" and the entity sheep of the "Wolf Sheep Simple 5" model (see Fig. 2), match the code "breed [sheep a-sheep]" and "sheep own [energy]". Questions such as "What are the temporal and spatial resolutions and extensions of the model?" are not semantically significant for the code. Using the final code, we distinguished the ODD elements that produce parts of the code from those that do not.

Identification of the Parts of NetLogo Code that Cannot Be Extracted from the ODD Specifications. It is possible that some information, essential to the code generation and conceptually relevant to the system does not appear in the ODD specifications. For example, there are three types of entities in NetLogo (turtles, patches, and links), but the distinction among them is not visible in an ODD specification. Conceptually, they display different properties. Intuitively, we categorise entities and we are able to associate each entity with a type, but the entity name by itself does not reflect this categorisation to enable automation of the process. We attempted to distinguish between higher-level information and low-level information, where low-level is part of the simulation model and should not be included in an ODD. The method to accomplish this was to formulate the information on the level of the ODD and check its conceptual validity.

Creation of Questions in the ODD Language to Accommodate Code Generation. To deal with the identified parts from the previous step, we designed questions to collect the relevant information. To follow up the previous example, to distinguish patches and turtles, we created questions on whether the entity is part of the environment or not.

We collected the questions in flow diagrams to visualize the order in which the user should input the answers. Then, they were incorporated in the editor description in a text format or in the editor structure. For example, general entities and environmental entities are placed in different sections of the specification, and this is how a question of whether an entity is general or environmental is reflected in the editor structure.

The same procedure applies to the rest of the model. The answers comprise the high-level formal model of Fig. 1, thus enabling code generation. The specifications with no semantic significance for the code generation, such as the Purpose statement (see Fig. 3), require an informal textual answer.

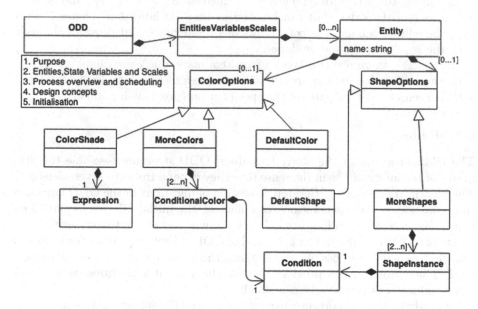

Fig. 3. UML class diagram of entities, state variables, and scales

Grouping Questions that Reappear. It is possible to ask the same questions in multiple positions of ODD. For example, to define environmental attributes and entity attributes we need the same information. Grouping this information reduces the time for the DSL development and enhances the visual representation of the specifications.

Extraction of the DSL Structure from the Diagram. Figure 3 illustrates part of the concepts of the DSL that relate to the ODD element "Entities, State Variables and Scales". Each user input corresponds to either a DSL concept (for example the concept `Entity`) or to a DSL concept attribute (for example the attribute `name` of the concept `Entity`).

Registration of Emerging Constraints. We made sure that specifications are meaningful and did not violate common sense. For this, we extracted the informal conditions placed on the concepts and formalized them as MPS constraints. If we take the example of the entity sheep (Fig. 4) of the "Wolf Sheep Simple 5" model, we read that it contains the attribute `energy` of type `float`. This will restrict the next line in the specification, which is the definition of the range of values, i.e. `float` values. If energy was of type `string`, then the editor would request a list of `string` values. Moreover, the editor will not allow to specify the range of a blank or unnamed attribute.

Similarly, the attribute type given in "Entities, State Variables, and Scales" will constrain the value that can be used in the "Initialisation" element. This way, the editor manages the constraints of the language and provides the user with the required help and guidance.

In general, there are two types of constraints: value constraints associated with the description in the specification and reference constraints associated with references to other parts of the specification (previous inputs).

3.3 Editor

The UML diagrams of the newly formalised ODD structure resemble the diagrams of the informal one in the sense that they expand from the seven elements. The identified questions of the step "Creation of questions in the ODD language to accommodate code generation" complement the initial ODD structure. The editor for ODD is providing textual and tabular syntax for the structural elements of ODD. The original look and feel of ODD is kept by putting the elements into text as much as possible and keeping the concepts at the same language level. The editor of MPS provides state-of-the-art editor facilities. Some more advanced features can be added manually.

It is particularly important when working with ODDs that the required input is very specific, except for answers with no semantic significance. For example, we can see in Fig. 4, that the editor description is "Color is defined for the entity". The initial text is "Color <Press Alt and Enter to choose to include or not include color> defined for the entity". When the user presses `Alt` and `Enter` the only choices are "is" and "is not".

The MPS editor provides auto-complete to help users identify possible continuations and lists where they need to define the possible answers, as well as

```
This is entity sheep a-sheep
Color  is  defined for the entity
Throughout the simulation, the  sheep a-sheep
has a default color which is White
Throughout the simulation, the  sheep a-sheep has a default shape which is sheep
Throughout the simulation, we  do not  track entity statistics
sheep a-sheep does contains the following attributes :
The attribute is named  Energy
The parameter is not stable for all  sheep a-sheep
Energy takes float values.
The estimated range of values for the  Energy is: ( 0 , 100 )
The attribute is named  Energy-gain-from-grass
The parameter is not stable for all  sheep a-sheep
Energy-gain-from-grass takes float values.
The estimated range of values for the  Energy-gain-from-grass is: ( 0 , 2 )
```

Fig. 4. Formalised ODD in MPS (MPS editor) (Color figure online)

static checks on the fly in order to avoid wrong inputs. For more complex inputs, the editor description indicates and checks the right way to configure the text. The editor does not show text that matches specifications not enabled in the current model. For example, in the previous example, when the user selects "is not", then the part where the user specifies the color method and the specific color choice, currently visible in Fig. 4, are not shown. The editor appearance is derived from the questions, which are similar to the corresponding concepts (see Fig. 3). Overall, the ODD elements are connected as shown in the UML diagram and the editor provides a rich user interface for creating an ODD document.

3.4   Executable Code Generation

Normally, code generation follows the flow of information as given in the ODD structure. Depending on the place in the generated code, it might be the case that information is collected from different parts of the specification. For example, even though we choose to specify whether an entity has a color in the "Entities State Variables and Scales" element, MPS uses these specifications to generate code for the Initialisation part of the editor.

Code generation requires the specification to be statically correct, i.e. all constraints should be satisfied. This is checked already in the editor and signalled to the user. Code generation is disabled as long as there are errors in the specification. Utmost care was applied to make sure that the code generation is correct whenever the specification is statically correct. For example, we can look at the generated code for the sections in Fig. 4, which is "sheep own [energy]". The editor requires the user to assign the attribute "energy" to the entity "sheep". If no entity has been defined, it will not be possible to define an attribute for it. Moreover, the name of the attribute has to be defined in order to enable generation of correct code.

In general, we can identify two categories of generated code: code that depends on the model definition and code independent of the specific model, but dependent on the platform of choice. The second type relates to the simulation platform we use, which is NetLogo in our case, and is automated for ODD2ABM.

4 Evaluation

We performed the eight-step procedure outlined in Sect. 3 for the four ODD elements: "Purpose", "Entity, State Variables, and Scales", "Process Overview and Scheduling", and "Initialisation" and verified the result using three NetLogo library models. Overall, we moved formality to the first stage of Fig. 1 and automated the rest of the steps with the metamodel.

4.1 Expressivity and Extension

Since we created our DSL based on relatively simple models, we cannot guarantee that ODD2ABM covers the range of social models. However, the concepts are carefully chosen to cover a broad range of applications and possible specifications. In the future, we will validate the DSL with more complex ABMs and introduce more specifications. For example, we plan to further develop the interaction part of our tool, and add the possibility of importing data from files external to the platform. The extensibility of our DSL is ensured by MPS and the conceptual framework we adopted.

4.2 ODD and Experts

The clear structure of the ODD protocol enabled us to enrich it as a DSL with some modifications without losing its accessibility for users with limited programming skills. The question remains whether the level of the language is high enough for thematicians to engage with it. Part of the concern lies in the fact that the original ODD targets modellers. We all use models (in a general sense) in our everyday lives. However, the concepts employed in the Agent-Based Modelling community, such as entities and attributes, may not be intuitively clear to all users. Therefore, even if the tool is very effective for modellers, experts not familiar with the ODD language may face difficulties in its use. In a next stage of development we will evaluate the usefulness of ODD2ABM.

5 Summary and Future Steps

The ODD2ABM tool described in this paper serves as a proof of concept for a methodology that incorporates DSL and MDD, uses the MPS platform, and enables experts to create and modify their ABMs, thereby providing a new way to enhance the reproducibility of results. During the construction of this tool, we were careful to ensure its user-friendliness and extensibility. We selected the ODD protocol as the basis for our DSL and NetLogo as our low-level language. The resulting DSL is original in its capabilities and properties as it accommodates a large range of modelling themes and enables automatic code generation from a formalized high-level model description. We plan to broaden ODD2ABM so that it allows more freedom in model creation. A next step would be to survey experts from different disciplines to discover whether our formalisation of the ODD protocol needs to be further abstracted.

References

1. Abar, S., Theodoropoulos, G.K., Lemarinier, P., ÒHare, G.M.: Agent based modelling and simulation tools: a review of the state-of-art software. Comput. Sci. Rev. **24**, 13–33 (2017). https://doi.org/10.1016/j.cosrev.2017.03.001
2. Garro, A., Parisi, F., Russo, W.: A process based on the model-driven architecture to enable the definition of platform-independent simulation models. In: Pina, N., Kacprzyk, J., Filipe, J. (eds.) Simulation and Modeling Methodologies, Technologies and Applications. Advances in Intelligent Systems and Computing, vol. 197, pp. 113–129. Springer, Heidelberg (2013). https://doi.org/10.1007/978-3-642-34336-0_8
3. Garro, A., Russo, W.: Easyabms: a domain-expert oriented methodology for agent-based modeling and simulation. Simul. Model. Pract. Theory **18**(10), 1453–1467 (2010). https://doi.org/10.1016/j.simpat.2010.04.004
4. Ghorbani, A., Bots, P., Dignum, V., Dijkema, G.: MAIA: a framework for developing agent-based social simulations. J. Artif. Soc. Soc. Simul. **16**(2), 9 (2013). https://doi.org/10.18564/jasss.2166
5. Grimm, V., Polhill, G., Touza, J.: Documenting social simulation models: the ODD protocol as a standard. In: Edmonds, B., Meyer, R. (eds.) Simulating Social Complexity. Understanding Complex Systems, pp. 117–133. Springer, Heidelberg (2013). https://doi.org/10.1007/978-3-540-93813-2_7
6. Hamill, L.: Agent-based modelling: the next 15 years. J. Artif. Soc. Soc. Simul. **13**(4), 11 (2010). https://doi.org/10.18564/jasss.1640
7. Hassan, S., Fuentes-Fernández, R., Galán, J.M., López-Paredes, A., Pavón, J.: Reducing the modeling gap: on the use of metamodels in agent-based simulation. In: 6th Conference of the European Social Simulation Association (ESSA 2009), pp. 1–13 (2009)
8. Janssen, M.A., Alessa, L.N., Barton, M., Bergin, S., Lee, A.: Towards a community framework for agent-based modelling. J. Artif. Soc. Soc. Simul. **11**(2), 6 (2008). http://jasss.soc.surrey.ac.uk/11/2/6.html
9. JetBrains: MPS Meta Programming System. https://www.jetbrains.com/mps/
10. Klügl, F., Davidsson, P.: AMASON: Abstract Meta-model for Agent-based SimulatiON. In: Klusch, M., Thimm, M., Paprzycki, M. (eds.) MATES 2013. LNCS (LNAI), vol. 8076, pp. 101–114. Springer, Heidelberg (2013). https://doi.org/10.1007/978-3-642-40776-5_11
11. Kubera, Y., Mathieu, P., Picault, S.: Interaction-oriented agent simulations: from theory to implementation. In: Proceedings of the 2008 Conference on ECAI 2008: 18th European Conference on Artificial Intelligence, pp. 383–387. IOS Press, Amsterdam (2008). http://dl.acm.org/citation.cfm?id=1567281.1567367
12. Netlogo dictionary. https://ccl.northwestern.edu/netlogo/docs/dictionary.html

13. Santos, F., Nunes, I., Bazzan, A.L.: Model-driven agent-based simulation development: a modeling language and empirical evaluation in the adaptive traffic signal control domain. Simul. Model. Pract. Theory **83**, 162–187 (2018). https://doi.org/10.1016/j.simpat.2017.11.006
14. Sargent, R.G.: Verification and validation of simulation models. J. Simul. **7**(1), 12–24 (2013). https://doi.org/10.1057/jos.2012.20
15. Wilensky, U.: Netlogo wolf sheep predation model. Report, Center for Connected Learning and Computer-Based Modeling, Northwestern University, Evanston, IL (1997). http://ccl.northwestern.edu/netlogo/models/WolfSheepPredation
16. Wilensky, U.: Netlogo home page. Center for Connected Learning and Computer-Based Modeling, Northwestern University, Evanston, IL (1999). http://ccl.northwestern.edu/netlogo/
17. Wilensky, U., Rand, W.: The Components of Agent-Based Modeling, 1st edn, pp. 203–282. The MIT Press, Cambridge (2015)

Towards a Representation of Cellular Automaton Using Specification and Description Language

Pau Fonseca i Casas$^{(\boxtimes)}$ (iD)

Universitat Politècnica de Catalunya, Barcelona 08034, CA, Spain
pau@fib.upc.edu

Abstract. Environmental simulation is complex, not only due to the inherent complexity of the phenomenon that we are facing but also to the fact that the personnel involved in this kind of projects belongs to different areas and specialties. In this scenario, the use of a formal language is needed since it simplifies the interaction between the parts. A key element that must be represented in an environmental simulation model is a Geographical Information System (GIS) data. This representation often uses Cellular Automaton structures since it allows to represent, not only the data but also its behavior inside the simulation model. In this work, we explore the use of SDL, that among other benefits we can remark that it is an ITU-T standard language and allows a complete graphical description of the models and several tools allows a semi-automatic implementation of the models.

Keywords: SDL · Cellular automaton · Formal representation · Fibonacci function

1 Introduction

The data used on environmental simulation models often can be dynamically modified by the behavior of the model, and usually, the results of the simulation model are mainly this dynamic modification of the data. As an example, for a decision support system related to forest fires [1, 2], the data representing the temperature for a geographical area can be both an output from the model and an input to the model. Therefore, the data and its structure is a key element of the model definition. Focusing on the conceptualization of a simulation model, to be able to do a complete and non-ambiguous representation of the system is necessary to represent:

1. The structure: that allows depicting the hierarchical decomposition of the model and the relation between all the different subcomponents and sub-models.
2. Behavior: that details the model processes and activities.
3. Data: that detail, not only the data, but its relationship with the model, and how the nature of the data modifies the structure of the model itself. On the paper, data declarations are made using C notation, conform to Z.104 Annex C clause C.1 C language binding.

P. Fonseca i Casas et al. (Eds.): SAM 2019, LNCS 11753, pp. 163–179, 2019.
https://doi.org/10.1007/978-3-030-30690-8_10

For environmental simulation, the problem with the data and its impact on the structure of the model is specifically how to represent a Cellular Automaton (CA), because CA are widely used to represent geographical and dynamical information in environmental simulation models [3–7].

Specification and Description Language (SDL) [8–10], is an ITU-T standard language, that allows a graphical, complete and unambiguous representation of a simulation model. The different concepts that the SDL covers are:

1. System structure: from the blocks to the processes and their related hierarchy.
2. Communication: signals, communication paths or channels, parameters that can be carried by the signals, etc.
3. Behavior: defined by different processes.
4. Data: based on Abstract Data Types (ADT).
5. Inheritance: useful to describe relations between objects and their properties.

In this paper we are focused on how SDL can be useful to describe the data related to an environmental model, using Inheritance, Data, and Communication in the diagrams.

1.1   Cellular Automaton

For the integration of a simulation model with Geographical Information System (GIS) data, that is often needed in an environmental model, it is useful to use a CA, due to its ability to effectively represent large-scale spatial dynamic phenomena [3, 4, 11].

CA is mainly a matrix and a set of rules that defines the matrix modifications over time. This behavior is completely specified in terms of a local relation. Table 1 shows one-dimensional CA after successive applications of the Wolfram's 30th rule. Table 1 shows the 30th rule using Wolfram's notation, see [12], where for each iteration we apply again the rule modifying the states of the cell.

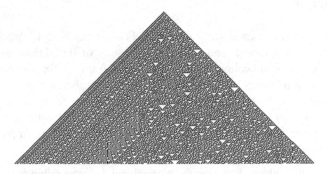

Fig. 1. One-dimension CA following Wolfram's 30th rule. Source Zhiming Wang [CC0]. Each row in the picture represents an evolution in the CA.

Table 1. Rule 30 CA.

Current pattern	111	110	101	100	011	010	001	000
New state for center cell	0	0	0	1	1	1	1	0

However, although this method of representing CA is simple, there are some clear limitations that we must consider:

1. Only one matrix (or vector in the rule 30 case) is considered, but in environmental simulation often there are several matrixes that are going to interact between them,
2. The evolution function that defines how the CA evolves is quite simple, the function can become more complex that cannot be represented with a simple pattern in a table. As an example of both limitations, in a simulation model representing a wildfire, it is needed to combine the data that represents the elevation, with the moisture, the wind direction, and other information, and calculate a complex function to be able to obtain a new state for the cell [2]. Also, on this function it is not considered how the time is going to be managed, there is no definition of the time needed to do the different operations (calculus).
3. The third constraint, that although is solved on our proposed CA is not detailed in this paper, is that we are restricted to a discrete state space (the matrix) while in environmental simulation, and specifically if we want to use continuous data (like the one represented on vector files i.e. representing rivers or territorial divisions), we must do always a rasterization of the data, losing some information in this process.

To solve these problems, we use a generalization of a cellular automaton that allows defining different layers on the same cellular automaton. We named this generalization m:n-CA^k, an initial proposal of this can be consulted on [13]. This generalization helps us to understand the complexity of the model we are going to face. Also, it simplifies the categorization of the different layers we are using, with a classification based on the existence or the absence of an intrinsic behavior on the layer. Main layers are those who have defined a specific behavior, this in our methodology is represented clearly because these layers have an SDL PROCESS representing this. Secondary layers are a simple matrix of data that are needed to perform a calculation, and because they do not own a specific behavior are fixed values.

1.2   Multi:N-Dimensional Cellular Automata (m:n-CA^k)

A multi:n-dimensional cellular automaton (m:n-CA^k) is a generalization of a cellular automata composed by m layers with n dimensions each one, see (1).

$$m : n - CA^k \tag{1}$$

Where

- m: is the automaton number of layers.
- n: is the dimension of the different layers.
- k: is the number of main layers (1 by default). If set to 0 we are using a matrix of cells, but no modification is applied to them.

A layer in an m:n-CA^k is a main layer if a transition function Λ is defined in order to modify its state. An m:n-CA^k automaton presents k main layers. Note that if k = 0 then we have an m:n-1, that is just a matrix of data, if k = 1 we have a usual CA (1:n-

CA is the same as an n-dimensional CA, a two-dimensional CA is represented as 1:2-CA). Some aspects to consider are:

1. Layers that modify their cell state are called **main layers**. The maximum number of main layers is m. The number of main layers is represented by k (m $\geq$ k). A given automaton may have more than one main layer. If k = 0 we have just a matrix of data.
2. The **combination function** Ψ allows state calculation in a main layer, it depends on the state of all the other layers of the automaton.
3. It is not needed that the data follows the raster format because all layers share the **same reference system**. Thus, vector data may be used in m:n-CA^k. The Ψ function determines the cell state independently of the structure of the layer data.

Vector data are quite usual in GIS, but in contrast to raster data (that is composed by a matrix containing the values), vector data presents a virtual continuous space that contains lines, polygons, etc. In this paper, we refer to vector data as an example of continuous information that can be used in a CA although in the examples we will be focused, for the sake of simplicity, on the raster case.

Extension of the Definition of a Neighborhood and the Concepts of Vicinity and Nucleus. In traditional cellular automata, the neighborhood function is defined to determine which cells are considered in the expression used to change the cell value, see Table 1. Because we accept vector data (continuous space) in our m:n-CA^k layer, the concept must be redefined without using cells and considering that all the layers share the same reference system, i.e. all the layers in a m:2-CAk starts on the same physical position, as example (0,0). Therefore, the space that characterizes a neighborhood must be defined without cell dependency.

From a position $x_1,..,x_n$, the **vicinity** function defines the points to be considered in the evolution function in new layer-state calculation.

From a position $x_1,..,x_n$, the **nucleus** function defines the environment to be modified after the evolution function is calculated. The concept of neighborhood is related to the concept of topology and formalizes a colloquial concept.

In the mathematical definition, a topological space is a nonempty set X with a defined topology. It is represented as (X, T). If (X, T) is a topological space and p is a point in X, a subset A of X is a neighborhood of p if an open U of the topology T exists such that p $\in$ U $\subset$ A.

The relationship between mathematical topology and the concepts of vicinity and nucleus allows us to formalize the ordination of points in layers on two levels. The first level represents the points considered in the calculation of a new state. The second level represents the points to be modified once the state changes.

The finest topology on X is the discrete topology, which implies the modification of points. The coarsest topology on X is the trivial topology, which consists of only two elements: T = {$\emptyset$, X}. In these two cases, the open sets that make up the space are defined by two topologies, nucleus and vicinity, which represent the points to be modified through a function Λ_k, named evolution function, that we will describe later, and the points to be considered in the calculation of a new state. Mathematical topology allows the explicit definition of neighborhoods for different points. Hence, in a raster layer (discrete space), a neighborhood can be explicitly defined for each point. For m:n-CA^k automata, these two topologies are defined as follows:

- **Vicinity topology** defines the set of points (neighborhood) of layer k to be considered in the calculation of Λ_k.
- **Nucleus topology** defines the set of points (neighborhood) of layer k to be modified by the calculation of Λ_k.

These two topologies define the neighborhood structures necessary for each point to establish the vicinity and the nucleus. However, not all neighborhoods can be used to represent the nucleus or the vicinity, and only one set can be used.

To define the set to be used for a point's neighborhood, a metric must usually be defined, based, for instance, on Euclidean distance (2).

$$d(x,y) = \sqrt{(x_1 - y_1)^2 + (x_2 - y_2)^2} \tag{2}$$

Distance d(x,y) allows for the definition of neighborhood bases as follows (3)

$$B(x,r) = \{y \in \mathfrak{R}^m / d(x,y) < r\} \tag{3}$$

This is the usual topology for RxR [14] and will become one of the most common topologies for an m:2-CA based on the RxR space defined by the usual distance, note that this is a continuous space. We can generally define a distance r from the point x by defining the **restrictions** of the selected neighborhood. A typical restriction rule is to calculate the minimum neighborhood that contains all points for which d(x,p) < r. For instance, in the usual topology presented in (3), B(x,r) is the minimum neighborhood that satisfies this restriction. In a more general topology, the restriction defines only one neighborhood for all the sets.

In an m:n-CA^k, two restriction rules must be defined: one for the vicinity topology and one for the nucleus topology. These two restriction rules are used to construct the vicinity and nucleus functions. We can now define the vicinity and nucleus functions.

- **Vicinity function** $vn_m(x_1,..,x_n)$ returns the minimum open set of the vicinity topology for the layer m, that contains point $x_1,..,x_n$ and includes the maximum points that satisfy the restriction and the minimum points that do not satisfy the restriction. If the restriction is defined by the usual distance, it represents a neighborhood that contains the maximum points that satisfy d(t,p) < r and the minimum points that satisfy $d(t,p) \geq r$.
- **Nucleus function** $nc_m(x_1,..,x_n)$ returns the minimum open set of the nucleus topology that contains point $x_1,..,x_n$ and includes the maximum points that satisfy the restriction and the minimum points that do not satisfy the restriction. Depending on the type of data in the different layers, the topology nucleus and neighborhood are defined over N^n or Z^n (in the raster case) or R^n (in the vector case). We can consider however working in other systems like the Complex or the Octonions.

With this redefinition of the vicinity and nucleus central concept in CA, we can go further to understand how the CA is going to modify its values following a specified rule

Combination Function (Ψ). Each cell of the matrix that defines an m:n-CA^k has a specific value. We define the number of possible states in the cell for the layer m with S_m, being a value that is not needed to be constrained in the body of the natural numbers, one can define S_m on the body of the Real or Octonions numbers (as an example) without any constraint. To combine the different S_m that belongs to the m:n-CA^k is needed to define a common reference, and a coordinate system, composed by n elements. With this, we can define the state of the cell in a m:n-CA^k as is presented on (4).

$$E_m(nc_m(x_1, .., x_n)) = S_i \qquad (4)$$

The function E_m represents the state of each cell (nucleus) in the different layers of the automaton. Note that if one considers only the state for the main layers, we can note this with E_k However, this state is not the global state of the automaton. For the coordinates $x_1,...,x_n$ the function E_G returns the global state of the automaton. To be able to calculate this E_G is needed to define the Combination function (Ψ), that returns the global state for a position using individual layer states, see (5).

$$\Psi\left(E_1(nc_1(x_1..x_n)),^{m-1)}, E_m(nc_m(x_1..x_n))\right) = E_G(x_1..x_n) \qquad (5)$$

The definition of the Ψ function depends on the structure of a given automaton. In a 1:n-CA, this function is the identity function, returning as E_G the nucleus of the single layer that exists (in that case main layer). This can grow in complexity in other scenarios, see (6).

$$\Psi(E_1(nc_1(x_1..x_n))) = E_1(nc_1(x_1..x_n)) = E_G(x_1..x_n) \qquad (6)$$

Evolution function (Λ_κ) in an m:n-CA^k In common cellular automata, the evolution function allows modify the E_m for each main layer, hence is focused on modify only the E_k, the main layers. Evolution function (Λ_κ) for a common cellular automata usually operate recalculating the E_k defining a Δt intervals, or, for a CA that does not define how to manage time, like the one presented on Fig. 1, calculating the new E_k from the previous E_k at a single step.

In m:n-CA^k automata, space can be represented as being continuous, but also time evolution can be considered as continuous, hence, the evolution function must also be (if needed) a continuous function. As we will see in our approach, the formal definition of the CA is based on SDL that will be agnostic on how the time is going to be updated, hence is possible to define an Activity Scanning [15] approach to model Λ_κ achieving if needed a good approximation to a continuous time evolution. In the example proposed in this paper, is not needed to use continuous time, hence Event Scheduling usual approach will be enough. Λ_κ is defined for main layer k to modify its state using the combination function Ψ.

The relationship between m:n-CA and common CA can now be established, being m:n-AC^k a generalization of a common cellular automaton, since 1:n-CA over Z_n defines a usual CA. We must establish a general method to define the CA structure and behavior (Ψ and Λ_κ functions). To do so we explore the use of SDL in the next sections.

1.3 Specification and Description Language

Specification and Description Language (SDL) is a standard object-oriented formal and graphical language defined by the International Telecommunications Union–Telecommunications Standardization Sector (ITU–T) (the Comité Consultatif International Telegraphique et Telephonique [CCITT]) on the Z. 100 recommendation. On its origins, SDL was designed for the specification of event-oriented, real-time and interactive complex systems. These systems might involve different concurrent activities that use signals to perform communication. SDL is based on the definition of four levels to describe the structure and the behavior of the models: system, blocks, processes and procedures. In SDL *blocks* and *processes* are named *agents*. The outermost block, the *system* block, is an agent itself. Figure 2 shows these levels hierarchy.

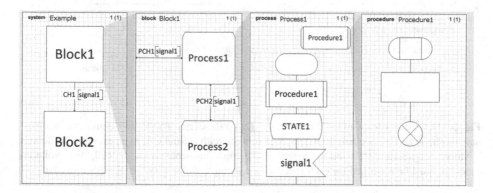

Fig. 2. A structural vision of an SDL model. 4 main different levels exist.

Although a textual SDL representation is possible (SDL/PR), this paper uses the graphical representation of the language (named SDL/GR). More details about the Specification and Description Language can be found in the recommendation Z.100 [16] or at the web site [17]. BLOCKS, PROCESS, and PROCEDURES define the basic structure and behavior of a simulation model, however, in order to represent environmental models, this is not enough. We need some structure in order to represent the data and its relationship with the simulation model, it is needed to detail, how the evolution of the simulation model modifies its surrounding data, and how this data influences on the model behavior. To do this we start with the definition of the cellular automatons following an m:n-CA^k over N^k numbers.

2   Representing m:n-CA^k on SDL

In order to solve the representation of CA (and specifically m:n-CA^k) with SDL we will define an AGENT TYPE to represent the layers of the CA, and a method to instantiate all the needed cells of the model, that will be represented also by a second AGENT TYPE. This allows representing graphically the interaction between the model and the data, and between all the layers that compose the CA. Starting with the needed information on each cell, we must define the neighborhood, the nucleus, the ID of the current cell, and define a method to modify the value of the matrix that contains the information of the CA, see Fig. 3. that represents the Λ_κ. Note that the state of the CA cell, in the case of a main layer, is going to be modified due to the inherent behavior of the PROCESS, however, one must want to obtain the initial value from the matrix or to write this value to the matrix that represents this layer.

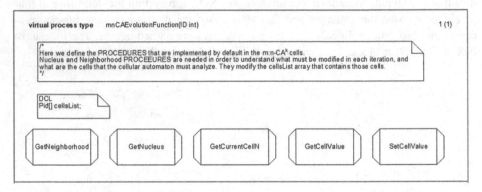

Fig. 3. Definition of the m:n-CAk on SDL. This PROCESS TYPE will define the nucleus, neighborhood and the needed PROCEDURES to work with a usual CA, as an example, by default a Moore neighborhood can be implemented. The specific behavior of the cell, the Evolution function, must be redefined for each specific case along with the PROCEDURES if needed.

This process will be rewritten adding the behavior of the Λ_κ that details how the cell behaves. Once the cell behavior is defined, the next step is to define its structure, mainly by several layers and cells. Again, this can be done using SDL agents. The layer is the element that (depending on the dimensions of the cellular automaton) creates all the needed cells. One can define this number of cells following a process like the one proposed in Fig. 4.

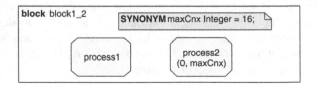

Fig. 4. A method to define the number of instances to be created, see [18]

In that case, the modeler must define, for each layer the number of cells that compose this layer. We prefer to avoid using this approach since we are focused on CA modeling and each one of the different layers of our CA must be defined using a file that usually can contain the dataset to be used and modified during the execution of the model. We propose to use the approach shown in Fig. 5, where the dimensions of the layers (the number of cells) are obtained from the dataset (represented in the simple case in a text file), assuring a coherence between the dataset to be used in each layer in the CA and the conceptual model definition of the CA. Also, we can establish a relation between the cell number and the PId. With this information later we can simplify send SIGNALS to a subset of the cells that compose the layer.

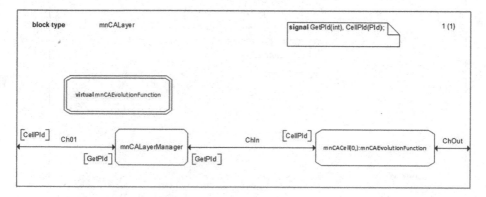

Fig. 5. Definition of a m:n-CAk layer on SDL. In this BLOCK the *mnCALayerManager* creates all the instances of the cells; each instance receives its number (N) that identifies it on the matrix, obtained by reading the data file that contains the state for each cell at the initial state. We store for each N the PId in a table contained in the *mnCALayerManager*. ChIn will be the usual communication CHANNEL between the manager and the cells of the CA. ChOut will be used to send SIGNALS to the redefined evolution function, only if needed, due to the combination function represented on the layers diagram. Ch01 will be used in case the mnCALayerManager is asked by some AGENT to obtain the PId of a specific cell "N" of the layer (outside the layer).

We can add *mnCALayer* to a package named **mnCA** that will be used to simplify the definition of a CA in SDL. The cells do not have a specific behavior defined. The user must define the specific behavior for the cells as is represented in the example of this paper in Figs. 11 and 12. This is a key element since the modelers can focus on this diagram in order to understand cellular automaton behavior.

All these agents can be packaged and can be included in any project that needs to represent a cellular automaton using SDL. As an example, we present the well-known Game of Life using this, because of its simplicity. The main idea is that for the representation of a model that uses a cellular automaton it is only needed to write the behavior of the cells and the relation of the cells with other cells of other layers. All can be done graphically as we see next (Fig. 6).

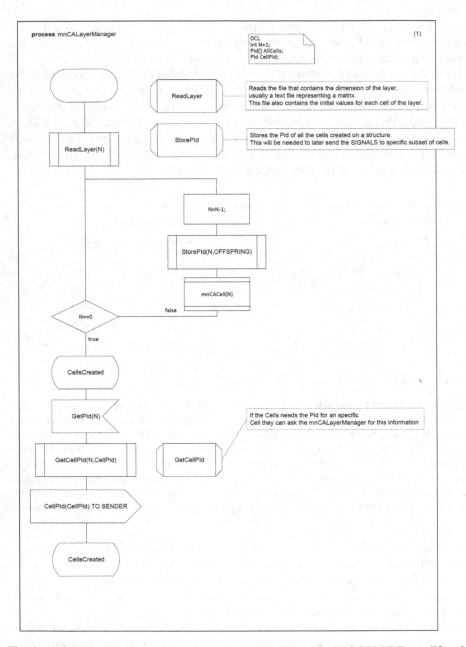

Fig. 6. Definition of the mnCALayerManager. ReadLayer(N) PROCEDURE modifies N according to the number of existing layers on the CA.

2.1   Extending the SDL to Define a Cellular Automaton

When we try to define the behavior of the cellular automaton two main issues need to be solved, the time management and the multiple instances management.

Regarding the time management, we use the feature of SDL-2010 that allows defining time and priority in the SIGNAL. Every SIGNAL that is output has an optional parameter that defines the *time* needed to travel to its destination, and an optional parameter defining the signal *priority* with respect to other signal instances in the destination input queue scheduled, for the same time. From this time parameter and the value of **now** at the time the signal is output, an availability time is calculated. It is needed also to comment that the communication path may include delaying channels, so this delay must also be added to the calculus. If the availability time is greater than arrival time, the signal remains unavailable until the availability time is reached. SIGNAL instances in the input port are ordered by the time of arrival. If the time parameter is omitted, then the *delay* is zero; When a signal is *output* and no signal priority is specified, it is given the priority value 0. When there are several signals available with different signal priority values, the signal with the lowest priority value is selected. The signals in the input port are scanned in the following order to determine whether there is a signal that is enabled: first, by the order of the arrival time in the priority inputs, and then, by the order of the arrival time for other (non-priority) inputs. For those signals that have the same arrival time, the signal *priority* determines which signal is processed first. If two signals have the same signal *priority,* then the order is arbitrary. In Fig. 7 is represented a SIGNAL and how it will be used in the context of the paper.

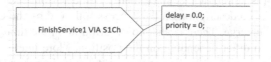

Fig. 7. Defining the delay, and the priority of the SIGNAL on SDL-2010.

The SIGNAL management in a CA differs from a usual process because all the cells of the nucleus will be updated by Λ_κ, hence it will be usual to send SIGNALS to a set of cells (PROCESS). In order to simplify this, we propose to extend the semantics of SDL allowing to send a SIGNAL to a MNCA that will receive as a parameter a list of cell arguments. The cell list parameter can be also the keyword ALL, representing that all the cells of the layer will receive the SIGNAL. On Fig. 8 is shown an example where a SIGNAL is sent to the same AGENT (itself).

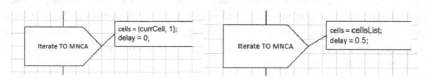

Fig. 8. Proposed extensions in order to define the cell that can receive a specific signal when the AGENT belongs to a cellular automaton. On the left side, we send the *Iterate* SIGNAL to two cells, one represented by the variable *currCell* and cell number 1. On the right side, we send the Iterate SIGNAL to all the cells on the cellist that *mnCAEvolutionFunction* owns by default.

On SDL one can send a SIGNAL to a list of destinations using "Iterate TO mnCACell[currCell] TO mnCACell [1]", or defining a list of String <PId> to be processed, but the proposed approach makes clear that the signal is sent to cells of the current CA (TO MNCA), simplifying its understanding. Also, notice that this extension can be implemented easily on SDL processing the signals to send one by one from the list but simplifies the lecture and the definition of the models; also, it allows to obtain improved codifications for this specific case.

2.2   The Game of Life

The Game of Life is a cellular automaton devised by the British mathematician John Horton Conway in 1970 [19]. The universe of the Game of Life is an infinite two-dimensional orthogonal grid of square cells, each of which is in one of two possible states, alive or dead. Every cell interacts with its eight neighbors.

The rules that define the evolution of the automatons are:

- If the neighborhood of the cell contains less than two live cells, the cell dies.
- If the neighborhood of the cell contains more than three life cells die.
- If the neighborhood of the cell contains three life cells, the cell becomes a living cell.

This description is not complete, since there is no description on the dimension of the CA, also, there is no description on the process followed by the CA that can cause different patterns to emerge. There is also no description on the time needed to do this modification, that can differ depending on the position. More interestingly, there is no method to connect with a specific dataset that contains an initial space of states of the CA or a method to connect with other models that will be using this CA. Although in this case (that is selected for the sake of simplicity, in order that the reader be used with the SDL representation), seems that the description of the CA following Wolfram's of textual representation is simple, there are clear advantages on the formalization of the CA. Some examples where without a formalization one cannot represent the behavior of the CA can be reviewed here [5, 13, 20]. Also, notice that from this description a codification must be done, a process that can introduce some errors that must be verified.

The structure of SDL allows to detail if we want to execute each one of the different cells in different computers. This is a decision that can be represented graphically because in SDL all the elements contained inside a BLOCK agent can be executed in parallel. This is what happens in our case, since the element that details this is a BLOCK, see Fig. 9. Note that this diagram just represents the dimension and the structure of the CA.

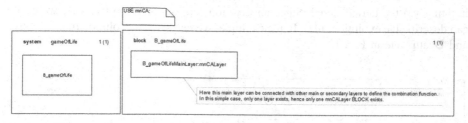

Fig. 9. Definition of a cellular automaton layer on SDL that represents the Conway's "Game of Life". In this simple case, only one main layer exists, however in other cases several layers are going to interact, and at this level, the formal representation of this interaction will be needed. This interaction defines the combination function that represents how the information is going to flow from one layer to another. Here the SIGNALS that will transport the information between the layers will be defined.

Inside the BLOCK agent, we find (in the "Game of Life" case) a complete description of the behavior that rules the agent's evolution. Since in a CA every cell behaves in the same manner, we only need to describe one single Process for each *Main Layer*. Thus, our *B_gameOflifeMainLayer* example Block will contain a single Process describing its nature, see Fig. 10. Notice that here one can represent the connection with other model elements that can interact with the CA during its execution.

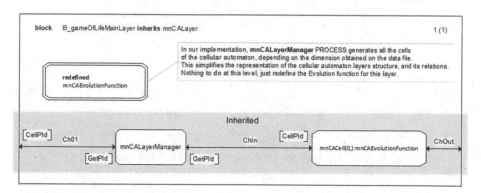

Fig. 10. The definition of the cellular automaton layer. Here we find the main elements that compose the layer, the cells, and any other PROCESS that must be defined to represent the dynamic behavior of the cellular automaton. The inherited elements need not be redefined.

In Figs. 11 and 12 we can see a simple example of this representation. A cell has three possible states: *Loading, Death* and *Alive*. Note that the behavior of a cell is the definition of Λ_κ. *Loading* state (Fig. 11) is used to initialize the CA, in the example, we assign the *Death* state by default with the exception of 5 concrete cells that will represent a Blister element. Once the model has been loaded, the PROCESS starts iterating via the Iterate signal. Since an iteration represents a step in a CA, we easily can describe the evolution rules. In the example, we can see the evolution rules of Alive and Death state in Fig. 12.

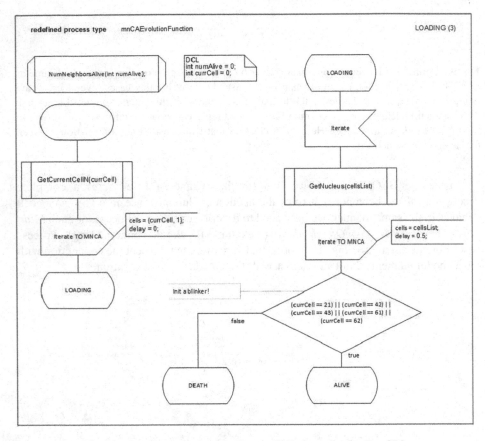

Fig. 11. Loading state for the *Game of Life* formalized using SDL.

To validate the model the experts can concentrate their efforts on the behavior described on the mnCAEvolutionFunction. Also, the implementation of the model can be based on the existing SDL tools. It is quite remarkable that the graphical definition we have of the model is complete and unambiguous. This model was successfully implemented on SDLPS [21, 22]. Some projects that implement this kind of solution are [1, 5, 13], where one can review that the definition encompasses not only the usual description of the rules of the CA, but also, the time needed to do the update on the cells, the relation of the data in each cell with other datasets, the relation of the CA with other models and the mechanism to combine the layers, among other elements that often are not represented in this kind of models.

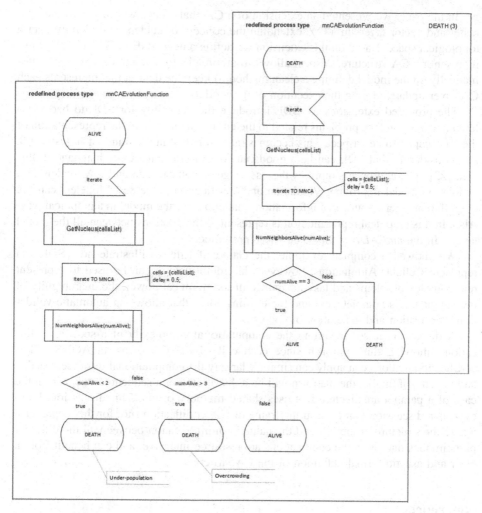

Fig. 12. *Alive* and *Death* states for the *Game of Life* formalized using SDL.

3 Concluding Remarks

Environmental models need geographical information that often must be modified dynamically. CA are widely used to represent this information and connect it with a simulation model. Since the behavior of the cellular automaton is a key issue it is desirable that this behavior can be represented in an unambiguous and formal way. Some alternatives exist in order to formalize a CA, however, none of them is based on a complete, unambiguous, standard, graphical and formal language like SDL. This fact simplifies the verification process of a simulation model since the implementation can be done automatically by the tools that understand SDL.

In the paper we presented an extension of a CA that allows working with multiple raster and vector layers in a CA, extending the concept of nucleus and vicinity over a topological space. Based on this extension we define a new AGENT TYPE that allows representing CA structure. Also, it allows to automatically use the data sources automatically on the model defining a clean method to keep the dataset that represents each CA layer updated during the execution of the model.

The proposed extensions for SDL introduce the capability for SDL to become a language that can face problems related to the environment, where the representation of the landscape is a key aspect. This becomes more relevant in the frame of Industry 4.0, and considering that SDL can be a good candidate to become a key language in this area [23]. The approach simplifies the use of geographical data and CA models in a simulation model improving Validation and Verification processes. Modelers can see the different layers (sources of information) that compose the model in a graphical way. Also, in this graphical representation is represented the relations between all the model layers. In the *mnCALayer* this is clearly represented.

We showed a complete example, the Game of Life, to illustrate how SDL can represent Cellular Automatons; however, this methodology can be used to represent real complex problems and take advantage of its graphical power, the unambiguity of the language, its completeness and the existing tools that allows an automatic validation, verification and generation of code.

A discussion arises regarding the computational complexity of a specific codification following this approach since each cell of the CA owns an AGENT. The codification that one can apply can simplify largely the computational resources needed and depends if finally, the platform will be a distributed or a sequential one, and in the case of a parallel architecture if it uses shared memory or not. This discussion, however, is a discussion that exist in the frame of CA codification (not for this approach), where the structure of the CA and the natural communication between all the different parts implies that often the codifications are resource-intensive, and can benefit from a clear and aseptic formal definition of the CA structure.

References

1. Jové, J.F., Fonseca i Casas, P., Petit, A.G., Casanovas, J.: FireFight: a decision support system for forest fire containment (2014). https://doi.org/10.1007/978-94-017-9136-6_19
2. Andrews, P.: BehavePlus fire modeling system: past, present, and future. In: Proceedings of 7th Symposium on Fire and Forest Meteorological Society (2007)
3. Benenson, I., Torrens, P.M.: Geosimulation. Wiley, Chichester (2004). https://doi.org/10.1002/0470020997
4. Andrews, G.: Cellular Automata and Applications, p. 29 (2008)
5. Fonseca, P., Colls, M., Casanovas, J.: A novel model to predict a slab avalanche configuration using m:n-CAk cellular automata. Comput. Environ. Urban Syst. **35**, 12–24 (2011). https://doi.org/10.1016/j.compenvurbsys.2010.07.002
6. Stephen, W.: Statistical-Mechanics-Cellular-Automata-Stephen-Wolfram-Article.pdf (1983). https://doi.org/10.1103/RevModPhys.55.601

7. Yue, H., Hao, H., Chen, X., Shao, C.: Simulation of pedestrian flow on square lattice based on cellular automata model. Phys. A Stat. Mech. Appl. **384**, 567–588 (2007). https://doi.org/10.1016/j.physa.2007.05.070

8. ITU-T: Specification and Description Language – Data and action language in SDL-2010 (2016)

9. ITU-T: Specification and Description Language – Overview of SDL-2010 (2011)

10. Doldi, L.: SDL Illustrated - visually design executable models (2001)

11. Wainer, G.A.: Advanced Cell-DEVS modeling applications: a legacy of Norbert Giambiasi. Simulation (2018). https://doi.org/10.1177/0037549718761596

12. Wolfram, S.: A New Kind of Science (2003)

13. Fonseca, P., Casanovas, J.: Simplifying GIS data use inside discrete event simulation model through M:N-AC cellular automaton. In: International Mediterranean Modeling Multiconference, I3 M 2005, European Modeling Simulation Symposium EMSS 2005, pp. 7–15 (2005)

14. Brendon, G.E.: Topology and Geometry (1993)

15. Law, A.M., Kelton, W.D.: Simulation Modeling and Analysis (1991)

16. ITU-T: Z.100. Specification and description language (SDL) (2016)

17. ITU-T: Specification and description language - overview of SDL-2010. http://handle.itu.int/11.1002/1000/12846%0A

18. Doldi, L.: Validation of Communications Systems with SDL. The Art of SDL Simulation and Reachability Analysis (2003)

19. Adamatzky, A., Durand-Lose, J.: Collision-Based Computing. Springer, London (2002). https://doi.org/10.1007/978-1-4471-0129-1

20. Fonseca i Casas, P., Colls, M., Casanovas, J.: Towards a representation of environmental models using specification and description language-from the fibonacci model to a wildfire model. In: KEOD (2010)

21. Fonseca i Casas, P.: Using specification and description language to define and implement discrete simulation models. In: Summer Computer Simulation Conference, SCSC 2010 - Proceedings of the 2010 Summer Simulation Multiconference, SummerSim 2010, pp. 419–426 (2010)

22. Fonseca i Casas, P.: SDL distributed simulator. In: 2008 Winter Simulation Conference (2008). https://doi.org/10.1109/WSC.2008.4736433

23. Sherratt, E., Ober, I., Gaudin, E., Fonseca I Casas, P., Kristoffersen, F.: SDL - the IoT language (2015). https://doi.org/10.1007/978-3-319-24912-4_3

Interoperability

Goal Model Integration: Advanced Relationships and Rationales Documentation

Malak Baslyman and Daniel Amyot[✉]

University of Ottawa and Institut du savoir Montfort, Ottawa, Canada
{mbas1071,damyot}@uottawa.ca

Abstract. Integrating new technology in a business environment raises many challenges such as ensuring that this technology meets stakeholder requirements and contributes to organizational goals. However, before analyzing the impact of technology on requirements and goals, goal models of the current context and of the proposed technology should be merged to reflect the whole context. Existing merging approaches mainly focus on merging partial views of a goal model, which belong to one context. However, merging different goal models to reflect one holistic context, such as in technology integration, is not addressed. This paper presents a *Goal Integration Method* targeting different initial contexts, enabling completeness and consistency analysis of the integrated goal model, and providing traceability to rationales and decisions made at integration time. The method introduces advanced relationships and procedures to capture newly added elements or raised conflicts that may occur during the integration. The method is presented with the help of a conceptual model and an algorithm. It also exploits the User Requirements Notation with tool support (jUCMNav) for building and integrating goal models. The feasibility of the method is illustrated through a case study. The method formalizes the integration of multiple goal models belonging to different contexts, and the accommodation of new requirements, while providing comprehensive traceability and rationales.

Keywords: Goal-oriented modeling · GRL · Model merging · Technology integration · User requirements notation

1 Introduction

In the context of technology integration, important goals are identified by different groups, such as technology providers and the organization where the technology is to be used. Stakeholder and system goals and their relationships can be captured with models. A global view of the technology-related and context-related goal models that enables holistic evaluations is needed to assess the potential impact of technology, before its acquisition and deployment. Integrating models often means merging partial views of structural or behavioral models,

© Springer Nature Switzerland AG 2019
P. Fonseca i Casas et al. (Eds.): SAM 2019, LNCS 11753, pp. 183–199, 2019.
https://doi.org/10.1007/978-3-030-30690-8_11

leading to one comprehensive view of the model. Much work has been done on the merging of behavioral models in the literature. However, goal model merging is still a challenging task due to many factors such as the usage of different vocabularies, stakeholder disagreements, semantic correctness, and inconsistency issues [7,18].

As a sample realistic context, let us assume that a hospital considers using a new technology to improve care quality. The hospital already has a goal model of the caregiver, administration, patient, and organizational goals along with performance objectives. In the absence of a goal model, one can be constructed according to existing guidelines such as those of Liaskos et al. [14], Akhigbe et al. [1], or Alwedian et al. [2]. Before deciding on purchasing and deploying the new technology under consideration, the impact of the candidate technology on the hospital's goals should be assessed and answers should be provided to many questions such as: *To what extent will the new technology contribute to the satisfaction of stakeholders' goals? Will the performance be affected? How can we help ensuring that agreement is actually reached?* To answer such questions, the goal model of the technology (produced by the technology provider or created according to the guidelines previously identified) and the goal model of the current context should be integrated. Existing work provides insights to solve, partially, this problem. However, there is no formal method describing how goal models of different contexts can be integrated and how new elements, relationships, or impacts, which may be introduced accordingly, will be captured.

The problem space of technology integration, considering goal models, overlaps the goal model merging domain as well as elicitation and validation aspects. In this paper, we propose a new *Goal Integration Method* to describe formally how goal models of different contexts can be integrated while enabling the analysis of consistency, completeness, and semantic correctness. The method introduces new relationships and procedures to follow in the cases of similarity, dissimilarity, and conflicts in the input models, and new added/changed elements resulting from the integration. In addition, the method systematically and iteratively validates the resulting integrated goal model and highlights opportunities for further elicitation. It also documents traceability of decisions made during the integration.

Although the ideas introduced here can apply to many goal-oriented modeling languages, a specific one is used to make the method concrete. We use the *Goal-oriented Requirement Language* (GRL) because GRL is part of an international standard (User Requirements Notation – URN [13]), it enables the modeling of stakeholders and their goals, and it supports indicators (for quantitative reasoning), contribution relationships, metadata, and evaluation strategies with various propagation algorithms. GRL is also well supported by the *jUCMNav* tool for evaluating the satisfaction of goals and actors under selected strategies [3,15].

The Goal Integration Method is used manually with jUCMNav at this time, but the verification of integration constraints is automated. Additional parts of the method will be automated in the future, but some parts will still require the input of experts, e.g., decisions regarding the similarity of model elements coming from different domains.

The rest of the paper is organized as follows: Sect. 2 provides an overview of related work, while Sect. 3 describes the proposed Goal Integration Method. Section 4 presents the formalization used to ensure well-formedness and consistency of the proposed method. Section 5 illustrates the usefulness of the integration method with the help of a healthcare-related case study. Section 6 discusses some challenges in this area, while Sect. 7 concludes and presents future work.

2 Related Work

Goal models have already been used in the context of technology selection, for instance for the justice system [2]. However, these approaches often just provide the goal model of the context of use, without any goal model describing the intent, stakeholders, benefits, and drawbacks of the new technology itself. Both models are actually needed for informed decision making.

Much work has been presented in the area of model merging. However, the focus was mainly on merging behavioral models (such as state machines) rather than structural models such as goal models [6,9,11,16]. The main challenge faced in merging structural models is to ensure consistency of definitions and of relations of combined elements while capturing and preserving correct semantics. Another challenge is modeling stakeholder disagreements and the evolution of their requirements over time.

Richards proposed a comprehensive methodology to lead the process of merging conceptual models [17]. Brunet et al. proposed a framework to define different merge operators based on algebraic properties [7]. Feng et al. discussed merging goal models of high semantic similarities using basic decomposition merge patterns [8]. One distinguished work done in goal model merging is from Sabetzadeh and Easterbrook [18], who proposed a framework that highlights incompleteness and inconsistency occurring in different partial views, designed by different modelers, of one goal model. They treated multiple views of a goal model as structured objects to map them back and forth during the merging process. They also created an algebraic algorithm for merging views to increase scalability and adaptability. The goal integration approach proposed in this paper is inspired by their three-way modeling approach.

One important concept that differentiates our method from the others is that we introduce relationships that go beyond the "similar" and "dissimilar" ones used by Sabetzadeh and Easterbrook [18] to denote inconsistency and incompleteness. The *transitive similarity, conflict, different, new,* and *approved* relationships in our goal integration method help define finer levels of integration but require deeper stakeholder engagement to reason about introducing new elements/relations and resolve conflicts as part of requirements elicitation and validation. Another key difference is that our approach provides comprehensive traceability to the integrated goal model during its evolution.

3 Goal Integration Method

This section introduces the method's conceptual model and relationships.

3.1 Conceptual Model

The conceptual model supporting the goal integration (Fig. 1) contains basic goal modeling concepts. A *Goal* (or an *Indicator*) belongs to a *GoalModel*, can be associated to a *Stakeholder*, and can have *Link*s of different types (e.g., *Contribution* or *Decomposition*) to other goals. The main novelty here is the *IntegrationRelation* class that identifies relationships between elements to be integrated in a goal model (see Sect. 3.2). In addition, the *Type* attribute in the GoalModel class is added for model consistency checking (to be discussed in Sect. 4).

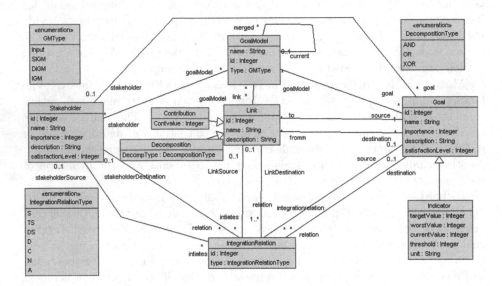

Fig. 1. Goal Integration Method's conceptual model

3.2 Relationships and Mapping Procedure

Our goal integration method has five main iterative phases, starting with the identification of similarities between the models to be merged. Then, the method requires analysts to identify dissimilarities between the input models. The method combines the identified similarities and dissimilarities of the input models into a new *Integrated Goal Model* (IGM), and then checks the new model to identify differences, conflicts, and new elements to be added. Table 1 explains the potential relationships that can be created between goal model elements to be integrated when applying the method and the condition for each case.

The procedures followed in the five phases are:

- **Phase 1** *Similarity identification:* the inputs of this phase are the goal models. The analyst, who is assumed to be a modeler and domain expert, identifies the similarities between the models to be merged, adds similar elements to

Table 1. Relationships and mapping conditions of the goal integration method.

Relationship	Elements involved	Conditions
S: Similar	- Stakeholder to Stakeholder - Goal to Goal - Task to Task - Relation to Relation	- Similar elements in the input goal models (GM1 and GM2) will be added to a new *Similar Integrated Goal Model* (SIGM) - The SIGM model's elements shall be mapped back to the input models to ensure coverage and consistency
TS: Transitive similarity	- Goal to Goal - Task to Task - Relation to Relation	The root elements element shall be similar first.
DS: Dissimilar	Elements that exist in one model but not in the other model: Goal, Task, Stakeholder, or Relation	The elements will be tagged (self-relation) with DS to be investigated for conflict or different representation.
C: Conflict	- Goal to Goal - Task to Task - Relation to Relation	- Similar goals/tasks with different representation/relations - Opposing/invalid effect of goals/relations in IGM
D: Different	- Goal to Goal - Relation to Relation - Goals and Relations	- Result of resolving conflicts - Result of refining the model
N: New	- New Goal - New Stakeholder - New Relation	Tagged (self-relation) in merged model when the element does not exist in the input models
A: Approved	All elements tagged with DS, C, D, or N	All elements are valid

a new *Similar Integrated Goal Model* (SIGM), and maps each element in the SIGM back to the original models through a Similar relationship. In addition, the sub-elements of the similar root elements should be added to SIGM and labeled with Transitive Similarity to the original models. If the sub-elements of similar roots have contradicting decomposition operators (AND or OR) in the original models, one decomposition operator is added directly to the root element in the SIGM, and a TemporaryElement is created to hold the other one (see Sect. 5). As for different vocabularies used by similar elements, the

analyst decides which one to keep in the merged model (often the organization's).

- **Phase 2** *Dissimilarity identification:* the procedure followed here is quite
  similar to Phase 1. However, dissimilarities are identified and the dissimilar
  elements are added to a *Dissimilarity Integrated Goal Model* (DIGM).
- **Phase 3** *Model combination*: the inputs of this phase are the SIGM and
  DIGM. The method combines them in a new *Integrated Goal Model* (IGM).
- **Phase 4** *Model investigation*: The analyst investigates the IGM model to
  identify different semantical or structural changes of the elements, which may
  exist or may be introduced, compared to the original models. Such differences
  could be changed representations of goals or relations (e.g., a different contribution level), or newly added elements (e.g., a new contribution link). All
  different elements have a relationship of type Different, and new elements
  are tagged with New. The method also identifies conflicting elements with a
  Conflict relationship.
- **Phase 5** *Model Validation:* The analyst and stakeholders collaborate to evaluate the IGM and resolve remaining issues. For contribution conflicts, the
  Analytic Hierarchy Process (AHP) method can be used to compute contribution levels [12]. In the end, each element involved in a Conflict, Different, New,
  or Dissimilar relation should be approved. Model investigation and validation
  can be performed iteratively, resulting in multiple versions of the IGM, until
  the fully approved version is obtained.

In Phases 1 and 2, the purpose of mapping the elements from SIGM and DIGM
back to the input models is to help assess *coverage* and *consistency*, and to
provide traceability back and forth to the original models. Further requirements
elicitation may also happen in Phase 4 (Model investigation) as differences and
gaps are discovered. All relationships to the original models and rationales are
stored in the approved version of the IGM, as described in the following section.

4   Formalization

We formalized the method using a conceptual model with constraints, a URN
profile with tool support, and a language-independent integration algorithm.

4.1   Goal Integration Conceptual Model Formalization

The goal integration conceptual model introduced in Fig. 1 was formalized using
the *UML-based Specification Environment* (USE) of Gogolla et al. [10] and OCL
constraints[1].

There are several groups of constraints required to ensure coverage and consistency. The first group ensures that all elements of the input SIGM and DIGM
are covered by the integrated goal model (Fig. 1). It is important to check this
constraint, especially in the first version of the IGM, before making any decision

---

[1] The model is available online at https://goo.gl/LLCE3m.

about adding, removing, or changing the elements in later versions of the IGM. The following OCL constraint ensures that all goals of an input model belong to an integrated goal model (similar OCL constraints were defined for links and stakeholders). Violations of these constraints would indicate missing elements (absent from the IGM but present in the SIGM or DIGM).

> **context** Goal
> **inv** GoalCoverage:
>   goalModel -> **select**(c : GoalModel | c.Type = GMType::IGM)
>   -> **size**() >= 1

Another important group of constraints is needed to check that if there exist IntegrationRelation instances between two elements, one of these instances has to be of type A (Approved, see Table 1). This must be checked for goals, link, and stakeholder elements, as formalized below. Violations of these constraints indicate integration relations that remain to be approved by the analyst and stakeholders. OCL constraints similar to the one below exist for links and stakeholders.

> **context** Goal
> **inv** GoalRelation:
>   self.integrationrelation.destination.relation->**size**() >= 1
>   **implies**
>   integrationrelation->**select**(c : IntegrationRelation | c.type =
>   IntegrationRelationType::A)
>   ->**size**() >= 1

Goal elements may have IntegrationRelation with Link and/or Stakeholder elements. In this case, it is also essential to check that these relations are also approved, leading to the next two OCL constraints.

> **context** Goal
> **inv** GoalLinkIntegrationRelation:
>   self.integrationrelation.LinkDestination.relation->**size**() >= 1
>   **implies**
>   integrationrelation->**select**(c : IntegrationRelation | c.type =
>   IntegrationRelationType::A)
>   ->**size**() >= 1
>
> **inv** GoalStakeholderIntegrationRelation:
>   self.integrationrelation.stakeholderDestination.relation->**size**() >= 1
>   **implies**
>   integrationrelation->**select**(c : IntegrationRelation | c.type =
>   IntegrationRelationType::A)
>   ->**size**() >= 1

4.2 URN Profile

This section presents a URN profile for the Goal Integration Method, which enables the use of URN (and particularly its GRL sub-language) as a concrete syntax to create goal models as instances of the goal integration conceptual model of Fig. 1. URN already possesses many of the goal integration conceptual model's elements as well as mechanisms to extend the language with additional concepts/attributes (using *metadata*) and relationships (using *URN links*). Table 2 shows the mapping between each conceptual model's element and its corresponding URN element.

Table 2. Mapping between the conceptual model elements and URN elements.

Conceptual model element	URN element	Existence	Missing attributes
Goal model	GRLgraph	Exists	Type
Goal	IntentionalElement (of type Goal)	Exists	-
Indicator	Indicator	Exists	-
Link	Link	Exists	-
Stakeholder	Actor	Exists	-
Integration Relation (goal model integration)	URN links	Does not exist	Integration-Relation

As shown in Table 2, almost all the conceptual model elements are covered by URN elements. The Type attribute of a goal model is captured using metadata on a GRLgraph in URN, where the metadata name is "Type" and the possible values are "Input", "SIGM", "DIGM", or "IGM". In addition, all relationships appearing between the goal model integration's elements (Table 1) are captured and mapped to URN relations through URN links and metadata on URN intentional elements. None of the types of relationships exists in URN, fully or explicitly, as URN does not support goal model integration out of the box. Therefore, the IntegrationRelation class is captured through URN links and the type of the relation is stored in the metadata of the URN links and, possibly, of the intentional elements. The reason for storing the IntegrationRelation type in additional metadata is that if element1 initially replaces element2, a URN link is used to capture the integration relation, of type Different. However, once element2 is deleted in some version of the integrated goal model, the URN link gets deleted as well and hence the integration relation will be lost. element1 is tagged, through metadata, with the integration relations to keep track of all integration relations that happened so far until the integration gets finally Approved.

We also used some user-selectable rules predefined in jUCMNav to further ensure the well-formedness of input models at design time such as *GRLactorNoCycle* (a GRL actor must not be part of a containment cycle).

4.3   Goal Integration Algorithm

In this section, a part of the algorithm is presented where Phases 1, 2 and 3 from Sect. 3 are covered. The complete algorithm can be found in [4].

The inputs are two goal models and the output is a goal model that integrates the input models, establish relationships, and allows the modeler to add new elements. The output integrated goal model is then ready for model investigation and validation (Phases 4 and 5 from Sect. 3).

Algorithm: GoalIntegration
Inputs: GM1, GM2: GoalModel
Output: IGM: GoalModel

SIGM: GoalModel = **new** GoalModel // *new intermediate similar goal model*
DIGM: GoalModel = **new** GoalModel // *new intermediate dissimilar goal model*

// *Phase 1: identify similar goals in the input models. The order of the input models is irrelevant*
for each G1:Goal **in** GM1 {
    for each G2:Goal **in** GM2 {
    // *isSimilar() is a user-defined function of return type Boolean; the function*
    // *requires the analyst to decide whether G1 and G2 are semantically similar.*
        if (G1.isSimilar(G2)) {
        // *merge the similar goals into one goal to be added in the SIGM.*
        // *merge() is done by the analyst. Could be G1, or G2, or some hybrid.*
            G:Goal = merge(G1,G2)
            SIGM.add(G)

            // *create an IntegrationRelation of type Similar between the source*
            //*(goal G in the SIGM) and the destination (G1 in GM1)*
            IG1:IntegrationRelation = **new** IntegrationRelation
            IG1.type = "S" // *Similar*
            IG1.source = G
            IG1.destination = G1

            // *create an IntegrationRelation of type Similar between the source*
            //*(goal G in the SIGM) and the destination (G2 in GM2)*
            IG2:IntegrationRelation = **new** IntegrationRelation
            IG2.type = "S" // *Similar*
            IG2.source = G
            IG2.destination = G2
}}} // *end if/for/for*

// *Phase 2: add dissimilar goals to DIGM*
for each GM:GoalModel **in** {GM1,GM2} {
    for each G:Goal **in** GM {

```
      if (!exists(G.relation.type = "S")) {
         Gds:Goal = G
         DIGM.add(G)
         IG1:IntegrationRelation = new IntegrationRelation
         IG1.type = "DS" // DisSimilar
         IG1.source = Gds
         IG1.destination = G
}}} // end if/for/for
```

// Similarities and dissimilarities of stakeholders and links of the input goal models are identified using a similar approach. See [4] for details.

```
// Phase 3: create the IGM
for each E:{Goal | Link | Stakeholder} in SIGM { IGM = IGM.add(E) }
for each E:{Goal | Link | Stakeholder} in DSGM { IGM = IGM.add(E) }
// add missing elements (relations: contributions and decompositions) of the
// input models (GM1 and GM2) to the IGM
for each E:{Goal | Link | Stakeholder} in GM1 {
   if (!IGM.contains(E)) { IGM = IGM.add(E) }
}
for each E:{Goal | Link | Stakeholder} in GM2 {
   if (!IGM.contains(E)) { IGM = IGM.add(E) }
}
return IGM
```

5   Illustrative Case Study

Montfort Hospital (in Canada) intends to deploy a new *Voice Recognition System* (VRS) to replace paper-based documentation/recording of patient information. Caregivers will record their notes using computers instead of writing or typing them. The VRS will recognize speech and present it as text for the caregiver to verify and sign electronically. Then, the recorded information will be fed automatically to the patient medical record (in the existing MediTech system). The administrative leaders expect the VRS to be beneficial for caregivers who prefer not to type directly into MediTech.

Currently, there are three alternatives for documenting patient reports and information: writing on paper, typing directly into MediTech, and using a voice recording system. The administrative leaders' objective is to evaluate the performance of each alternative on goal achievement and needs fulfillment, in order to choose the best one. The goal model of the current context contains the stakeholders with their goals and needs, and the contribution of the current documentation alternatives to the goals. The current model and the VRS model should be merged to assess the performance of the VRS on the achievement of stakeholders' goals. Figures 2 and 3 contain the goal models of the current context and the proposed VRS before applying the goal integration method.

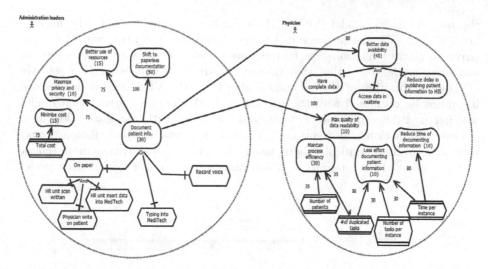

Fig. 2. Current patient report documentation goal model (in GRL)

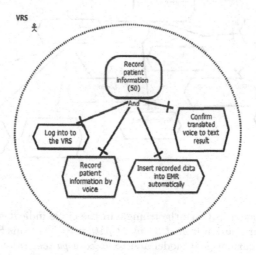

Fig. 3. Proposed VRS goal model (in GRL)

The first phase in the goal integration method is to identify similarities between the two goal models and combine the similar elements in the similarity model (SIGM). The goals "Document patient information" in the hospital actor and "Record patient information" in the VRS actor are similar. Both are about documenting patient information; however, the Record patient information goal is more specified in terms of the technology used to document patient information. Therefore, in the similarity model, the Document patient information goal is used to represent both goals. Similarity relationships are added between the two goals in the original models and the Document patient information goal in the new similarity model (SIGM). The tasks of the two goals in the hospital actor and the VRS actor are added to the similarity model too, with TS (transitive similarity) relationships to the source elements. Figure 4 illustrates the similarity model. Note that the structural TemporaryTask is used to hold the AND-decomposition of the subtasks added from the VRS goal model because it cannot be combined with the subtasks added from the current goal model, which has a different type of decomposition (OR) with the goal "Document patient information". As mentioned in Sect. 3, a TemporaryTask plays a temporary structural role until it gets replaced with another task that is more related to the context of the integration, which cannot be done in the similarity model.

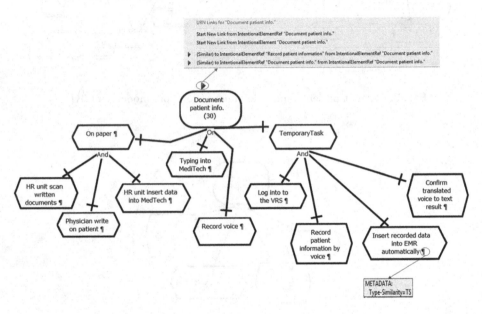

Fig. 4. Similarity model (SIGM): the triangle in the circle indicates, in jUCMNav, the presence of a Similar relation from *Document patient info.* in this SIGM to *Document patient info.* in the current goal model and to *Record patient information* in the VRS goal model. The transitive similarity (TS) metadata is also attached to all tasks

The second phase in the goal integration method is to create the dissimilarity model (DSGM). In this case, the actor VRS from the proposed VRS goal model and all elements in the current context goal model, which are not in the similarity model, are added to the dissimilarity model (see Fig. 5). Following this, the similarity and dissimilarity models are merged in the integrated goal model (IGM). In the IGM, the actor VRS does not have any goal. In fact, in the integration context, the VRS is one of the alternatives for documenting patient information. Therefore, the VRS is modeled as a task and a Different relationship is added between the VRS task and the VRS actor (IGM-V1, not shown here). In addition, the VRS task replaces the TemporaryTask, which is not needed anymore.

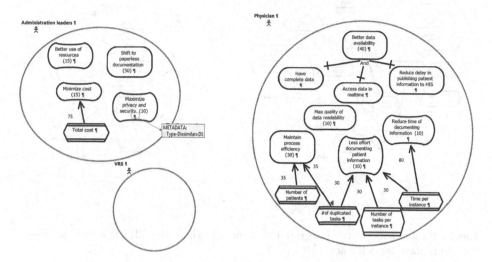

Fig. 5. Dissimilarity model (DSGM): all elements were tagged with the DS type

After ensuring that there are no conflicts between the merged models in the IGM, the relationships from the original models (current context and proposed VRS) are added to the IGM-V1 (Fig. 6), resulting in IGM-V2 (Fig. 7). For all added relationships in IGM-V2, the representation of the VRS actor as a task is approved by the domain experts. The added relationships are not different from the relationships in the original models so no conflict or different context has occurred. The IGM-V2 was validated with the stakeholders where no issue was raised. Accordingly, the IGM-V2 is the approved goal model to be used for evaluation and analysis. The conformance and well-formedness of the resulting IGM were checked using the USE tool and jUCMNav as suggested in Sect. 4. It is worth mentioning that real stakeholders and domain experts were not only involved in the validation phase, but also in all other phases to ensure that the context is logically correct.

6 Discussion

Our *Goal Integration Method* integrates goal models of the organization and of the new candidate technology, in order to reflect the global integration context. While surveying existing work, we noticed that goal model merging refers to partial views of a goal model where essentially the same elements exist in both models but with different vocabularies or with extra information. In our work, we preferred to use the term *integration* rather than *merge* to distinguish the problem context of our approach from the others. In the technology integration

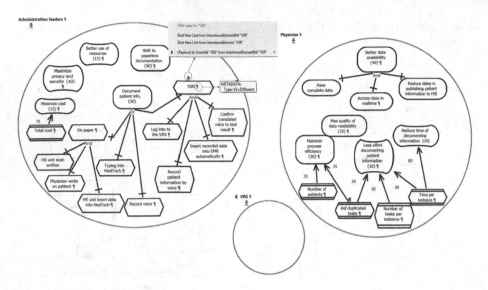

Fig. 6. First version of the integrated goal model, where the VRS is represented as a task to replace the VRS actor (IGM-V1)

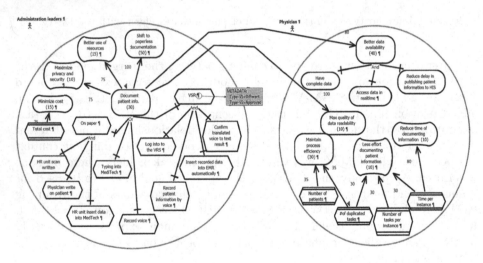

Fig. 7. Second version of the integrated goal model (IGM-V2), where all types of relations have been approved by the stakeholders.

context, for example, goal models should be integrated in a way that supports the elicitation of new requirements or goals while capturing introduced or conflicting relationships, as well as ensuring consistency and completeness of the resulting integrated goal model. Hence, the output of our integration method is a new goal model that preserves the semantics and properties of the input models and, at the same time, brings new realizations to reflect a new context, which is the integration context. However, this does not limit our approach to the technology integration context only; we see an opportunity for the method to be used in other goal model merging contexts. Other application domains for our method include the process integration and decision support contexts [4,5].

In addition, the Goal Integration Method aims to provide a holistic view of the context (after integration) for a comprehensive analysis and to support decision making before technology deployment and implementation. For example, in the illustrative case study, the method presented the VRS as an alternative that complements three other alternatives. The impact of each alternative, on the goal model, could be investigated closely using the corresponding KPIs' (Key Performance Indicator) data, such as the number of duplicated tasks and others in Fig. 2. Although no specific contributions were identified here from the VRS tasks, new ones or modified ones could be identified in other case studies.

Although the proposed method is promising, there are several limitations and threats to validity. For example, our method requires engaging stakeholders into multiple iterations of validation, especially in Phases 4 and 5. This is caused by parts of the goal integration method hitting, iteratively, elicitation of new requirements and validation of results. On the positive side, the validity of the intermediate integration results is always assessed with stakeholders; on the other hand, it could be costly, in terms of effort and time, to engage stakeholders intensively in the validation the method suggests. In our case study, the Montfort Hospital collaborators were sufficiently patient and available to validate several iterations of model integrations (even on larger case studies), but this may not be always the case in other organizations.

Another limitation relates to tool support. jUCMNav was used effectively to build the goal models and to check well-formedness rules. However, the tool does not permit the representation of stakeholder disagreements or the evolution (different representations) of an element during the integration. This was, partially, handled through having multiple versions of the integrated goal model and storing the evolution history in the metadata or URN links of the element. Much manual work was encountered, which makes the task prone to errors. More appropriate tool support is needed to accommodate changes happening to goal models during the integration and to further automate the method, especially in Phases 1, 2 and 3.

Another challenging point with jUCMNav was the representation of self-relations such as the relation between the same goal in the original goal model and dissimilarity model. The relationship was captured using metadata because URN links from/to the same element are not permitted by the tool, even if allowed by URN (see Sect. 4).

It is worth mentioning that even though the case study illustrated effectively the application of the integration method, it may not reflect the complexity of real-world problems in other contexts [4].

7   Conclusion

In this paper, we proposed a new *Goal Integration Method* to integrate goal models belonging to different contexts such as technology-related models and organization models constructed individually and independently by different groups. The method proposes new relationships to capture the types of changes introduced, i.e., whether a new element was added or the representation of an element was changed, during the integration. The method also highlights disagreements and conflicts, helps ensuring consistency and completeness, and provides traceability to rationales and decision made until the final version of the integrated goal model is obtained. The goal integration method was presented formally with a conceptual model, OCL constraints, and an algorithm. The interactive method was implemented with a URN profile, with tool support provided by jUCMNav (model creation and analysis) and USE (verification of integration constraints). In addition, the feasibility of the method was successfully assessed through a *Voice Recognition System* illustrative case study, in collaboration with a real hospital.

For future work, we will conduct further evaluation with more complex case studies to assess scalability and effectiveness, as well as generalization to other contexts. In addition, we will focus on providing better tool support and investigating the opportunity to further automate the implementation of the method.

Acknowledgment. The authors are thankful to Dr. E. M. Bouattane for his help with the case study. This work was supported in part by the Saudi Government and its Ministry of Education, NSERC (Discovery), and the Institut du savoir Montfort.

References

1. Akhigbe, O., et al.: Creating quantitative goal models: governmental experience. In: Yu, E., Dobbie, G., Jarke, M., Purao, S. (eds.) ER 2014. LNCS, vol. 8824, pp. 466–473. Springer, Cham (2014). https://doi.org/10.1007/978-3-319-12206-9_40
2. Alwidian, S., Amyot, D., Babin, G.: Evaluating the potential of technology in justice systems using goal modeling. In: Aïmeur, E., Ruhi, U., Weiss, M. (eds.) MCETECH 2017. LNBIP, vol. 289, pp. 185–202. Springer, Cham (2017). https://doi.org/10.1007/978-3-319-59041-7_11
3. Amyot, D., Mussbacher, G.: User requirements notation: the first ten years, the next ten years. J. Softw. (JSW) **6**(5), 747–768 (2011). https://doi.org/10.4304/jsw.6.5.747-768
4. Baslyman, M.: Activity-based process integration framework to improve user satisfaction and decision support in healthcare. Ph.D. thesis, University of Ottawa, Canada (2018). https://doi.org/10.20381/ruor-22359
5. Baslyman, M., Almoaber, B., Amyot, D., Bouattane, E.M.: Activity-based Process Integration in Healthcare with the user requirements notation. In: Aïmeur, E., Ruhi, U., Weiss, M. (eds.) MCETECH 2017. LNBIP, vol. 289, pp. 151–169. Springer, Cham (2017). https://doi.org/10.1007/978-3-319-59041-7_9
6. Ben-David, S., Chechik, M., Uchitel, S.: Merging partial behaviour models with different vocabularies. In: D'Argenio, P.R., Melgratti, H. (eds.) CONCUR 2013.

LNCS, vol. 8052, pp. 91–105. Springer, Heidelberg (2013). https://doi.org/10.1007/978-3-642-40184-8_8

7. Brunet, G., Chechik, M., Easterbrook, S., Nejati, S., Niu, N., Sabetzadeh, M.: A manifesto for model merging. In: Proceedings of the 2006 International Workshop on Global Integrated Model Management, pp. 5–12. ACM (2006)

8. Feng, Z., He, K., Peng, R., Wang, J., Ma, Y.: Towards merging goal models of networked software. In: SEKE, pp. 178–184 (2009)

9. Fischbein, D., Uchitel, S.: On correct and complete strong merging of partial behaviour models. In: Proceedings of the 16th ACM SIGSOFT International Symposium on Foundations of Software Engineering, pp. 297–307. ACM (2008)

10. Gogolla, M., Büttner, F., Richters, M.: Use: a UML-based specification environment for validating UML and OCL. Sci. Comput. Program. 69(1–3), 27–34 (2007)

11. Hackenberg, G., Bytschkow, D.: Towards early emergent property understanding. In: Proceedings of the 1st Extreme Modeling Workshop at MODELS 2012 (2012)

12. Ishizaka, A., Nemery, P.: Multi-criteria Decision Analysis: Methods and Software. Wiley, Hoboken (2013)

13. ITU-T: Recommendation Z.151 (10/18) User Requirements Notation (URN) - Language definition (2018). https://www.itu.int/rec/T-REC-Z.151/en

14. Liaskos, S., Jalman, R., Aranda, J.: On eliciting contribution measures in goal models. In: 2012 20th IEEE International Requirements Engineering Conference (RE), pp. 221–230 (2012). https://doi.org/10.1109/RE.2012.6345808

15. Mussbacher, G., Amyot, D.: Goal and scenario modeling, analysis, and transformation with jUCMNav. In: 31st International Conference on Software Engineering - Companion Volume, pp. 431–432. IEEE CS (2009). https://doi.org/10.1109/ICSE-COMPANION.2009.5071047

16. Nejati, S., Sabetzadeh, M., Chechik, M., Easterbrook, S., Zave, P.: Matching and merging of statecharts specifications. In: 29th International Conference on Software Engineering (ICSE 2007). IEEE CS (2007). https://doi.org/10.1109/ICSE.2007.50

17. Richards, D.: Merging individual conceptual models of requirements. Requir. Eng. 8(4), 195–205 (2003)

18. Sabetzadeh, M., Easterbrook, S.: View merging in the presence of incompleteness and inconsistency. Requir. Eng. 11(3), 174–193 (2006)

Union Models: Support for Efficient Reasoning About Model Families Over Space and Time

Sanaa Alwidian and Daniel Amyot$^{(\boxtimes)}$

School of EECS, University of Ottawa, Ottawa, Canada
{salwidia, damyot}@uottawa.ca

Abstract. For a given modeling language, a model family is a set of related models, with commonalities and variabilities among family members, that results from the variation/evolution of models over the space and time dimensions. With large model families, the analysis of individual models becomes cumbersome and inefficient. This paper proposes *union models* as a paradigm supporting the representation of model families (for time and space dimensions) using one generic model. Elements of a union model are annotated with information about time and space using a new *spatio-temporal annotation language* (STAL) in order to distinguish which element belongs to which model. We demonstrate empirically the usefulness of union models for analyzing a family of models, *all at once*, compared to individual models, *one model at a time*. Our experiments suggest that the use of union models facilitate efficient analysis in several contexts.

Keywords: GRL · Model analysis · Model evolution · Model family · Property checking · Union model

1 Introduction

In Model-Based Engineering (MBE), models are first-class artifacts used to represent and abstract knowledge and activities that govern a particular domain [1]. Models often undergo continuous change due to, for example, modifications in requirements or standards, or enhanced understanding of the domain to be modeled. Such change could happen over the course of *time* (i.e., evolution), resulting in one model evolving into a set of related versions. A model could also vary over the *space* dimension, where there could be several variants of the same model, all existing at the same time (e.g., to reflect different products or configurations). In both scenarios, a family of related models in the same language, where commonalities and variabilities between family members exist, is called a *model family*.

Change in an MBE context is inevitable. Hence, raising awareness to the phenomena of model families is of particular importance, especially in variant-rich domains such as cyber-physical systems, smart systems, or regulatory environments (where slightly different regulations need to be modeled for different regulated parties and jurisdictions). In any of these domains, models that are used to capture the domain's dynamic nature are subject to frequent variation and evolution. In other words, a modeler may start with an initial model version (v_0), which over *time* needs to

© Springer Nature Switzerland AG 2019
P. Fonseca i Casas et al. (Eds.): SAM 2019, LNCS 11753, pp. 200–218, 2019.
https://doi.org/10.1007/978-3-030-30690-8_12

be updated into a slightly different version (v₁) to reflect a changing requirement. This version may further evolve into versions v_2, v_3, and so on. In the space dimension, two or more modelers may need, *at the same time*, to create slightly different variations of an initial model to reflect different spaces called *configurations*. In such contexts, modelers often end up having a family of model versions and/or variations. *Analyzing and reasoning* about such models requires the modeler to load into a tool, analyze, and report on analysis results of each individual model, *separately*. This is a time-consuming and laborious process that becomes more critical as the number of models to analyze gets larger.

To alleviate these challenges, we propose to capture the set of individual models in a family using one generic model called *union model (M_U)*. M_U represents the union of all elements found in all family members, in both the space and time dimensions. The purpose behind the creation of M_U is to support efficient reasoning and analysis of a family of models, all at once, compared to analyzing individual models separately. At the core of M_U is the annotation of elements, which we realize by proposing a *spatio-temporal annotation language (STAL)*. The main purpose of STAL is to annotate elements of M_U with information about space and time, so as to distinguish which element belongs to which member model in the model family.

The rest of this paper is organized as follows: Sect. 2 discusses the motivation behind our work. Section 3 provides necessary background and formalisms that we rely on to formalize union models. In Sect. 4, we discuss how union models are formalized, constructed, and annotated. The potential benefits of using union models for reasoning and analysis are discussed in Sect. 5. Section 6 reports on experiments conducted to validate the potential efficiency of union models. Related work is discussed in Sect. 7. Finally, Sect. 8 concludes the paper and provides future directions.

2 Motivation

To explain and motivate our approach, we use a simple proof-of-concept example of a smart home environment, where we use the Goal-oriented Requirement Language (GRL) [2, 3] as a modeling language. In a smart home environment, stakeholders' goals, importance of goals, means to achieve goals and relationships between goals (e.g., contributions or decompositions) vary. This variation stems mainly from the existence of different configurations of a smart home that also evolve over time. In this example, we distinguish between two different configurations:

- Configuration A (*confA*): A smart home that is lived in by students who spend about 8 h of the day out of home.
- Configuration B (*confB*): A smart home that is lived in by retired senior persons (most likely sick), who spend most of their daytime and nighttime at home.

In these two configurations (see Fig. 1), a student's goals are slightly different from a senior's goals. For example, a student is more concerned about getting fresh air in her room by opening windows so as to reduce energy consumption (since a student's budget is usually tight). A retired senior, on the other hand, may focus more on getting her room's atmosphere refreshed using the most convenient option (regardless of cost), e.g., by having the ventilator turned on most of the time. Also, the importance of achieving the "refresh air inside" goal differs between a senior person (100) and a student (80). Furthermore, to keep a senior's smart home secure, the home central operator could give the illusion that the house is lived in using several options, one of them being to keep lights always on. However, this may not be a feasible option for a student, since turning lights on all the time consumes energy beyond a student's budget affordability.

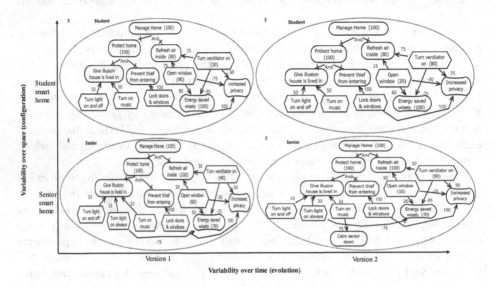

Fig. 1. Goal model family for smart home environments varying according to space and time

In addition to these "space-based" variations, goal models (in both configurations) could also evolve over time. In this example, we illustrate the evolution of models after several months (however, evolution could also happen over shorter periods of times). In such time-based evolution, goals and the means to achieve them (i.e., tasks) may differ between version 1 (produced in the summer) and version 2 (produced in the winter), due to changes in temperature, humidity, daylight duration, etc.

For a student's smart home (i.e., *confA*), the importance of goals/tasks and their impacts (i.e., contribution values) on other goals evolved from version 1 to version 2. For instance, the importance of task "Open window" in version 1 is 90 while it is 20 in version 2, as a student is able to open the window more often in the summer (assuming these models were produced in a Nordic country). Also, the impact of opening a window on the goal "energy saved wisely" is higher in the summer version (with contribution value = 90) than in the winter version (60). Finally, opening a window often in the summer has a higher negative impact on the "increased privacy" softgoal.

The previous evolutions are also applicable in the senior smart home environment (i.e., *confB*). As Fig. 1 shows, the "Open window" task is almost neglected at winter time (with importance = 10) compared to summer time (importance = 60). This is because a senior person is more vulnerable to get cold in the winter. Also, in version 2 (winter), the possibility for seniors to get depressed and anxious is higher (due to snow fall and short daylight duration). In this version, a smart home operator may calm the senior down by turning on soft music.

One important **challenge** implied by Fig. 1 is related to the complexity and effort required to analyze such family of models. Note that past versions may require analysis in case old versions of a product remain used by customers in the field. Assume a modeler plans to conduct satisfaction analysis (using the GRL forward propagation algorithm [2]) on each individual model, by assigning initial values to particular leaf goals, in order to study the impact of its satisfaction on the satisfaction of upper-level goals. She would end up running the same evaluation algorithm four times (in this example only), even though there are *many* common elements and computations among the four models. Intuitively, if there are M individual models in a model family, and each model has E elements, then the complexity of running a satisfaction propagation algorithm on all models would be in order of $M \times O(E)$. Such complexity becomes more significant if there are hundreds of models (or more), with hundreds of elements (or more) in each model. Moreover, the effort of loading a model into a tool, analyzing the model, saving analysis results, and then moving to the next model is *not negligible* in practice.

We aim to improve analysis complexity and reduce the effort of analyzing model families in arbitrary modeling languages (not only goal models), for both the space and time dimensions. This objective motivates us to find a way of representing model families other than using separate individual models. In this paper, we propose the use of a union model (M_U) as a single generic model that captures the entirety of a model family (in both dimensions of variability), in a comprehensive and exact way, such that all (and only) individual members of a family can be represented and analyzed.

3 Foundations

This section introduces relevant notations and background concepts related to graph-based modeling and propositional logic encodings.

3.1 Graph-Based Formalization of (Meta)Models

We formalize metamodels (resp. models) as type graphs (resp. typed graphs), as illustrated in Fig. 2.

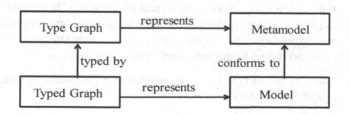

Fig. 2. Relationship between (meta)models and their graph representation

The following definitions, based on previous work by Ehrig et al. [4], are used as a basis for further formal definitions of model families and their union models.

Definition 1–Graph: A graph is a tuple $G = (N_G, E_G, src_G, tgt_G)$, where N_G is a set of graph nodes (or vertices), E_G is a set of graph edges, and functions $src_G, tgt_G: E_G \rightarrow N_G$ associate to each edge a source and a target node, respectively, such that e: x $\rightarrow$ y denotes an edge e with $src_G(e) = x$ and $tgt_G(e) = y$.

In graph theory (as in typed programming languages, where each element is assigned a type), it is often useful to determine the well-formedness of a graph by checking whether it conforms to a so-called *type graph*. A type graph is a distinguished graph containing all the relevant types and their interrelations [4]. This is analogous to the relationship between models and metamodels in MDE [5], where each model needs to conform to a metamodel, as depicted in Fig. 2.

Definition 2–Type graph (metamodel): A type graph TG is a distinguished graph, where $TG = (N_{TG}, E_{TG}, src_{TG}, tgt_{TG})$, and N_{TG} and E_{TG} are types of nodes and edges.

Definition 3–Typed graph (model): A typed graph is a triple $G_{typed} = (G, type, TG)$ such that G is a graph (Def. 1) and type: $G \rightarrow TG$ is a graph morphism called the *typing morphism*. For example, the state machine model shown in Fig. 3 (right) is typed with the metamodel shown in Fig. 3 (left).

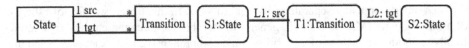

Fig. 3. Type graph (left) and typed graph (right)

The *vocabulary* (or scope) of a typed graph G_{typed} is a set $Voc = \{N_G \cup E_G\}$ of its typed nodes and edges [4]. For example, the vocabulary of the model in Fig. 3 (right) consists of nodes S1 and S2 of type *State*, node T1 of type *Transition*, and edges L1 and L2 of types *src* association (referred next as *srcAssoc*) and *tgt* association (referred next as *tgtAssoc*), respectively. We refer to the set of nodes and edges that are in the vocabulary of a model as the *elements* of that model.

3.2   Propositional Encoding of Models

In order to facilitate reasoning about models, and also to define a simple graph union, we represent typed graphs (i.e., models) as logical propositions. To encode a model in propositional logic, we first map elements in their vocabulary into propositional variables and then conjoin them. The mapping of graph elements into propositional variables is performed according to the following naming conventions:

- A node element $n \in N_G$ of type $t \in N_{TG}$ is mapped to a propositional variable *"n-t"*. Formally: *n-t iff* $\exists n \in N_G \wedge type(n) = t$

- An edge element $e \in E_G$ of type $t \in E_{TG}$ with source node x and target node y is mapped to a propositional variable "*e-x-y-t*". Formally: *e-x-y-t iff* $\exists e \in E_G \wedge$ type $(e) = t \wedge \text{src}_G (e) = x \wedge \text{tgt}_G (e) = y$.

For instance, the propositional encoding *(PE)* of the model *(m)* in Fig. 3 (right) is the conjunction of its propositional variables, described as follows:

```
PE(m)  =  S1-State ∧ T1-Transition ∧ S2-State ∧
          L1-S1-T1-srcAssoc ∧ L2-T1-S2-tgtAssoc
```

4   Union Models

The union model M_U of a model family (MF) is the union of all elements in all individual models of that family. The subsequent sections formally define union models (based on Defs. 1 to 3 and Sect. 3.2), and discuss how to construct an M_U and how to distinguish its elements by means of annotations using our annotation language (STAL).

4.1   Union Model Formalism

Definition 4–Union Model (M_U): Let MF be a model family with two models (i.e., typed graphs), such that MF = {G1, G2}, where G1 = ((N_{G1}, E_{G1}, src_{G1}, tgt_{G1}), type_{G1}, TG) and G2 = ((N_{G2}, E_{G2}, src_{G2}, tgt_{G2}), type_{G2}, TG). Their union model is a typed graph M_U = ((N_U, E_U, src_U, tgt_U), type_U, TG), such that: $N_U = N_{G1} \cup N_{G2}$, $E_U = E_{G1} \cup E_{G2}$, and the functions src_U, tgt_U, and type_U are:

$$\text{src}_U(e) = \begin{cases} \text{src}_{G1}(e), \text{if } e \in E_{G1} \\ \text{src}_{G2}(e), \text{if } e \in E_{G2} \end{cases} \qquad \text{tgt}_U(e) = \begin{cases} \text{tgt}_{G1}(e), \text{if } e \in E_{G1} \\ \text{tgt}_{G2}(e), \text{if } e \in E_{G2} \end{cases}$$

$$\text{type}_U(elem) = \begin{cases} \text{type}_{G1}(elem), \text{if elem} \in V_{G1} \cup E_{G1} \\ \text{type}_{G2}(elem), \text{if elem} \in V_{G2} \cup E_{G2} \end{cases}$$

We can apply the above definition of graph union to sets of typed graphs of arbitrary sizes. Note however that even if the typed graphs used to construct union models are well-formed, there is no guarantee that their M_U is also a well-formed model. In fact, a union model M_U could respect the typing constraints imposed by the TG, but not the multiplicity constraints of attributes or association ends, or OCL constraints. We have already highlighted this general issue in [6], which is outside the scope of this paper.

4.2   Union of Propositional Encodings of Models

Given the propositional encoding of models discussed in Sect. 3.2, the union operation simply becomes the union of the propositional encodings of individual models.

Definition 5–Proposition Encoding Union (PE$_U$): Let MF = {G1, G2} be a model family, where G1 and G2 are typed graphs with the same metamodel TG, and PE(G1) and PE(G2) be their propositional encodings, such that they satisfy these conditions:

- *Cond. 1*: If two nodes have the same name and type, then these nodes are considered identical. We assume here that each node and each edge have its own unique identifier. For simplicity, we express this identity by means of a unique name.
- *Cond. 2*: If two edges have the same name and type and connect between the same source and target nodes, then edges are considered identical.

Then, the union of their propositional encoding becomes: `PE`$_U$ `= PE(G1) ∪ PE(G2)`.

Again, provided that the two conditions are satisfied, we can generalize the propositional encoding union (Def. 5) to a set of arbitrary encoded models.

4.3   Spatio-Temporal Annotation Language (STAL)

The challenging part of constructing a union model is not in the union operation itself (as expressed in Def. 5), but in being able to distinguish to which models a particular element belongs. To address this challenge, we propose a *spatio-temporal annotation language (STAL)* to annotate elements of each individual model with space/time information in the form of <*ver$_{num}$, conf$_{info}$*> , where *ver$_{num}$* denotes the version number of a particular model (e.g., 1st version, and so on), while *conf$_{info}$* denotes space dimension-related information (e.g., smart home configuration, organization type or size, etc.).

Syntax and Semantics of STAL. In the time dimension, models can evolve (independently and asynchronously) over distinct *timepoints*. Since timepoints can be corelated and compared, they naturally form a *chronological order*. Given this inherent chronological nature of models' evolution, a sequence of versions of a particular model can be annotated with sequential version numbers: *ver$_1$, ver$_2$, ver$_3$... ver$_n$*. This creates an implicit *temporal validity* between model versions. For instance, we can say that ver$_1$ happened before ver$_2$. The timing information embedded with the *ver$_{num}$* format in STAL could represent version numbers or dates, or ranges thereof.

The space dimension, on the other hand, is different and somewhat more complex. This stems from the fact that the space dimension is flat and has neither a chronological order nor a hierarchical nature (except in very specific domains, such as in provinces and their cities). In STAL, we use the naming conventions *conf$_X$, conf$_Y$, ..., conf$_Z$* (instead of *conf$_1$, conf$_2$, ..., conf$_n$*) to reflect the lack of ordering semantics.

If a configuration is simple, we use its syntactical description as a name for that configuration. For example, in Fig. 1, we used the names conf$_A$ = "Student smart home" and conf$_B$ = "Senior Smart home" as the names of the two different configurations of smart homes. However, it is worth mentioning that information about configurations could be composite (i.e., consists of several pieces of information). For example, if we want to model different configurations or types of smart houses (similar to TYPE1, TYPE2, and TYPE3 in [7]), where each type refers to a home of a specific size, location, and occupant kind, then we need to take these information into consideration. For instance, TYPE1 refers to homes that are of medium size, located in Ontario, and meant for seniors. To represent this type of composite information in STAL, in a way that keeps annotated models as simple as possible, we propose the use of *look-up tables* (see Table 1), which provide mappings between configuration names and their real descriptions. Please note that in this example, the numbering suffixes of TYPEs do not hold any ordering meanings and they are just descriptions of the configuration.

Table 1. Mapping configurations to their descriptions

Configuration	Description
TYPE1	Size = Medium, Location = Ontario, Occupants = Seniors
TYPE2	Size = Large, Location = Ontario, Occupants = Students
TYPE3	Size = Medium, Location = Quebec, Occupants = Seniors

Annotating the Propositionally-Encoded Models. We annotate the propositional encodings of model elements with information about their versions and/or configurations. For example, assume that the model m in Fig. 3 (right) represents a second version (ver_2) and a configuration X ($conf_X$) of a particular model. Then, the propositional encoding of m with annotation $PE(m_{annot})$ of this model becomes:

```
PE(m        )= S1-State-<ver ,  conf > ∧ T1-Transition-<ver ,  conf > ∧
     annot                 2       x                      2        x
               S2-State-<ver ,  conf > ∧ L1-S1-T1-srcAssoc-<ver ,
                            2       x                         2
               conf > ∧ L2-T1-S2-tgtAssoc-<ver ,  conf >
                   x                          2       x
```

Given a set of annotated, propositionally-encoded models and based on Def. 5, the union of these models is the union of their annotated propositional variables:

$$PE_{Uannot} = PE(G1_{annot}) \cup PE(G2_{annot}) \ldots \cup PE(Gn_{annot})$$

Annotating the Union of Propositionally-Encoded Models with STAL. In a model family, it is possible one model element belongs to several or all family members. For instance, assume that there is a model family with one model configuration ($conf_A$) that evolves into five versions (i.e., ver_1 to ver_5). Assume also a node n that belongs to the five versions of that model. Now, to construct a union model, we need to unify the annotated propositional variables of these five versions. In this case, n will be annotated in the union model with five annotations: $<ver_1, conf_A>$, $<ver_2, conf_A>$, $<ver_3, conf_A>$, $<ver_4, conf_A>$, $<ver_5, conf_A>$. Such style may lead to large amounts of annotations.

To simplify annotations of union models, STAL represents a sequence of version annotations as a range of values (*[start:end]*). In the above example, the annotation of n becomes $<[ver_1: ver_5], conf_A>$. Many sequences can also be used, e.g., for ver_1 to ver₇ skipping ver₄, we get:$<[ver_1: ver_3]$ $[ver_5: ver_7]$, conf$_A>$. If an element belongs to all versions and all configurations of a family, we annotate it with the keyword *ALL*.

Example. We use a simple state machine example, with two versions of a model, as shown in Fig. 4. The union model combining these two versions is expressed as follows:

$$PEU_{annot} = \texttt{S1-State\_<ALL>} \wedge \texttt{T1-Transition-<ver>}_1 \wedge \texttt{S2-State-<ALL>}$$
$$\wedge \texttt{T2-Transition-<ver}_2\texttt{>} \wedge \texttt{L1-S1-T1-srcAssoc-<ver}_1\texttt{>}$$
$$\wedge \texttt{L2-T1-S2-tgtAssoc-<ver}_1\texttt{>} \wedge \texttt{L1-S1-T2-srcAssoc-<ver}_2\texttt{>}$$
$$\wedge \texttt{L2-T2-S2-tgtAssoc-<ver}_2\texttt{>}$$

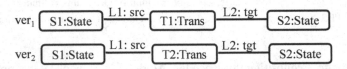

Fig. 4. Two versions of a state machine diagram

In this paper, we limit ourselves to simple type graphs, where attributes of model elements have to be expressed structurally with named nodes and edges. In future work, we will also assess the benefits of extending the definitions of basic type and typed graphs with explicit attributes, for instance using Ehrig's attributed type graphs (or E-graphs) [4], where special edges are used for attributes.

5   Reasoning and Analysis with Union Models

This section explores the research question: *How efficient is reasoning and analysis with a group of models, all at once, using M_U in comparison to the use of individual models?* To answer this research question, we consider three reasoning tasks (RTs), namely: property checking (which is already known in the literature), trend analysis, and significance analysis (which we proposed for this work). Then we compare the performance of the three RTs using M_U as opposed to using individual models.

Although these kinds of analyses can still be performed using individual models (several times, one model at a time), our objective is to try to make these analyses more efficient using M_U. In addition, we aim to reduce the effort of loading each model into a tool, analyzing the model, saving analysis results, and then moving to the next model, especially that this effort *cannot* be neglected with a large number of models. These manual steps are however not considered in our results, so our results are conservative.

RT1: Property Checking. Property checking on models aims to verify if a model satisfies a particular property or not. Given a model m and a property p, the result of property checking is either True if m satisfies p, or False otherwise. For instance, a modeler may want to check whether a group of state machine diagrams contains self-looping edges or not, or she may check if there exist two or more different actors in a

GRL model family that contain the same goal. In these scenarios, property checking is beneficial to help modelers understand, for example, what is common between model versions or variations that violate a property.

In this paper, we limit ourselves to language-independent, syntactic properties (which describe the structure of models) other than semantic properties (which describe the behavior of models, e.g., traces). The rationale behind this scoping is because our approach aims to be applicable to any metamodel-based modeling language. However, while there exists a standard approach for defining the syntax of a modeling language (i.e., through metamodeling), there is no common approach for specifying semantics. So, we limit our approach to checking those properties related to language syntax, independently from any language specificity. Hence, "property" here means "syntactic property". To perform property checking, we assume that a property p (expressed in any constraint language such as FOL or OCL) can be grounded over the vocabulary of models. Hence, a corresponding propositional formula Φp can be obtained. For example, given a well-formedness constraint $\Phi c: \forall t: \texttt{Transition} \, \exists s: \texttt{State} | \texttt{t.src=s}$, it can be grounded over the vocabulary of the model in Fig. 5. as follows:

T1-S1-S2-Transition$\Rightarrow$ S1-State $\wedge$ T2-S2-S3-Transition$\Rightarrow$ S2-State

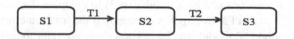

Fig. 5. An example of propositional encoding of a property

It is important to emphasize here that the example in Fig. 5. is just a proof of concept and it does not adhere to our formalization of typed graphs (Sect. 3). As can be noted, the example considers the graphical representation of the state machine presented in the canonical form in Fig. 3. (right), where Transitions T1 and T2 are represented here as directed edges between states, and not as nodes.

Formally speaking, given the propositional encoding of both models (Sect. 3.2) and properties, the task of property checking can be defined as follows:

Definition 6–Property Checking: Given model m and a property p, and their propositional encodings Φm and Φp, respectively, we check if the expression $\Phi m \wedge \Phi p$ is satisfiable or not using a SAT solver.

RT2: Trend Analysis. The idea of this analysis is to search for a particular element across members of a model family and study the *trend* of that element. By "trend" we mean the behavior of elements over space/time. In other words, a trend analysis studies how properties of elements change over the course of time or across configurations. For instance, a modeler may need to search for a particular goal in all members of a GRL family to conduct a trend analysis about the properties of that goal (e.g., its importance value, or satisfaction value) and observe how that value changes across model version/variations to get some insights about its evolution pattern.

RT3: Significance Analysis. We suggest this type of analysis to enable modelers to check for those elements that are common in all (or part) of versions (i.e., time) or variations (i.e., space) of a model family. Elements that are common among all models can be inferred to be essential or significant. For example, if a modeler is investigating several design options of a particular system, and she needs to know which elements are significant (i.e., mandatory for design) in all design options, then she would conduct this analysis *once* using the M_U of the model family she has at hand (instead of doing a pairwise search on each version/variation of individual models).

6   Experiments

We assess the feasibility of reasoning using M_U empirically. We ran experiments with parameterized random inputs that simulate different settings of various reasoning and analysis categories. In this paper, we build on the formal semantics of union models (Sect. 3) and use formalized GRL models and state machine models. However, our approach is also applicable to other metamodel-based languages.

6.1   Methodology

We ran two experiments (named Exp.1 and Exp.2) to evaluate the feasibility of using M_U with RT1, RT2, and RT3. In Exp.1, we measured the total time needed to perform one task on each individual model, one model at a time. We refer to this time as T_{ind}. In Exp.2, we measured the time needed to accomplish the same task with M_U. We refer to this time as T_{MU}. Then, we compute improvements with a metric called time *speedup* (as used in [8]), defined originally as: speedup_old = T_{ind}/T_{MU}. However, to be fairer and more realistic in our experiments (especially for large models), we decided not to neglect the time needed to construct M_U (although it is quite small and can performed once before being amortized over multiple analyses). We call $T_{construct}$ the time needed to construct M_U, and the time speedup is then calculated as: speedup = $T_{ind}/(T_{construct + TMU})$. A speedup larger than 1 is a positive result, and the larger the speedup, the better.

For both experiments, we considered the following experimental parameters: (1) the size of individual models (*SIZE*), which represents the number of elements (i.e., nodes and edges) in each individual model and (2) the number of individual models in a model family (*I*). To control the possible combinations of parameters SIZE and I, we discretized their domains into categories (following Famelis' methodology [8]). For parameter SIZE, we defined four categories based on the number of nodes and edges, as follows: small (S), medium (M), large (L), and extra-large (XL). To calculate the ranges of each size category, we performed experiments with a seed sequence (0, 5, 10, 20, 40). The boundaries of each category were calculated from successive numbers of the seed sequence using the formula $n \times (n + 1)$. Using the same formula, we calculated the representative exemplar of each category by setting n to be the median of two successive numbers in the seed sequence. The ranges of the categories and the selected exemplars for each category are shown in Table 2. These numbers are in line with our own experience dealing with goal models and state machines of various sizes.

We followed the same methodology for the number of individual models, I, using a seed sequence (0, 4, 8, 12, 16). The four size categories (S, M, L, XL) are shown in Table 3.

Table 2. Categories of parameter SIZE (size of a model)

#elements/model (*SIZE*)	(0, 30]	(30, 110]	(110, 420]	(420, 1640]
Exemplar	12	56	240	930
Category	S	M	L	XL

Table 3. Categories of parameter I (number of individual members in a model family)

# of individual models (*I*)	(0, 20]	(20, 72]	(72, 156]	(156, 272]
Exemplar	6	42	110	210
Category	S	M	L	XL

To evaluate the property checking task (RT1), we encoded each annotated individual model m in a model family MF as a propositional logic formula $\Phi m = \bigwedge e_i \in PE$ (m_{annot}). We also encoded a union model M_U of that MF as $\Phi M_U = \bigwedge e_i \in PE_{Uannot}$. Furthermore, the property to be checked was encoded into a propositional formula Φp. Then, a SAT solver was used to check if the encodings of each of the individual model and their union model satisfy (or not) the property. In particular, for each individual model, we constructed a formula $\Phi m \wedge \Phi p$. The property is said to hold in any model if and only if this formula is satisfiable. Similarly, we constructed the formula $\Phi M_U \wedge \Phi p$ and checked whether the property was satisfiable. In both experiments (using the same computer), we recorded the time it took to check a property on individual models (T_{ind}) and compared it to the time needed to do the check on union models (T_{MU}).

6.2   Implementation

To validate our approach, we had a prototype implementation in Python 3.6 to represent models (GRL and state machine models) as typed graphs (based on Defs. 3 and 4), and construct their M_U according to Def. 5. We used NetworkX 2.2 [9] to implement typed graphs, and we implemented our own union algorithm to construct M_U by adapting NetworkX's built-in union function as a building block. NetworkX is a Python package for the creation, manipulation, and study of the structure, dynamics, and functions of complex graphs [9]. It is enriched with a variety of features from the support of graph data structures and algorithms to analysis measures to visualization options. We used NetworkX's graph generators to randomly generate valid typed graphs (with different parameters SIZE and I) with likely evolutions. We checked a sample of the generated graphs manually to make sure that we are generating likely changes to existing models rather than generating independent models. Then, we assigned attributes to nodes and edges of these generated graphs to reflect attributions and typing information of real models. We then constructed G_U from the generated graphs using our union algorithm. G_U is the union of a set of typed graphs, and hence G_U corresponds to M_U.

For RT1, we manually generated propositional formulas for state machine diagrams (both individual models and their M_U). We checked the "*cyclic composition property*" inspired from [10], which ensures that "the model does not contain self-looping edges". A propositional formula was also generated for this property. The propositional encodings were generated according to the rules discussed in Sect. 3.2, and they were fed as literals to the MiniSAT solver included in the SATisPY package [11]. SATisPy is a Python library that aims to be an interface to various SAT solver applications.

6.3   Results

This section is organized according to the experiments conducted to evaluate RT1, RT2, and RT3. All figures illustrated in this section represent the average results of 15 runs.

Results for RT1. Figure 6 illustrates the time speedup of performing property checking, first with a set of individual state machine diagrams (represented as typed graphs) and then with their M_U. In this experiment, we checked the satisfiability of the cyclic composition property (Sect. 6.2). Figure 6 shows that the use of M_U for property checking achieves a significant time speedup compared to performing the same task on a set of individual models separately. The highest speedup (=365) was observed with a large number of individual models (i.e., I = L) that are of a small size (i.e., SIZE = S). The smallest speedup (=2.54), on the other hand, was observed when both I, and SIZE parameters are of category XL. In addition, for all categories of I, there is a noticeable pattern of speedup degradation as the number of elements per individual model (i.e., SIZE) increases. This is due in part to the increase of $T_{construct}$ as the SIZE increases. Nevertheless, the speedup never went below 1, which means that even with very large models (with I = XL and SIZE = XL), the time to perform property checking on a

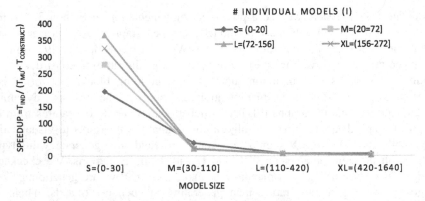

Fig. 6. Average speedups achieved by using MU to perform property checking (RT1)

group of such models (using M_U), with considering the time to construct M_U, is still better than performing property checking on individual models.

Results for RT2. In this experiment, we conducted a trend analysis on an element named GoalX from a set of GRL individual models and their M_U. The purpose of this analysis is to study the trend of this goal's *importance value* attribute and analyze how this value changes over time. To perform this analysis on M_U, we simply searched for and retrieved an element named X of type Goal, annotated with any version number (i.e., X-Goal-<{ver_i}>), where {ver_i} reflects the set of versions that the element may belong to. With individual models, the search for and retrieval of X-Goal involve each individual model, where the (laborious) process in reality involves opening each individual model, searching about the desired element, observe its importance value, and close the current model, iteratively for each model. Figure 7 illustrates the time speedup gained in this experiment. The results illustrated in this figure show a pattern close to the results of RT1 (i.e., property checking). This is somewhat expected as both the property checking task and the searching task (which is the core of trend analysis) have a linear time complexity. From Fig. 7, it can be noticed that the use of M_U reduces the time to search for elements that belong to a group of models instead of traversing each individual model, separately. The highest speedup (=296) was achieved when I = XL and SIZE = S, and the lowest (=5.9) when I = S and SIZE = XL. The decrease pattern of speedup gained in this experiment is almost close to the one illustrated in Fig. 6.

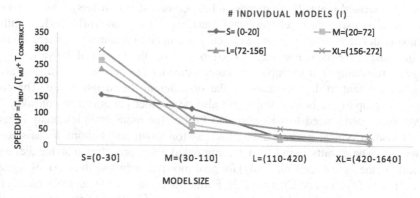

Fig. 7. Average speedups achieved by using MU to perform trend analysis (RT2)

Results for RT3. Figure 8 shows the time speedup for significance analysis on a set of GRL models and their M_U. In this experiment, we searched for all elements that are common between all model versions. This is a tedious task, especially when the number and the size of models increase. Searching a set of M individual models, with N elements each to find elements in common between all models has a complexity of O $(M \times N^2)$. However, with M_U, we only use one model to search elements in common, where the search task is reduced here into searching for elements annotated with <ALL> . The time speedup gained in this experiment is more significant than in the

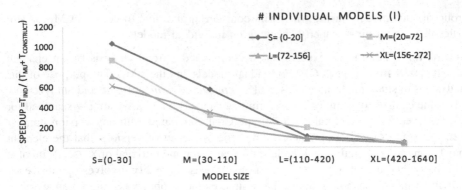

Fig. 8. Average speedups achieved by using MU to perform significance analysis (RT3)

experiments for RT1 and RT2, as the potential gain here is quadratic rather than linear. Again here, there is a decrease in the speedup as the model SIZE increases.

We noticed in some experiments with particular settings (related to variation of models, size, number of models in a family) that the time saving achieved from using M_U was a few minutes (about 15 min for some model families).

6.4   Threats to Validity

One major threat to the validity of our empirical evaluation stems from relying on randomly generated inputs (both graphs and experimental parameters). This threat can be alleviated by using more realistic parameters, e.g., from real-world model families.

Another threat to validity is related to the experimental parameters, where we used only *SIZE* and *I*. We recognize that we need to examine the impact of the variability of models on reasoning. For example, we could consider the number of different annotations per element to describe how similar or different the members are. The complexity of a property to be checked might also be another parameter to consider.

Our experiments need to be elaborated further for more complex analysis techniques found in typical goal modeling such as top-down and bottom-up satisfaction propagation. The results could also be compared to approaches that handle some variability in the time dimension (only) for goal models, including the work of Aprajita et al. [12] and of Grubb and Chechik [13]. Furthermore, the current analysis covers two modeling language (goal models and state machines) and it should be extended to other types that are more structural (e.g., class diagrams) or behavioral (e.g., process models).

Finally, the usefulness of our approach needs to be assessed and demonstrated with more significant examples or real-world case studies.

7   Related Work

There are few approaches proposed in the literature to support *model families*. Shamsaei et al. [7] defined a generic goal model family (using GRL) for various types of organizations in a legal compliance domain. They annotate models with information about organization types to specify which ones are applicable to which family member. Different from our work, the work of [7] handles only variation of models in the space dimension and does not consider evolution over time. Also, the authors focused only on maintainability issues and did not propose union models to improve analysis complexity and reduce analysis effort. Palmieri et al. [14] elaborated further on the work of [7] to support more variable regulations. The authors integrated GRL and feature models to handle regulatory goal model families as software product lines (SPLs), by annotating a goal model with propositional formula related to features in a feature model. Unlike [7], Palmieri et al. considered further dimensions such as the organization size, type, the number of people, etc. However, they did not consider evolution of goal models over time, and did not introduce union models.

Our work has strong conceptual resemblances with the domain of SPL engineering, which aims to manage software variants to efficiently handle families of software [15]. Although both of our work and the SPL domain have the concept of "families", their usages are different. In essence, the goal of SPL engineering is to plan for "proactive reusability", which means to strategically maintain a set of modeling artifacts (with high-level features) to exploit what variants have in common to derive or create new desirable products. The goal of our work, however, is not to plan for reusability but to analyze families of models more efficiently using union models.

The notion of a *feature* is central to variability modeling in SPL, where features are expressed as variability points. Feature models (FMs) [16] are a formalism commonly used to model variability in terms of optional, mandatory, and exclusive features organized in a rooted hierarchy, and associated with constraints over features. FMs can be encoded as propositional formula defined over a set of Boolean variables, where each variable corresponds to a feature. FMs characterize the valid combinations of features as a configuration. A configuration defines, at a conceptual level, one product which can be extracted from the SPL. Yet, a FM is different from an M_U in both usage and formalism. A FM represents variability at an abstract "feature level" which is separate from the software artifacts (like a grammar of possible configurations), whereas M_U represents variability of all existing models at the "artifact level" itself.

To express variability, annotative approaches are commonly used in the literature, as in the work of Czarnecki and Antkiewicz [17], where variability points are represented as presence conditions. These conditions are propositional expressions over features. Annotations of features can be used as inputs to a variability realization mechanism to derive or create a concrete software system as variant of the SPL. Using a negative variability mechanism [17], annotative approaches define a so-called 150% model that superimposes all possible variations of for the entire SPL. The 150% model is used to derive a particular variant, while other irrelevant parts are removed. While union models have some similarities to 150% models, the usage of both models, the domains they are used in, and the way of annotating them are different.

The approaches proposed by Seidl et al. [18] and Lity et al. [19] are closely related to ours. They considered variation of software families in space and time, and explicitly annotated variability models with time and space information to distinguish between the different versions and variations of software artifacts. However, this work is done from the SPL perspective (where FMs are essential), while FMs are not used here.

Famelis et al. [20] proposed partial models to capture a set of possible alternative design models with uncertainty. While the idea of capturing models in one partial model is close to our idea of representing models of a family in one union model, our proposed approach is different in two major aspects: the context and the purpose. In essence, we propose union models to enable a more efficient reasoning of multiple models compared to individual models. Partial models, however, are used to describe the observable behavior of a system and to reduce design-time uncertainty.

Mussbacher [21] and Aprajita et al. [12] extended the metamodel of GRL to document explicit changes (additions/deletions) of model elements to specific versions of a metamodel. Although a model family can then be captured, this approach is specific to one language and currently incomplete in the kinds of changes to versions it can accommodate.

Grubb et al. [22] introduced the concepts of "dynamic intentions" into goal models to model alternatives on multiple time scales. The authors proposed a tool-supported method for specifying changes in intentions over time which uses simulation for asking a variety of 'what if' questions about models that evolve over time. Unlike our work, Grubb's approach is limited to goal models (Tropos and i^* in particular), and does not cover variations of models over the space dimension.

The concept of difference and union/merging of models is well investigated in the context of version control systems [23, 24]. For instance, Alanen and Porres [25] proposed an approach to calculate the difference between two models, represented as a sequence of operations, and then extend the difference calculation to form a union algorithm. The union algorithm calculates the union of two models based on their differences from a given original/base model, where two separate modifications are made to a base model, and the union algorithm combines both differences into one model by interleaving the operations from the latter difference with the former difference. For example, given a base model M_{base} and two alternative model versions M_1 and M_2, the union of these models, denoted as M_{final}, is calculated as: $M_{final} = M_{base} + (M_1 - M_{base}) + (M_2 - M_{base})$. This mechanism, known as *three-way merge*, is mainly concerned with tracking and highlighting the changes that happen across models, and calculates the final model based on the *differences* from the original model, without backward traceability to the source of the changes. This is different from our union algorithm, where we calculate the union model by taking all elements that belong to all versions of models, with an additional feature that annotates elements to indicate to which version they belong.

8   Conclusion and Future Work

This paper proposed union models as a modeling paradigm to support the representation of model families (for time and space dimensions) using one generic model. Elements of a union model are annotated with information about time and space using a new spatio-temporal annotation language (STAL) in order to distinguish which element belongs to which model. The paper is contributing a formalization of union models that simplifies the creation of such models while enabling several types of efficient analyses.

Our experiments indeed demonstrate the usefulness of union models for analyzing a family of models, all at once, compared to individual models.

For future work, we plan to extend our empirical evaluation by having more experimental inputs, parameters, and tasks, by using existing model families, and also by considering other categories of analysis techniques (such as GRL top-down propagation) and other modeling languages. We expect that some analysis techniques will need to be adapted from a single-model context to a model-family context; the circumstances imposing such adaptation and the effort required to adapt the analysis techniques need to be identified and better understood. Usable tool support is also being developed.

Acknowledgement. We would like to thank the anonymous reviewers, as well as Prof. Michalis Famelis, for their comments and feedback, which helped us improve the presentation of this paper. We also thank the Ontario Trillium Scholarship program, the NSERC Discovery program, and the BMO Financial Group Graduate Bursaries for their financial support.

References

1. Micouin, P.: Model Based Systems Engineering: Fundamentals and Methods. Wiley, Hoboken (2014)
2. ITU-T: Recommendation Z.151 (10/18) User Requirements Notation (URN) – Language definition (2018). https://www.itu.int/rec/T-REC-Z.151/en
3. Amyot, D., Mussbacher, G.: User requirements notation: the first ten years, the next ten years. J. Softw. **6**(5), 747–768 (2011)
4. Ehrig, H., Ehrig, K., Prange, U., Taentzer, G.: Fundamentals of algebraic graph transformation. Monographs in Theoretical Computer Science. An EATCS Series. Springer, Heidelberg (2006). https://doi.org/10.1007/3-540-31188-2
5. Kent, S.: Model driven engineering. In: Butler, M., Petre, L., Sere, K. (eds.) IFM 2002. LNCS, vol. 2335, pp. 286–298. Springer, Heidelberg (2002). https://doi.org/10.1007/3-540-47884-1_16
6. Alwidian, S., Amyot, D.: Relaxing metamodels for model family support. In: 11th Workshop on Models and Evolution (ME 2017), vol. 2019, pp. 60–64. CEUR-WS (2017)
7. Shamsaei, A., et al.: An approach to specify and analyze goal model families. In: Haugen, Ø., Reed, R., Gotzhein, R. (eds.) SAM 2012. LNCS, vol. 7744, pp. 34–52. Springer, Heidelberg (2013). https://doi.org/10.1007/978-3-642-36757-1_3
8. Famelis, M.: Managing design-time uncertainty in software models. Doctoral dissertation, University of Toronto, Canada (2016)
9. NetworkX. https://networkx.github.io/. Accessed 05 June 2019
10. Van Der Straeten, R., Mens, T., Simmonds, J., Jonckers, V.: Using description logic to maintain consistency between UML models. In: Stevens, P., Whittle, J., Booch, G. (eds.) UML 2003. LNCS, vol. 2863, pp. 326–340. Springer, Heidelberg (2003). https://doi.org/10.1007/978-3-540-45221-8_28
11. SATisPY Solver. https://github.com/netom/satispy. Accessed 15 June 2019
12. Aprajita, Luthra, S., Mussbacher, G.: Specifying evolving requirements models with TimedURN. In: Proceedings of the 9th International Workshop on Modelling in Software Engineering, pp. 26–32. IEEE Press (2017)

13. Grubb, A.M., Chechik, M.: Modeling and reasoning with changing intentions: an experiment. In: 2017 IEEE 25th International Requirements Engineering Conference (RE), pp. 164–173. IEEE CS (2017)

14. Palmieri, A., Collet, P., Amyot, D.: Handling regulatory goal model families as software product lines. In: Zdravkovic, J., Kirikova, M., Johannesson, P. (eds.) CAiSE 2015. LNCS, vol. 9097, pp. 181–196. Springer, Cham (2015). https://doi.org/10.1007/978-3-319-19069-3_12

15. Pohl, K., Böckle, G., van der Linden, F.J.: Software Product Line Engineering: Foundations, Principles and Techniques. Springer, Heidelberg (2005). https://doi.org/10.1007/3-540-28901-1

16. Schobbens, P.Y., Heymans, P., Trigaux, J.C., Bontemps, Y.: Generic semantics of feature diagrams. Comput. Netw. 51(2), 456–479 (2007)

17. Czarnecki, K., Antkiewicz, M.: Mapping features to models: a template approach based on superimposed variants. In: Glück, R., Lowry, M. (eds.) GPCE 2005. LNCS, vol. 3676, pp. 422–437. Springer, Heidelberg (2005). https://doi.org/10.1007/11561347_28

18. Seidl, C., Schaefer, I., Aßmann, U.: Integrated management of variability in space and time in software families. In: Proceedings of the 18th International Software Product Line Conference (SPLC), vol. 1, pp. 22–31. ACM (2014)

19. Lity, S., Nahrendorf, S., Thüm, T., Seidl, C., Schaefer, I.: 175% modeling for product-line evolution of domain artifacts. In: Proceedings of the 12th International Workshop on Variability Modelling of Software-Intensive Systems (VaMoS), pp. 27–34. ACM (2018)

20. Famelis, M., Salay, R., Chechik, M.: Partial models: towards modeling and reasoning with uncertainty. In: 34th International Conference on Software Engineering (ICSE), pp. 573–583. IEEE CS (2012)

21. Mussbacher, G.: TimedGRL: specifying goal models over time. In: IEEE International Requirements Engineering Conference Workshops (REW), pp. 125–134. IEEE CS (2016)

22. Grubb, A.M., Chechik, M.: Looking into the crystal ball: requirements evolution over time. In: 24th International Requirements Engineering Conference (RE), pp. 86–95. IEEE CS (2016)

23. Altmanninger, K., Seidl, M., Wimmer, M.: A survey on model versioning approaches. Int. J. Web Inf. Syst. 5(3), 271–304 (2009)

24. Förtsch, S., Westfechtel, B.: Differencing and merging of software diagrams–state of the art and challenges. In: Filipe, J., Helfert, M., and Shishkov, B. (eds.) Second International Conference on Software and Data Technologies (ICSOFT), pp. 90–99. INSTICC Press (2007)

25. Alanen, M., Porres, I.: Difference and union of models. In: Stevens, P., Whittle, J., Booch, G. (eds.) UML 2003. LNCS, vol. 2863, pp. 2–17. Springer, Heidelberg (2003). https://doi.org/10.1007/978-3-540-45221-8_2

Facilitating the Co-evolution of Standards and Models

Philip Makedonski[✉] and Jens Grabowski

Institute of Computer Science, University of Göttingen,
Göttingen, Germany
{makedonski,grabowski}@cs.uni-goettingen.de

Abstract. The Information Model (IM) specified by the Network Function Virtualisation (NFV) Industry Specification Group (ISG) at the European Telecommunications Standards Institute (ETSI) provides a consolidated view of all information elements used in the various interfaces defined in the NFV standards. Its purpose is to enable quick identification of gaps and inconsistencies in the standards and in implementations of the standards. As the standards are increasing in volume, manual approaches for ensuring their consistency and their co-evolution with the IM are becoming unsustainable, especially considering the rapid release cycles. In this article, we present a model-based approach for facilitating the co-evolution of standards and models and the current state of its prototypical implementation put into place to support the work within the NFV Interfaces and Architecture (IFA) working group. The initial results from the application of the approach were reported to the NFV IFA working group and are expected to contribute towards maintaining the high quality of the standards as they continue to evolve.

Keywords: Model evolution · Validation · Maintenance · Standards · Traceability

1 Introduction

Modelling is gaining ground in standardisation. The Network Function Virtualisation (NFV) Industry Specification Group (ISG) at the European Telecommunications Standards Institute (ETSI) has adopted the Unified Modeling Language (UML) for the Specification of an Information Model (IM) for NFV. The IM provides a consolidated view on all information elements used in the various interfaces defined in the different NFV standards. It enables a quick identification of gaps and inconsistencies in the standards and in implementations of the standards. The IM consolidates information elements from more than 14 different NFV Interfaces and Architecture (IFA) working group Specification spanning more than 1000 pages that provide input to the information model. The size of the model has grown to more than 200 classes, 250 data types and 250 associations and continues to grow with the rapid release cycle resulting from the intense work within the ISG.

© Springer Nature Switzerland AG 2019
P. Fonseca i Casas et al. (Eds.): SAM 2019, LNCS 11753, pp. 219–232, 2019.
https://doi.org/10.1007/978-3-030-30690-8_13

While machine readable models can aid the standardization work and provide added value during both the standards development and the use of the standards, human readable Specification are still the main outcome of standardisation. Thus, it is necessary that both the specifications and the models co-evolve in a consistent manner.

So far the consistency checking and co-evolution of the standards and the model has been performed manually. This process can be very time consuming, tedious, and error-prone, to the point of becoming unsustainable with the increasing volume of the standards and the IM, especially considering the rapid release cycles, and the growing interconnectedness in the domain with different organisations coming together to evolve the standards further. At the same time, having an up-to-date IM becomes more and more important in order to ensure that the standards are consistent. Thus, some automation of the consistency checking is highly desirable in order to ensure the usefulness of the IM and enable the maintenance team to focus on the adaptation of the IM. Automation in this area can also benefit the allocation of highly specialised expertise that is required to maintain the standards by enabling experts to dedicate more time on technical matters instead of manual consistency checking.

Since standards are highly (and sometimes also formally) structured documents, it is feasible to extract a model from the document. This model can then be checked against the IM at various levels of detail to ensure that any incoming changes to the documents are reflected in the IM. Additionally, checks for the internal consistency of both the IM and the documents can be realised by model constraints, for example. In this article, we outline our approach for facilitating the co-evolution of standards and models and the current state of its prototypical implementation put into place to support the work within the NFV IFA working group, some initial results from the application of the approach, as well as our vision for future work in this area.

The rest of this article is structured as follows: In Sect. 2, we summarise some of the background information regarding the peculiarities of the application domain. In Sect. 3, we present the model-based approach for facilitating the co-evolution of standards and models. In Sect. 4, we showcase the current state of the prototypical implementation of the presented approach as well as some initial findings from its application. In Sect. 5, we discuss related work in the area. Finally, in Sect. 6, we conclude this article by providing a short summary and an outlook on future work in this area.

2 Background

The NFV ISG undertakes work in 2-year phases (release cycles) during which a new release is developed. Within a release cycle, new IFA specifications and maintenance revisions of existing IFA specifications are typically approved every six months and provided as new versions within "release drops". During the ongoing work on the specifications, the draft versions of the specifications and the IM need to be continuously aligned. The draft versions are provided for discussion during IFA meetings before publication, in order to identify potential misalignments and be able to take timely corrective actions and coordinate with the work on other related NFV IFA specifications.

The NFV IM was conceived as means to obtain a consolidated view on all information elements present in the descriptors and interface specifications. Such consolidated view enables a quick identification of gaps and inconsistencies in the standards and implementations of the standards. It also provides means to check the consistency and validity of new features and changes during the drafting of related specifications. Thus, the IM is an important tool for ensuring the consistency among specifications. Having the consolidated IM in a machine-readable format also eases the sharing of the model with external stakeholders. By relying on tools and formats commonly used in the broader community, the use of the ETSI NFV IM as a basis becomes more appealing, as it is easy to build custom solutions on top of it. To continue to be useful, the IM needs to be maintained and aligned with changes in the related specifications.

The ETSI NFV specifications are referenced and used by operators, vendors, and open source communities involved in NFV deployments. The availability of the ETSI NFV IM representation is essential for the quick development of high-quality specifications and for making ETSI NFV the industry reference for management and orchestration standards. Furthermore, it also helps the faster adoption of ETSI specifications by other standards organizations and open source projects as it offers a well-defined "entry point" to understand the relationship among the different concepts, artefacts, functionality, interfaces, etc.

While the information elements described in the IM are focused on the management of the virtualisation aspects, other models, defined by other organizations, such as the Open Networking Foundation (ONF), TM Forum, and the 3rd Generation Partnership Project (3GPP) focus on other aspects in the domain. To provide an end-to-end model view, interaction points between the IM selected models from other organizations are described in a separate report (IFA024[1]). This allows all organizations to extend their models based on the interaction points as needed.

3   Methodology

Due, in part, to the increasing overhead associated with the maintenance of the IM, its latest published version is v3.1.1. In the meantime, two updated versions of related specifications were prepared, v3.2.1 and v3.3.1. We collected the updated versions of the relevant specifications since the last published update to the IM as input material. The specifications included: IFA005, IFA006, IFA007, IFA008, IFA011, IFA012, IFA013, IFA014, IFA030, IFA031, IFA032 (See footnote 1).

Consequently, we started with more than 2000 pages of standards documents for the two versions since the last published version of the IM. Luckily, the documents were also available with change marks. The first step was to investigate

---

[1] See https://www.etsi.org/technologies/nfv.

the extent and type of changes between the versions. This already provided us with an initial overview, where newer versions of some of the documents only included minor changes, whereas other documents featured more substantial modifications. The next step was to migrate the changes to the IM. The first obvious challenge was to identify where the relevant elements are located. The IM is structured in different nested packages and there are a total of 64 diagrams where the elements may be represented. Due to the lack of traceability links, this proved to be a rather challenging task. More importantly, it quickly became apparent that there are more differences between the standards and the IM than the ones indicated by the change marks. Thus, relying on the change marks alone would not be sufficient.

Considering the amount of documents that need to be aligned with the IM, as well as the inherent complexity of the domain and the rapid release cycles, it became evident that the maintenance process for the IM can benefit from some automation to quickly identify inconsistencies and enable the maintainers to focus on the important tasks. Inconsistencies emerge for a number of reasons. New information elements are added to the standards as part of ongoing maintenance activities. Similarly, existing elements are refined where their descriptions and attribute definitions are modified. In rare cases, information elements are also removed from the standards. Certain information elements are exposed through multiple interfaces, thus their definitions appear in the specifications for each of those interfaces and need to be kept consistent whenever changes to the information elements are introduced. While there is an established process for mirroring changes to these information elements across all relevant specifications, given the growing volume of the specifications, it is important to monitor and ensure the consistency of the mirrored definitions. Both the standards and the IM abide by certain conventions, which need to be checked and enforced over time. After examining the standards and the IM further, the following challenges emerged:

1. **Validation of the standards against the IM:** whether all elements exist in the IM (detect new elements), whether the attributes and descriptions match (detect mismatching attributes and descriptions);
2. **Validation of the IM against the standards:** whether all elements exist in the standards (detect obsolete elements), whether elements are described in multiple standards (detect duplicate specifications);
3. **Internal consistency of the standards:** whether conventions within the individual standards are followed, whether there are inconsistencies between different standards and different versions of standards;
4. **Internal consistency of the IM:** whether conventions within the IM are followed, whether the structure of the IM and its elements is consistent;
5. **Establish traceability links:** document where an element is represented in the standards, the IM, and the diagrams.

To illustrate these challenges, consider the *VnfVirtualLinkResourceInfo* information element. Comparing its definition in IFA008 v3.2.1, shown in Fig. 1, and in the IM, shown in Fig. 1, we can observe that the *reservationId* attribute from

9.4.5   VnfVirtualLinkResourceInfo information element

9.4.5.1   Description

This information element provides information on virtualised network resources used by an internal VL instance in a VNF.

9.4.5.2   Attributes

The VnfVirtualLinkResourceInfo information element shall follow the indications provided in table 9.4.5.2-1.

Table 9.4.5.2-1: Attributes of the VnfVirtualLinkResourceInfo information element

Attribute	Qualifier	Cardinality	Content	Description
virtualLinkInstanceId	M	1	Identifier	Identifier of this VL instance.
vnfVirtualLinkDescId	M	1	Identifier (Reference to VnfVirtualLinkDesc)	Identifier of the VNF Virtual Link Descriptor (VLD) in the VNFD.
networkResource	M	1	ResourceHandle	Reference to the VirtualNetwork resource.
vnfLinkPort	M	0..N	VnfLinkPortInfo	Links ports of this VL.
metadata	M	0..N	KeyValuePair	Metadata about this resource.

Fig. 1. *VnfVirtualLinkResourceInfo* information element in IFA008 (excerpt from standard)

the IM is not present in the corresponding definition in IFA008 v3.2.1. Assuming that the standards are the primary point of reference, we might conclude that it needs to be removed from the IM as the definition in IFA008 v3.2.1 does not include such attribute. However, a more thorough examination reveals that the same information element is also defined within IFA007 v3.2.1 and IFA013 v3.2.1. The corresponding excerpts are shown in Figs. 3 and 4, respectively. Considering the definitions for *VnfVirtualLinkResourceInfo* in IFA007 v3.2.1 and IFA013 v3.2.1, we can observe that the *reservationId* attribute is indeed present in these definitions. This raises the question which definition is to be considered correct. Without, further information, it is impossible to tell, so such inconsistencies need to be discussed with the NFV IFA working group. Alternatively, looking at the history of changes and the related change requests may reveal further hints regarding which definition is the correct one. Beyond this obvious inconsistency, a closer look reveals further differences in the attribute descriptions, ranging from the definition of an acronym in the description for the *vnfVirtualLinkDescId* attribute in IFA007 v3.2.1 to additional information in the *networkResource* attribute description in IFA007 v3.2.1 and additional requirements in the *vnfLinkPort* attribute descriptions in IFA007 v3.2.1 and IFA013 v3.2.1. While such inconsistencies are not very common in the standards and in the IM, checking for them manually requires substantial effort and might still fail to detect them due to the sheer volume of content that needs to be continuously examined.

To address these challenges, we first needed to extract the relevant information from the standards. Since the standards have a highly structured format, we defined a minimal meta-model to capture the essential relevant concepts, comprising of *standards*, containing *information elements*, which in turn contain

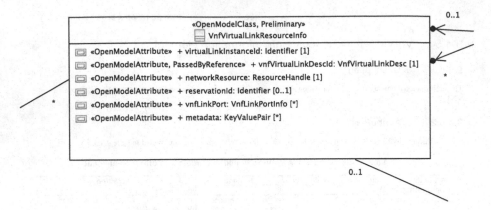

Fig. 2. *VnfVirtualLinkResourceInfo* information element in IM (excerpt from diagram)

attributes. The meta-model is summarised in Fig. 5. Then, we defined a mapping from the standards to the meta-model, enabling us to construct model instances from the standards documents. Following a model-based approach allows us raise the level of abstraction and capitalise on existing modelling technologies and approaches.

Next, we defined a set of model transformations for establishing traceability links between the information elements in the standards models, the IM, and the diagrams, resulting in a trace model. Finally, we defined a set of constraints for checking the consistency of the IM and the standards models which take advantage of the trace model in order to address the first four challenges listed above. The overall approach is summarised in Fig. 6.

4   Implementation and Evaluation

In this section, we discuss the realisation of the approach, its current status, as well as its initial evaluation.

4.1   Overview

Eclipse and associated technologies were chosen as the base platform for the implementation as it is one of the most widely used modeling platforms today. Another reason for the adoption of Eclipse was the fact that the IM has been specified and maintained in the form of a UML model within the Papyrus modeling environment[2], which is also part of the Eclipse ecosystem. In addition to end-user modelling capabilities, Eclipse also provides Application Programming Interface (API) for developers allowing the programmatic access of UML models and resources. Associated modelling technologies, such as implementations of OCL, provide higher level access to the UML models as well. This enabled us to inspect and process the IM.

8.5.5   VnfVirtualLinkResourceInfo information element

8.5.5.1   Description

This information element provides information on virtualised network resources used by an internal VL instance in a VNF.

8.5.5.2   Attributes

The VnfVirtualLinkResourceInfo information element shall follow the indications provided in table 8.5.5.2-1.

Table 8.5.5.2-1: Attributes of the VnfVirtualLinkResourceInfo information element

Attribute	Qualifier	Cardinality	Content	Description
virtualLinkInstanceId	M	1	Identifier	Identifier of this VL instance.
vnfVirtualLinkDescId	M	1	Identifier (Reference to VnfVirtualLinkDesc)	Identifier of the VNF Virtual Link Descriptor (VLD) in the VNFD.
networkResource	M	1	ResourceHandle	Reference to the VirtualNetwork resource. Information about the resource is available from the Virtualised Network Resource Management interface.
reservationId	M	0..1	Identifier	The reservation identifier applicable to the resource. It shall be present when an applicable reservation exists.
metadata	M	0..N	KeyValuePair	Metadata about this resource.
vnfLinkPort	M	0..N	VnfLinkPortInfo	Links ports of this VL. Shall be present when the linkPort is used for external connectivity by the VNF (refer to VnfLinkPortInfo in clause 8.5.11). May be present otherwise.

Fig. 3. *VnfVirtualLinkResourceInfo* information element in IFA007 (excerpt from standard)

8.3.3.6   VnfVirtualLinkResourceInfo information element

8.3.3.6.1   Description

This information element provides information on virtualised network resources used by an internal VL instance in a VNF.

8.3.3.6.2   Attributes

The VnfVirtualLinkResourceInfo information element shall follow the indications provided in table 8.3.3.6.2-1.

Table 8.3.3.6.2-1: Attributes of the VnfVirtualLinkResourceInfo information element

Attribute	Qualifier	Cardinality	Content	Description
virtualLinkInstanceId	M	1	Identifier	Identifier of this VL instance.
vnfVirtualLinkDescId	M	1	Identifier (Reference to VnfVirtualLinkDesc)	Identifier of the VNF VLD in the VNFD.
networkResource	M	1	ResourceHandle	Reference to the VirtualNetwork resource.
reservationId	M	0..1	Identifier	The reservation identifier applicable to the resource. It shall be present when an applicable reservation exists.
vnfLinkPort	M	0..N	VnfLinkPortInfo	Links ports of this VL. Shall be present when the linkPort is used for external connectivity by the VNF (refer to VnfLinkPortInfo in clause 8.3.3.20). May be present otherwise.
metadata	M	0..N	KeyValuePair	Metadata about this resource.

Fig. 4. *VnfVirtualLinkResourceInfo* information element in IFA013 (excerpt from standard)

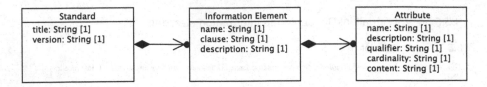

Fig. 5. Minimal meta-model for capturing relevant information from standards

The standards are available in Word and Portable Document Format (PDF) formats. Apache POI[3] provides API for accessing the contents of various kinds of documents, among which also Word documents. We defined a custom mapping by using the Apache POI API to extract relevant information from the standards documents and construct standards model instances. The meta-model for the standards documents was also defined in Papyrus.

The transformation scripts were defined by means of the Epsilon Object Language (EOL)[4] [10] and the Epsilon Transformation Language (ETL) [5] [11]. EOL is a domain-specific language for creating, querying, and modifying models. It supports the access and modification of multiple models. ETL is a domain-specific language for hybrid, rule-based model transformations built on top of EOL. It provides common transformation capabilities, as well as the ability to transform many input to many output models. The transformations are defined by means of both declarative and imperative transformation specifications, allowing for sophisticated transformation logic, as well as abstraction and reuse. Based on previous experiences, we selected the Epsilon family of languages as the most convenient solution. The constraints were realised with the help of the Epsilon Validation Language (EVL) (See footnote 5). EVL provides means for the implementation of add-on constraints and extends the capabilities of OCL, e.g. by providing additional facilities for the specification of guards on constraints.

4.2 Current Status

We implemented the essential steps for the mapping, transformation, and validation as a prototype. To support the ongoing maintenance work of the NFV IFA working group, we provided a basic Graphical User Interface (GUI) indicating the main aspects of interest. An example of the GUI is shown in Fig. 7. On the top right, a document browser allows the users to select the standard that needs to be evaluated and inspected. After the users select a standard, its content is loaded in a hierarchical tree in the top middle portion of the GUI. Matched information elements are highlighted with green background. Mismatched information elements are highlighted with red background. Additionally in the bottom right area of the GUI a list of all the mismatched information elements is

---

[2] See https://www.eclipse.org/papyrus/.
[3] See https://poi.apache.org.
[4] See https://www.eclipse.org/epsilon/doc/eol/.
[5] See https://www.eclipse.org/epsilon/doc/etl/.

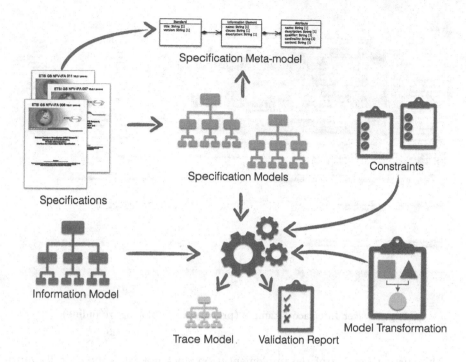

Fig. 6. Approach overview

provided for reference. The large number of mismatched information elements is due to the fact that IFA032 is a new standard currently under development. Upon selecting an information element in the content area, its content is shown in the bottom portion of the GUI for quick reference. Additionally, if there is a matching element in the IM, it is automatically selected in the IM tree shown on the top right area of the GUI, and its description and the diagrams in which it is displayed are shown in the middle right area of the GUI. The bottom part of the GUI shows detailed matching information for the attributes found in the standard (bottom left) and the corresponding attributes found in the IM (bottom right), both in a tabular and textual format. The mismatching attributes and their characteristics are highlighted in red in the tabular format. The textual format is used for a textual comparison (bottom middle part), providing a quick overview of all the changes in one place. In this case we can immediately notice that the attribute *endTime* may have been renamed to *stopTime*. This way the users can quickly inspect and compare the descriptions of the elements as well as their attributes. They are also directed to the relevant diagrams where they may want to perform further inspection or modification of the IM. Finally, on the very top, a search bar enables the users to check for similarly named elements in the IM in order to verify that a mismatched element is really missing rather than renamed.

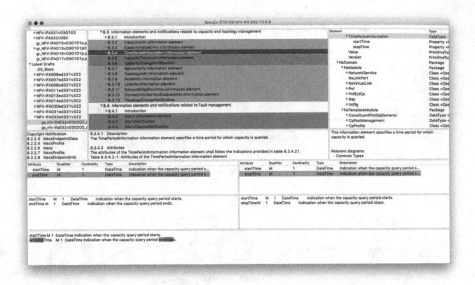

Fig. 7. User Interface Example (prototype) (Color figure online)

The current version of the implementation does not yet support fully automated inspection of attributes as well as bi-directional validation. In particular, it does not indicate whether there are duplicated clauses in multiple documents describing the same element of the IM, or whether certain elements of the IM are no longer present in the standards. We are working to add support for these consistency checks to the prototypical implementation in order to streamline the work of the NFV IFA working group further and ensure the high quality and consistency of both the standards and the IM.

The extraction of the models from the standards relies on consistent structure of the documents. Thus, some constraints were defined to check whether the models are extracted properly, e.g. whether attributes can be extracted reliably. These constraints revealed inconsistencies in the table headings and clause names in some cases. During the study and validation of the IM, some issues with the way associations were displayed within diagrams in Papyrus became apparent. In some cases, the same association is displayed with swapped labels for the multiplicities (and roles) at the respective ends. An example is illustrated in Fig. 8. This can be confusing to both users and maintainers of the IM. Upon further investigation it became apparent that in some of the cases, in an effort to get the correct labels to be displayed, the IM was modified in a way that resulted in inconsistencies with the standards. As part of the study, we determined that the actual problem arose due to mismatching the source and target shapes in the diagram model. It is still unclear whether this occurred due to bugs in Papyrus or due to compatibility issues between different versions. This observation led to the definition of a constraint checking for such inconsistencies.

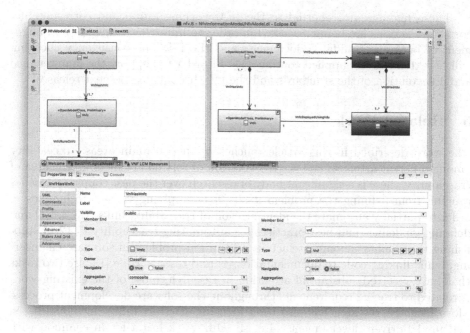

Fig. 8. Inconsistent association label display

4.3   First Results

During the manual inspection and with the help of the prototypical implementation of the approach we collected some initial findings demonstrating how the proposed approach can be useful. The initial findings indicated the following inconsistencies:

Inconsistent naming: different naming was used in some cases, which presented some challenges for the naming conventions which we relied on for the identification of the relevant clauses within the standards documents, e.g. different suffixes, Network Service Descriptor vs Nsd, VNFD vs Vnfd;

Inconsistent descriptions: differences in the descriptions and attributes of related elements may need some alignment upon further examination;

New/Mismatched elements: we identified 40 new information elements, initial search did not yield reliable matches for similarly named and similarly structured elements in the IM, these elements need further inspection, many of them are the result of recent activities within NFV IFA;

Typos/Renames: we identified 6 elements that appear to be renamed or contain typos both in the standards and in the IM;

Potentially duplicated elements: we identified multiple elements which are described in multiple standards (this is part of the working procedures at NFV IFA), these need to be aligned where applicable, with the implementation of the approach helping to keep track of these for future changes.

These findings are reported to the IFA working group and corresponding corrective actions are being discussed in order to improve the quality and alignment of both the standards documents and the IM. The consistency checking will be extended and applied continuously in order to support the maintenance and co-evolution of the standards and the IM throughout the next releases.

5   Related Work

The work described in this article touches upon two main areas: traceability among different artefacts and the co-evolution of related artefacts. In the area of traceability, there is a significant body of research over the past couple of decades ranging from defining the problem itself [9] to applying various techniques in order to partially automate the identification of traceability links [1,3,4,6,8] and defining guidelines and best practices for automating traceability [5,12]. Establishing traceability among artefacts is a common problem in software engineering, while linking code to documentation [1] and tests to code [13] are two tasks that have received substantial attention in research, most of the existing work is related to tracing requirements throughout the software development process. More recently, research has also been focusing on traceability in model-based and model-driven development [4,8,14]. Our work has a lot in common with previous approaches. We refine some of the techniques to the specific domain of co-evolution of standards and models. Standards are requirements specifications, thus the application of requirements traceability approaches is appropriate.

Regarding co-evolution of artefacts, some work has been done on the co-evolution of code and tests [7,14], as well as the co-evolution of different components [2,15]. Our work is concerned with the co-evolution of related standards and models. It is similar to the co-evolution of related components where a family of standards can be perceived as related components, however some peculiarities still require adaptation and refinement of existing approaches.

6   Conclusion

The NFV IM provides a consolidated view on all information elements present in the interface specifications, enabling a quick identification of gaps and inconsistencies in the implementations of the standards. With the increasing volume of the NFV IFA specifications, the maintenance of the IM required considerable overhead. This lead to an increasing risk that the IM falls behind and becomes less useful for the further development of the specifications.

We proposed a model-based approach to aid the maintenance of both the IM and the specifications by automating some of the consistency checks and establishing traceability links between the specifications, the IM and the relevant diagrams for the IM. With the help of a prototypical implementation of the approach, we obtained some promising initial results, indicating potential inconsistencies in the IM and the specifications as a first step towards the continued maintenance of the IM.

The approach its realisation enable the NFV IFA working group to maintain its rapid release cycle and continue to deliver high quality specifications, despite the increasing volume of both the specifications and the IM. With the help of the prototypical implementation, the IM can be maintained and developed further in a timely manner and with lower overhead, increasing the confidence in the specifications and paving the way to their adoption.

Future work includes the specification and realisation of further consistency checks, as well as the refinement of existing consistency checks. From a user's point of view, it is desirable to include support for comparing suspected duplicates, annotations enabling users to mark intentional deviations in certain cases, as well as the generation of change logs for documenting and tracking the progress of the alignment. Ultimately, some automation for the alignment is also desirable, in order to relieve the maintainers from transferring trivial updates from the specifications to the IM, such as fixing typos, updating descriptions, or renaming attributes. In a broader context, this work can be a first step towards a more generic approach for similar scenarios in supporting the evolution and maintenance of standards as highly structured and formalised documents.

Acknowledgements. Part of the work discussed within this article has been funded by the ETSI in the context of the Specialist Task Force (STF) 570.

References

1. Antoniol, G., Canfora, G., Casazza, G., De Lucia, A.: Information retrieval models for recovering traceability links between code and documentation. In: Proceedings 2000 International Conference on Software Maintenance, pp. 40–49, October 2000. https://doi.org/10.1109/ICSM.2000.883003
2. Berardinelli, L., Biffl, S., Maetzler, E., Mayerhofer, T., Wimmer, M.: Model-based co-evolution of production systems and their libraries with AutomationML. In: 2015 IEEE 20th Conference on Emerging Technologies Factory Automation (ETFA), pp. 1–8, September 2015. https://doi.org/10.1109/ETFA.2015.7301483
3. Borg, M., Runeson, P., Ardö, A.: Recovering from a decade: a systematic mapping of information retrieval approaches to software traceability. Empirical Softw. Eng. **19**(6), 1565–1616 (2014). https://doi.org/10.1007/s10664-013-9255-y
4. Cleland-Huang, J., Hayes, J.H., Domel, J.M.: Model-based traceability. In: 2009 ICSE Workshop on Traceability in Emerging Forms of Software Engineering, pp. 6–10, May 2009. https://doi.org/10.1109/TEFSE.2009.5069575
5. Cleland-Huang, J., Settimi, R., Romanova, E., Berenbach, B., Clark, S.: Best practices for automated traceability. Computer **40**(6), 27–35 (2007). https://doi.org/10.1109/MC.2007.195
6. David, J., Koegel, M., Naughton, H., Helming, J.: Traceability ReARMed. In: 2009 33rd Annual IEEE International Conference on Computer Software and Applications (COMPSAC 2009), vol. 1, pp. 340–348 (2009). https://doi.org/10.1109/COMPSAC.2009.52
7. Ens, B., Rea, D., Shpaner, R., Hemmati, H., Young, J.E., Irani, P.: ChronoTwigger: a visual analytics tool for understanding source and test co-evolution. In: 2014 Second IEEE Working Conference on Software Visualization, pp. 117–126, September 2014. https://doi.org/10.1109/VISSOFT.2014.28

8. Galvao, I., Goknil, A.: Survey of traceability approaches in model-driven engineering. In: 11th IEEE International Enterprise Distributed Object Computing Conference (EDOC 2007), p. 313, October 2007. https://doi.org/10.1109/EDOC.2007.42

9. Gotel, O.C.Z., Finkelstein, C.W.: An analysis of the requirements traceability problem. In: Proceedings of IEEE International Conference on Requirements Engineering, pp. 94–101, April 1994. https://doi.org/10.1109/ICRE.1994.292398

10. Kolovos, D.S., Paige, R.F., Polack, F.A.C.: The epsilon object language (EOL). In: Rensink, A., Warmer, J. (eds.) ECMDA-FA 2006. LNCS, vol. 4066, pp. 128–142. Springer, Heidelberg (2006). https://doi.org/10.1007/11787044_11. (cited by 0118)

11. Kolovos, D.S., Paige, R.F., Polack, F.A.C.: The epsilon transformation language. In: Vallecillo, A., Gray, J., Pierantonio, A. (eds.) ICMT 2008. LNCS, vol. 5063, pp. 46–60. Springer, Heidelberg (2008). https://doi.org/10.1007/978-3-540-69927-9_4

12. Maro, S., Anjorin, A., Wohlrab, R., Steghöfer, J.: Traceability maintenance: factors and guidelines. In: 2016 31st IEEE/ACM International Conference on Automated Software Engineering (ASE), pp. 414–425, September 2016

13. Parizi, R.M., Lee, S.P., Dabbagh, M.: Achievements and challenges in state-of-the-art software traceability between test and code artifacts. IEEE Trans. Reliab. 63(4), 913–926 (2014). https://doi.org/10.1109/TR.2014.2338254

14. Winkler, S., von Pilgrim, J.: A survey of traceability in requirements engineering and model-driven development. Softw. Syst. Model. 9(4), 529–565 (2010). https://doi.org/10.1007/s10270-009-0145-0

15. Yu, L.: Understanding component co-evolution with a study on Linux. Empirical Softw. Eng. 12(2), 123–141 (2007). https://doi.org/10.1007/s10664-006-9000-x

Concurrency, Data Integrity

Adapting Integrity Checking Techniques for Concurrent Operation Executions

Xavier Oriol$^{(\boxtimes)}$ and Ernest Teniente

Department of Service and Information System Engineering,
Universitat Politècnica de Catalunya – BarcelonaTech, Barcelona, Spain
{xoriol,teniente}@essi.upc.edu

Abstract. One challenge for achieving executable models is preserving the integrity of the data. That is, given a structural model describing the constraints that the data should satisfy, and a behavioral model describing the operations that might change the data, the integrity checking problem consists in ensuring that, after executing the modeled operations, none of the specified constraints is violated.

A multitude of techniques have been presented so far to solve the integrity checking problem. However, to the best of our knowledge, all of them assume that operations are not executed concurrently. As we are going to see, concurrent operation executions might lead to violations not detected by these techniques.

In this paper, we present a technique for detecting and serializing those operations that can cause a constraint violation when executed concurrently, so that, previous incremental techniques, exploiting our approach, can be safely applied in systems with concurrent operation executions guaranteeing the integrity of the data.

Keywords: Integrity checking · Concurrent operations · UML/OCL

1 Introduction

One of the main challenges for achieving executable models is ensuring data integrity [1]. That is, given a structural model describing the data and its integrity constraints, such as an UML diagram with OCL invariants; and a behavioral model describing the operations that can change this data, like OCL operation contracts for instance, the integrity checking problem consists in assessing whether the particular execution of a given operation in the current data state may induce a constraint violation. The difficulty of this problem is clear since, in the context of SQL databases, the integrity checking problem was already defined more than 25 years ago (under the form of SQL assertions checking [2]) and, still, none of the current major database management systems has implemented a solution for it (Oracle, SQL Server, DB2, PostgreSQL, MySQL).

As an example, consider the structural model described in Fig. 1, written in UML/OCL, of a system for managing a research group. In this system, we have

© Springer Nature Switzerland AG 2019
P. Fonseca i Casas et al. (Eds.): SAM 2019, LNCS 11753, pp. 235–248, 2019.
https://doi.org/10.1007/978-3-030-30690-8_14

some *researchers* who *work in* some *projects*. Moreover, some of these researchers *lead* some of these projects, although a project might have a maximum of two leaders. The OCL invariants states that researchers and projects are identified by their name (*ResercherPK*, and *ProjectPK* invariants), a leader of a project is also a member of the project (*LeaderIsMember* invariant), and that the salary of a leader of a project is higher than the salary of all its members (*LeaderEarnsMore* invariant). Note that these constraints might be violated because of the actions of the operations, as they are specified in the behavioral model.

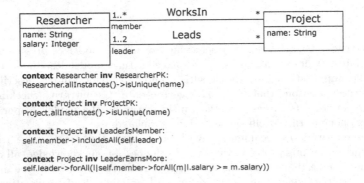

context Researcher **inv** ResearcherPK:
Researcher.allInstances()->isUnique(name)

context Project **inv** ProjectPK:
Project.allInstances()->isUnique(name)

context Project **inv** LeaderIsMember:
self.member->includesAll(self.leader)

context Project **inv** LeaderEarnsMore:
self.leader->forAll(l|self.member->forAll(m|l.salary >= m.salary))

Fig. 1. Structural model of a research group management system

In Fig. 2, we show a fragment of the behavioral model for this system. In this model, we show the operation contracts, written in OCL, of four operations. The first one is required for adding new researchers (*hireResearcher*), the second one for assigning a leader to a project (*addLeader*), the third one for including a member in a project (*addMember*), and the last one for removing a member from a project (*removeMember*)[1].

Depending on the current state of the information base, executing some of these operations with certain parameters can lead to a constraint violation. For instance, if we execute *addLeader* with parameters *Mary* and *ModelsProject*, but *Mary* is not currently a member of *ModelsProject*, the execution of the operation violates the *LeaderIsMember* constraint. The difficulty of this problem scales rapidly when complicating the operations and constraints involved.

To solve this problem, several proposals have been made in the modeling community based on incremental techniques [3–7]. Briefly, incremental integrity checking techniques are based on the idea that, assuming that the current data

---

[1] This behavioral schema is oversimplified in purpose for the seek of facilitating the explanation of the method. More in general, our method can deal with operations applying several insertions/deletions at the same time, and not just one. In addition, our method is independant with the preconditions defined, thus, more complicated contracts are allowed. The unique requirement, as it will be explained laterly, is that OCL postconditions should be rewrittable in first-order logics (i.e., no aggregation nor transitive closure are allowed in postconditions).

Op hireResearcher(name: String, salary: Integer)
post: Researcher.allInstances()->exists(r|r.oclIsNew() and r.name = name and r.salary = salary)

Op addLeader(rName: String, pName: String)
pre: Researcher.allInstances().name->includes(rName)
pre: Project.allInstances().name->includes(pName)
post: Project.allInstances()->select(p|p.name = pName).leader.name->includes(rName)

Op addMember(rName: String, pName: String)
pre: Researcher.allInstances().name->includes(rName)
pre: Project.allInstances().name->includes(pName)
post: Project.allInstances()->select(p|p.name = pName).member.name->includes(rName)

Op removeMember(rName: String, pName: String)
pre: Researcher.allInstances().name->includes(rName)
pre: Project.allInstances().name->includes(pName)
post: Project.allInstances()->select(p|p.name = pName).member.name->excludes(rName)

Fig. 2. Behavioral model of a research group management system

state satisfies all the constraints, they check whether the data updated by an operation execution leads to a violation without inspecting the rest of the data. For instance, following our previous example, we would only need to check whether *Mary* is a member of *ModelsProject* and, thus, there is no need to check other project leaders such as *John*, since *John* is not affected by the update.

However, to the best of our knowledge, all the presented techniques assume that operations are executed isolatedly, and thus, are not able to detect integrity violations when two operations executed concurrently interacts in a way that cause a constraint violation. For instance, assume that in our current data state *Mary* is a member of *ModelsProject*. In this situation, executing the operation to make *Mary* a leader of the project does not violate a constraint. In the same situation, executing, instead, an operation to remove *Mary* from the *ModelsProject* does not violate a constraint either. However, when executing both operations simultaneously, both interacts in a way to reach a new state in which *Mary* leads a project where she is not a member of. Thus, they raise a constraint violation.

This means that, right now, if we use the previous incremental techniques with systems that admit concurrent operation executions, some violations are going to be missed (i.e., previous incremental checking techniques are not complete when considering concurrency). Clearly, the problem can be solved by forcing all the operations to be executed in a serialized manner, but this might heavily penalize the runtime efficiency of the system.

Fortunately, not all operations must be executed in a serialized manner to avoid these violations. Indeed, not all operations can interact to cause a constraint violation. For instance, operations *addLeader* and *removeMember* can interact to violate *LeaderIsMember* and must be serialized, but operations *addLeader* and *hireResearcher* cannot interact to violate any constraint, and thus, can be executed concurrently.

In this paper, we define a method for identifying, and serializing, those operation executions that can interact to cause a constraint violation, permitting the rest of operations to be executed concurrently. In this way, we allow using the previous incremental techniques in systems with concurrent operations, without the penalization of serializing every execution, neither loosing completeness. Our technique has been implemented in a tool [8] for executing UML/OCL models, thus, showing that it is feasible in practice. In any case, since the core of our technique is fully based on logics, it can be adapted and implemented in other model executor tools using UML/OCL [9,10] or other modeling languages, provided that they can be translated into logics. In particular, our technique can be adapted to first-order expressive languages (aka relational algebra equivalent) such as SQL, and SPARQL.

It is worth to mention that our work is, somehow, similar to the one in [11]. In particular, [11] detects operations invoked in a wrong order due to CRUD inconsistencies (e.g. reading some information deleted). We argue that our method and theirs can be combined, since both deal with different problems due to concurrency. Note, additionally, that our work is about checking a constraint on runtime assuming concurrency, and not on verifying/validating the models at compile time such as [12].

2   Basic Concepts and Notation

We review some key concepts and the basics of the notation used in the paper.

Terms, Atoms and Literals. A *term* t is either a variable or a constant. An *atom* is formed by a n-ary *predicate* p together with n terms, i,e. $p(t_1, ..., t_n)$. We may write $p(\bar{t})$ for short. If all the terms $\bar{t}$ of an atom are constants, we call the atom to be *ground*. A literal l is either an atom $p(\bar{t})$, a negated atom $\neg p(\bar{t})$, or a built-in literal $t_i \ \omega \ t_j$, where ω is an arithmetic comparison (i,e. $<, \leq, =, \geq, >, \neq$).

Derived/Base Predicates. A predicate p is said to be *derived* if the boolean evaluation of an atom $p(\bar{t})$ depends on some derivation rules, otherwise, it is said to be *base*. A *derivation rule* has the form: $\forall \bar{t}. \ p(\bar{t_p}) \leftarrow \phi(\bar{t})$ where $\bar{t_p} \subseteq \bar{t}$. In the formula, $p(\bar{t_p})$ is an atom called the *head* of the rule and $\phi(\bar{t})$ is a conjunction of literals called the *body*. We suppose all derivation rules to be safe (i.e. all the variables appearing in the head or in a negated or built-in literal of the body also appears in a positive literal of the body) and non-recursive. Given several derivation rules with predicate p in its head, $p(\bar{t})$ is evaluated to true if and only if one of the bodies of such derivation rules is evaluated to true.

Logic Formalization of the UML Schema. As proposed in [13] we formalize each class C in the class diagram with attributes $\{A_1, \ldots, A_n\}$ by means of a base atom $c(Oid, A_1, ..., A_n)$, each association R between classes $\{C_1, \ldots, C_k\}$ by means of a base atom $r(C_1, \ldots, C_k)$ and, similarly, each association class R between classes $\{C_1, \ldots, C_k\}$ and with attributes $\{A_1, \ldots, A_n\}$ by means of a base atom $r(Oid, C_1, \ldots, C_k, A_1, \ldots, A_n)$.

Roughly speaking, when an object/relation encoded as $P(\bar{x})$ exists in some data state, the ground literal $P(\bar{x})$ evaluates to true in such data state. Conversely, when an object/relation encoded as $P(\bar{x})$ does not exists in some data state, the ground literal $P(\bar{x})$ evaluates to false in such data state.

3   Our Approach

Our approach is based on the notion of structural events. A structural event is an elementary change in the population of the data, that is, an insertion or deletion of a class/association instance. For instance, inserting *Leads(Mary, ModelsProject)*, or deleting *WorksIn(Mary, ModelsProject)* are structural events. For our purposes, we encode insertion structural events with the prefix *ins*, and deletion structural events with the prefix *del*, e.g., the previous structural events are encoded as *ins_Leads(Mary, ModelsProject)*, and *del_WorksIn(Mary, ModelsProject)*, respectively. Attribute updates can be seen as an insertion/deletion of the same object.

Executing an operation leads to structural events in the data, and these structural events might change the evaluation of a constraint, that is, the structural events might violate a constraint, or even repair a constraint that was going to be violated. For instance, executing the operation *addLeader* causes the structural event *ins_Leads* that might violate *LeaderIsMember*; on the contrary, executing the operation *add_Member* causes the structural event *ins_WorksIn* that might repair such violation.

The operations that must be serialized depend on the time where the chosen integrity checking technique takes place. In essence, the integrity checking techniques can be applied *before* executing the structural events (such as [3]), which we refer as *precondition-time checking*; or *after* it (such as [7]), which we refer as *postcondition-time checking*. In the first case, we need to serialize two operations O_1, O_2 that can interact to cause a violation; on the second, we need to serialize two operations O_1 and O_2 if the structural events of O_1 might compensate the effects of O_2, since a rollback of O_1 might affect the consistency of O_2.

For instance, consider the operations *addLeader*, *removeMember*, and *addMember* from our running example. Using a preconditiom-time checking, the operations *addLeader* and *removeMember* should never be applied concurrently since they might interact to cause a constraint violation, and the checking technique will not realize of it since it makes the analysis separately. Note, however, that a postcondition-time checking will find the violation since, at the time of performing the analysis, both operations have been executed and all their effects are in the information system (and thus, at the time of checking the consistency of the data, the postcondition-time checking can find a leader not being a member of its project). However, in the case of a postconditiom-time checking, the operations that should not be executed (or at least analyzed) together are *addMember* and *addLeader*, since a rollback (or not) of the first might imply a violation (or not) of the second operation. Indeed, if we execute *addMember* and *addLeader*, and analyze together the consistency of the data, we might find that *addLeader* does not violate the *LeaderIsMember* constraint because the operation *addMember* adds the new leader as a member for the project, but if *addMember* violates any other constraint and must rollback, this rollback makes *addLeader* violate the *LeaderIsMember*. Thus, we should analyze the consistency of *addLeader* after the consistency analysis of *addMember*. Note that this problem does not occur in precondition-time checking techniques.

Formally, when dealing with integrity checking in systems with concurrent operations, we identify two kinds of concurrency interactions between operations that must be taken into account:

- *Potential concurrency violation.* There is a potential concurrency violation between two operations O_1 and O_2 if, for some constraint C, the structural events applied by O_1 and O_2 might violate C.
- *Potential concurrency compensation.* There is a potential concurrency compensation from O_1 to O_2 if, for some constraint C, the structural events applied by O_1 might repair a violation of C caused by the structural events of O_2.

In the case of *precondition-time checking*, we must serialize two operations O_1 and O_2 if they have a potential concurrency violation; in the case of *postcondition-time checking*, two operations O_1 and O_2 must be serialized if O_1 has a potential concurrency compensation with O_2.

In this paper we focus on detecting this kind of interactions, and we suggest a serialization to deal with the problems they can carry out. Other approaches different than serialization, or a more refined versions of serialization, can be studied, but they are left for further work.

To detect this kind of interactions, we apply the following steps: (1) given all the operation contracts $\mathcal{O}$, we detect the kind of structural events applied by each operation $O \in \mathcal{O}$, (2) given all constraints $\mathcal{C}$, we detect all the kind of structural events that can violate/repair each $C \in \mathcal{C}$, (3) for each pair of operations O_1, O_2, and each constraint C, we use the structural events to analyze if there is any kind of interaction between them w.r.t. C. Note that all these analysis can be performed at compile time since they purely rely on the model specification of the operations and constraints.

3.1   Detecting the Kind of Structural Events Applied by Some Operation

Given an OCL operation contract, it is possible to identify, at compile time, which are the kind of structural events applied by the operation [14,15]. For our purposes, we rely on the approach of [14] to detect them. In essence, the idea behind this approach is to translate any operation contract to an equivalent logic formula that, intuitively, states that executing of an operation implies the application of certain structural events.

In particular, the previous operations from Fig. 2 can be encoded by means of the following logic formulas:

```
ins_Researcher(R, Name, Salary) :- hireResearcher(Name, Salary)
ins_Leads(R, P) :- addLeader(RN, PN), Researcher(R, RN, S),Project(P, PN)
del_WorksIn(R, P) :- removeMember(RN, PN), Researcher(R, RN, S),Project(P, PN)
ins_WorksIn(R, P) :- addMember(RN, PN), Researcher(R, RN, S),Project(P, PN)
```

Intuitively, the first formula states that invoking the operation *hireResearcher* with parameters *Name*, *Salary* causes the structural event of *ins_Researcher(R,*

Name, Salary) to happen, where *R* is a new object identifier value. The second one states that, when invoking the operation *addLeader* with parameters *RN* and *PN*, there is a structural event *ins_Leads(R, P)* provided that R and P are the researcher and project identified by *RN* and *PN*, respectively. Similarly, the third formula states that, when invoking the operation *removeMember*, there is a *del_WorksIn(R,P)* structural event.

The rationale behind such translations can be sketched as follows. OCL operations such as *includes*, and *includesAll*, when used in a postcondition, are used to specify insertions on associations [15]. The source of such operations represent the association where the insertion takes place, and the body of such operations represents the value/s inserted. Thus, the logic translation consists in, roughly speaking, (1) identifying these OCL operations, (2) generate an insertion rule for each one of them, and (3) put, in the generated logic rule, the OCL logic translation of the objects where the insertion takes place. For this last step, we have to translate into logics the source of the OCL operation (i.e., the objects where the insertion takes place), and translate the body of the OCL operation (i.e., the objects inserted). That is, if the source/body of the OCL operation is an object/s *x*, we have to build an OCL logic translation that retrieves all those *x*. In general, if OCL obtains some objects *x* by means of *n* navigation steps, the logic translation consists in a conjunction of *n* non-ground ordinary literals, each one representing one step of the navigation. A similar approach is taken with OCL *oclIsNew()* and *excludes* operations as detailed in [14].

Thus, and thanks to this translation which is already implemented [16], the structural events implied by each operation become explicit in the head of each rule. Hence, we can build a program that reads this translation, and realizes that executing *hireResearcher* implies the structural event *ins_Reseracher*, *addLeader* implies *ins_Leads*, and *removeMember* implies *del_WorksIn*.

Note that, in general, an operation will apply more than one kind of structural event when executed. For instance, we could specify an operation that creates a new researcher and adds his membership associations. In this case, and following [14], an operation is translated into several logic formulas, each one implying a different structural event. Thus, the structural events implied by such operation is the union of all the structural events appearing in all the formulas.

3.2 Detecting the Structural Events that Violate/Repair a Constraint

Given a constraint *C*, it is possible to determine, at compile time, which are the kind of structural events that might violate a constraint, and also those that may repair it [7,17]. For our purposes, we use the approach defined in [17] since it is based on logics in a similar way as we did in previous section.

In essence, we first translate the UML and OCL constraints into logic denials, that is, logic formulas stating the condition that rise a constraint violation. Following, for instance, the automatic translation of UML/OCL constraints to denials defined in [13], our running example would bring the following logic formulas:

```
:- Researcher(R1, N, S1), Researcher(R2, N, S2), R1<>R2
:- Project(P1, N), Project(P2, N), P1<>P2
:- Leads(R,P), not(WorksIn(R,P))
:- WorksIn(R,P), Leads(L,P), Researcher(R,RN,RS), Researcher(L,LN,LS),RS>LS
```

The first and second formulas, encode that, if there are two different researchers or projects with the same name, there is a constraint violation. The third one states a constraint violation if R leads a project P where s/he does not work in. The last formula asserts a violation if for some project P, there is a leader L that earns less than a worker R.

The rationale behind such translations can be summarized as follows. Like in the previous section, every OCL value/set expression that retrieves an object/s x is translated into a conjunction of ordinary literals. This conjunction of ordinary literals contains a variable x that, roughly speaking, represents any object x that can be retrieved from the navigation. Then, every OCL boolean operator that combines two OCL value/set expressions to retrieve a boolean value is translated as two conjunctions of ordinary literals (one for each OCL value/set expression) together the translation of the OCL operator. In the easiest case, like an OCL equality operator, the translation consists in a logic built-in literal. Other cases require more complex treatment, like the definition of derivation rules, as detailed in [13].

Given the logic formulas, we can realize which structural events might make these formulas true (and thus, rise a violation), and which of them might make them false (and thus, repair the violation).

To do so, we rely on the event rule equivalences [18]. The event rule equivalences define when a structural event makes a literal true/false in the new state of the data after applying the events. In particular, consider P^N to be the literal P evaluated in the new data state. Then, the event rule equivalences tells us that:

$$P^N(\overline{x}) \equiv ins\_P(\overline{x}) \vee (P(\overline{x}) \wedge \neg del\_P(\overline{x}))$$
$$\neg P^N(\overline{x}) \equiv del\_P(\overline{x}) \vee (\neg P(\overline{x}) \wedge \neg ins\_P(\overline{x}))$$

Intuitively, the literal $P(\overline{x})$ is true in the new state after applying the structural events if we have inserted $P(\overline{x})$ through some insertion structural event, or $P(\overline{x})$ was already true in the data state and we have not deleted it. Similarly, $\neg P(\overline{x})$ is true in the new state after applying the structural events if we have deleted $P(\overline{x})$ through some deletion structural event, or $P(\overline{x})$ was already false in the data state and we have not inserted it.

Applying the previous equivalences to our logic denials, by means of applying all the possible literal substitutions (aka unfoldings) given by the event rule equivalences, we obtain what we call event-dependency constraints (EDCs), that is, denials that tells which structural events rise a constraint violation. For instance, for the first denial we obtain:

```
:- ins_Researcher(R1, N, S1), ins_Researcher(R2, N, S2), R1<>R2
:- ins_Researcher(R1,N,S1), Researcher(R2,N,S2), not del_Researcher(R2,N,S2),
      R1<>R2
:- Researcher(R1,N,S1), not del_Researcher(R1,N,S1), ins_Researcher(R2,N,S2),
      R1<>R2
:- Researcher(R1,N,S1), not del_Researcher(R1,N,S1), Researcher(R2,N,S2),
      not del_Researcher(R2,N,S2), R1<>R2
```

The first EDCs states that there is a constraint violation if we apply two different structural events for inserting a researcher with the same name. The second and third one specify that if we insert a new researcher with a name N, and this name N belongs to some researcher in the current data, but we do not remove this researcher, there is a constraint violation. Finally, the last rule tells us that if we have two researchers with the same name and we do not remove any of them, there is a constraint violation.

Intuitively, the structural events that appear positively in an EDC are the structural events that might cause a violation, while those that appear negatively in an EDC are the structural events that might repair the violation (since they make the body of the EDC, which detects the violation, to evaluate to false). For instance, *ins_Researcher* is a structural event that can cause a violation of the *ResearcherPK* constraint, while *del_Researcher* is a structural event that can repair it.

It is worth to highlight that the number of EDCs obtained from one denial grows exponentially with the length of the denial encoding. However, some optimizations can be applied to reduce the number and size of the denials [3]. Indeed, considering the classical optimization that the initial data state does not violate any constraint, and that there is homomorphism between denials two and three, the unique EDCs required are:

```
:- ins_Researcher(R1, N, S1), ins_Researcher(R2, N, S2), R1<>R2
:- ins_Researcher(R1,N,S1), Researcher(R2,N,S2), not del_Researcher(R2,N,S2),
      R1<>R2
```

3.3 Detecting Operations and Constraints Interactions Through the Structural Events

At this point, we want to analyze, using the structural events previously determined, which kind of interactions might have two operations w.r.t. some constraint. To do so, and benefiting from the fact that all our approach is based on logics, we are going to use an unfolding technique. In essence, our idea is to unfold the body of the EDCs obtained in Sect. 3.2, which tells us which structural events cause a violation/repair, with the rules from Sect. 3.1, which specifies which structural events are implied by the operations. As a result, we obtain some new rules that directly define which operations can violate/repair some constraint.

For instance, if we unfold the previous EDCs with the logic rules that tells that hiring a researcher makes an insertion structural event of a researcher, we obtain:

```
:- hireResearcher(N, S1), hireResearcher(N, S2)
:- hireResearcher(N, S1), Researcher(R2,N,S2), not (del_Researcher(R2,N,S2)),
        R1<>R2
```

Intuitively, the first rule states that two executions of *hireResearcher* can interact to rise a constraint violation (i.e., a violation of *ResearcherPk* constraint). The second rule tells us that, *hireResearcher* might be compensated with an operation that deletes researchers. However, since there is no operation to delete researchers, there is no interaction according to this rule.

We now bring an example of a detection of a *compensation interaction*. Consider the EDCs obtained from the *LeaderIsMember* constraint:

```
:- ins_Leads(R,P), del_WorksIn(R,P)
:- ins_Leads(R,P), not (WorksIn(R,P)), not (ins_WorksIn(R,P))
:- Leads(R,P), not (del_Leads(R,P)), del_WorksIn(R,P)
```

Intuitively, the first EDC states that there is a violation if we insert that R is going to lead a project P s/he is leaving. The second asserts a violation if we insert that R is going to lead a project P s/he is not working in and that he is not going to work in. Finally, the third EDC detects a violation if we delete R from working in P, when R is leading P and we do not delete R as a leader of P.

Then, when unfolding the EDCs according to the rules from Sect. 3.1, which encodes the operations behavior, we have:

```
:- addLeader(RN,PN), Researcher(R, RN, S), Project(P, PN), removeMember(RN,PN)
:- addLeader(RN,PN), Researcher(R, RN, S), Project(P, PN), not(WorksIn(R,P)),
        not (addMember(RN,PN))
```

Roughly speaking, these rules are saying which operations can interact to cause/compensate a violation. For instance, the first rule says that, when applying the *addLeader* operation, between a researcher with name RN and project named PN, over a database that contains that researcher and project, while applying the operation or *removeMember* with the same parameters, then, there is a constraint violation. Differently, the second rule says that, when applying the *addLeader* operation with the same parameters, over a database where the researcher does not work for the project, and without applying the *addMember* operation, then, there is another constraint violation.

In general, two operations that appears positively in the same denial have a potential concurrent violation, whereas two operations, where one appears in a negated literal, have a potential concurrent compensation. Indeed, we can identify that the operations *addLeader* and *removeMember* has a potential concurrent violation interaction with *LeaderIsMember*, since they both appear positively in the body of the first denial, while *addLeader* and *addMember* has a potential compensation interaction, since *addMember* appears negatively and *addLeader* positively in the same denial. Hence, *addLeader* and *removeMember* should be serialized for precondition-time checking techniques, whereas *addMember* and *addLeader* should be serialized (preferably in this order) for postcondition-time techniques.

Finally, we can summarize all the above with the following statement: *a precondition-time checking technique should serialize those operations appearing positively in the unfolded EDCs, whereas a postcondition-time checking technique should serialize those operations appearing, one as a positive literal and the other as a negative literal, in the unfolded EDCs.*

4 Implementation

We have implemented our approach in OpExec [8], an artifact-centric business process model executor. Briefly, this tool is capable of loading the structural and behavioral models of the system at compile time, encoded in logics, and, at runtime, execute the operations invoked by the user into a relational database.

In OpExec, we integrated an implementation of a precondition-time checking technique [19]. This technique assumed that all operations were executed isolatedly, i.e., not concurrently, and thus, required an automatic serialization technique as the one we have discussed in this paper.

The implementation of our technique is summarized in Fig. 3. In OpExec, a user loads, in compile time, the structural and behavioral models into a *Controller*. Then, when the user wants to execute the models, the user uses the Controller to create a *ProcessExecutor*. The ProcessExecutor contains an artifactID, which is an id number to identify all the information related to such process. At runtime, the user invokes an operation from the behavioral model through the ProcessExecutor. This processExecutor, then, creates an OperationExecThread, which is a new Thread that will execute the operation invoked by the user into the database.

The integrity checking part is implemented in the *OperationExecThread* which, intuitively, checks whether its structural events are going to violate any constraint according to the current contents of the data. In case that there is any constraint violation, the OperationExecThread does not commit any change into the database, otherwise, the database is updated accordingly.

In order to enable multiple users invoke OpExec concurrently, and to guarantee that the integrity checking part detects all possible violations, we implemented the *OperationExecThreadManager*. When a new OperationExecThread is created, this Thread is enqueued in the OperationExecThreadManager, which is responsible of executing it as soon as it is safe to execute it, i.e., when it is guaranteed that it will not interact, with any other currently running OperationExecThread, to cause a violation.

The technique discussed in our paper is fully implemented in the OperationExecThreadManager class. That is, at compile time, it receives the models and performs our interaction analysis to detect which operations can collaborate to raise a constraint violation. Then, at runtime, if we try to execute an operation which might interact with another operation which is currently being executed, the OperationExecThreadManager delays the execution of the first untill the second has finished.

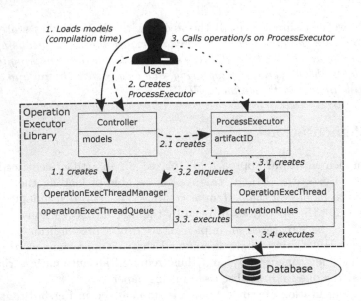

Fig. 3. Architecture of a model executor with an integrity checking technique

Although our implementation is thought for a precondition-time integrity checking, we understand that it might not be difficult to adapt it to work with a postcondition-time integrity checking such as those presented in [4–7].

5   Conclusions

We have presented an approach for adapting integrity checking techniques to systems with concurrent operations. Indeed, current integrity checking techniques do not take into account concurrent operation executions and, as we have seen, this concurrency might cause violations which cannot be detected by these techniques.

To solve this situation, we have defined an approach for identifying which operations can bring problems to the integrity checking techniques when executed concurrently. As we have seen, the kind of operations that might bring problems depend on the kind of integrity checking technique applied. On the one hand, integrity checking techniques performed at precondition time should avoid concurrent executions of operations that might collaborate to cause a violation. On the other, integrity checking techniques performed at postcondition time should avoid analysing concurrently two operations if one compensates a violation from the other. Our approach can detect both kinds of interactions and thus, can be applied for both kinds of integrity checking techniques. To show the feasibility of our approach, we have implemented it in the OpExec model executor.

As further work, we would like to highlight the necessity of defining a UML/OCL benchmark for experimenting with concurrent operations, and thus, enable comparative efficiency experiments with other methods.

References

1. Olivé, A., Cabot, J.: A research agenda for conceptual schema-centric development. In: Krogstie, J., Opdahl, A.L., Brinkkemper, S. (eds.) Conceptual Modelling in Information Systems Engineering, pp. 319–334. Springer, Berlin (2007). https://doi.org/10.1007/978-3-540-72677-7_20
2. ANSI Standard: The SQL 92 Standard (1992)
3. Oriol, X., Teniente, E.: Incremental checking of OCL constraints with aggregates through SQL. In: Johannesson, P., Lee, M.L., Liddle, S.W., Opdahl, A.L., López, Ó.P. (eds.) ER 2015. LNCS, vol. 9381, pp. 199–213. Springer, Cham (2015). https://doi.org/10.1007/978-3-319-25264-3_15
4. Bergmann, G.: Translating OCL to graph patterns. In: Dingel, J., Schulte, W., Ramos, I., Abrahão, S., Insfran, E. (eds.) MODELS 2014. LNCS, vol. 8767, pp. 670–686. Springer, Cham (2014). https://doi.org/10.1007/978-3-319-11653-2_41
5. Uhl, A., Goldschmidt, T., Holzleitner, M.: Using an OCL impact analysis algorithm for view-based textual modelling. ECEASST **44** (2011)
6. Groher, I., Reder, A., Egyed, A.: Incremental consistency checking of dynamic constraints. In: Rosenblum, D.S., Taentzer, G. (eds.) FASE 2010. LNCS, vol. 6013, pp. 203–217. Springer, Heidelberg (2010). https://doi.org/10.1007/978-3-642-12029-9_15
7. Cabot, J., Teniente, E.: Incremental integrity checking of UML/OCL conceptual schemas. J. Syst. Softw. **82**(9), 1459–1478 (2009)
8. De Giacomo, G., Oriol, X., Estañol, M., Teniente, E.: Linking data and BPMN processes to achieve executable models. In: Dubois, E., Pohl, K. (eds.) CAiSE 2017. LNCS, vol. 10253, pp. 612–628. Springer, Cham (2017). https://doi.org/10.1007/978-3-319-59536-8_38
9. Object Management Group (OMG): Unified Modeling Language (UML) Superstructure Specification, version 2.4.1 (2011). http://www.omg.org/spec/UML/
10. Object Management Group (OMG): Object Constraint Language (UML), version 2.4 (2014). http://www.omg.org/spec/OCL/
11. Combi, C., Oliboni, B., Weske, M., Zerbato, F.: Conceptual modeling of interdependencies between processes and data. In: Proceedings of the 33rd Annual ACM Symposium on Applied Computing. SAC 2018, New York, NY, USA. ACM, pp. 110–119 (2018)
12. Przigoda, N., Hilken, C., Wille, R., Peleska, J., Drechsler, R.: Checking concurrent behavior in UML/OCL models. In: 18th ACM/IEEE International Conference on Model Driven Engineering Languages and Systems, MoDELS 2015, Ottawa, ON, Canada, 30 September–2 October 2015, pp. 176–185 (2015)
13. Queralt, A., Teniente, E.: Verification and validation of UML conceptual schemas with OCL constraints. ACM TOSEM **21**(2), 13 (2012)
14. Queralt, A., Teniente, E.: Reasoning on UML conceptual schemas with operations. In: van Eck, P., Gordijn, J., Wieringa, R. (eds.) CAiSE 2009. LNCS, vol. 5565, pp. 47–62. Springer, Heidelberg (2009). https://doi.org/10.1007/978-3-642-02144-2_9

15. Cabot, J.: From declarative to imperative UML/OCL operation specifications. In: Parent, C., Schewe, K.-D., Storey, V.C., Thalheim, B. (eds.) ER 2007. LNCS, vol. 4801, pp. 198–213. Springer, Heidelberg (2007). https://doi.org/10.1007/978-3-540-75563-0_15

16. Oriol, X.: Verificació i validació d'esquemes conceptuals UML/OCL amb operacions (2012)

17. Oriol, X., Teniente, E., Tort, A.: Computing repairs for constraint violations in UML/OCL conceptual schemas. Data & Knowl. Eng. **99**, 39–58 (2015). Selected Papers from the 33rd International Conference on Conceptual Modeling (ER 2014)

18. Olivé, A.: Integrity constraints checking in deductive databases. In: Proceedings of the 17th International Conference on Very Large Data Bases (VLDB), pp. 513–523 (1991)

19. Oriol, X., Teniente, E., Rull, G.: TINTIN: a tool for incremental integrity checking of assertions in SQL server. In: Proceedings of the 19th International Conference on Extending Database Technology, EDBT 2016, Bordeaux, France, 15–16 March 2016, pp. 632–635 (2016)

Eventual Consistency Formalized

Edel Sherratt[1(✉)] and Andreas Prinz[2]

[1] Department of Computer Science, Aberystwyth University,
Aberystwyth SY23 3DB, Wales, UK
eds@aber.ac.uk
[2] Department of ICT, University of Agder, Grimstad, Norway
Andreas.Prinz@UIA.no

Abstract. Distribution of computation is well-known, and there are several frameworks, including some formal frameworks, that capture distributed computation. As yet, however, models of distributed computation are based on the idea that data is conceptually centralized. That is, they assume that data, even if it is distributed, is consistent. This assumption is not valid for many of the database systems in use today, where consistency is compromised to ensure availability and partition tolerance. Starting with an informal definition of eventual consistency, this paper explores several measures of inconsistency that quantify how far from consistency a system is. These measures capture key aspects of eventual consistency in terms of distributed abstract state machines. The definitions move from the traditional binary definition of consistency to more quantitative definitions, where the classical consistency is given by the highest possible level of consistency. Expressing eventual consistency in terms of abstract state machines allows models to be developed that capture distributed computation and highly available distributed data within a single framework.

Keywords: Distributed state · Eventual consistency · Formality · Abstract state machine

1 Introduction

Over time, and particularly since the invention of the Internet, computation has more and more become distributed. Today, almost all computation is achieved by cooperating computing entities communicating over a network. There are numerous frameworks to support distributed computing, and formal methods have provided the means to study distributed computation in depth.

In the public Internet, data is central to computation. This represents a change from the earliest days, where computers were thought of primarily as computing engines. Nowadays, persistent data forms the heart of almost all computation. In terms of distribution, the leading idea is still that we want to distribute the computation. This means both distribution of processing and distribution of data.

P. Fonseca i Casas et al. (Eds.): SAM 2019, LNCS 11753, pp. 249–265, 2019.
https://doi.org/10.1007/978-3-030-30690-8_15

Current formal models of distributed computation [2,8,10,16,17,21–23] rely on data given by a centralized state, i.e. data that is *not* distributed. However, reality is different [1,25]. This is also captured in the Java memory model [19]. Data really is distributed and it is possible to have several copies of the same data that are not consistent.

This means we need to come to an agreement about distributed state in addition to distributed computation, see also [24]. Both of them are closely connected. When we talk about distributed state, we want to do this on the right level of abstraction. This is needed in order to be able to handle the complexity involved. The abstraction cannot mean that we have to look into all the existing copies of data entities and their updates by connected servers. This is obviously too detailed. It is also not enough to look at a centralized data model - that would be too coarse. The right level of abstraction lets us see possible states of the data without going too deep into detail of how these come about.

In noSQL databases, such an understanding is evolving and it is revolving around the term of *eventual consistency*. This means that data can be stored in the system with a certain amount of inconsistency, but that this is resolved over time and finally, the system is consistent. This paper aims at making this idea more formal, based on an understanding of state changes in the presence of distributed data.

We base our discussion on the model of Abstract State Machines (ASM) [8], because they provide a high-level and abstract view of computation. ASM can be considered formalized pseudo-code, such that ASM programs are readable even without much introduction. ASM are using a centralized state model, and we will combine this model with data that is distributed over several locations.

This paper starts with an introduction of eventual consistency and abstract state machines in Sect. 2. In Sect. 3, we define distributed state in ASM. After than, we look into ways to quantify inconsistency in Sect. 4. Afterwards, we define eventual consistency in Sect. 5. We discuss related work in Sect. 6 before we conclude in Sect. 7.

2 Background

2.1 Distributed Data and Eventual Consistency

A first idea of handling data for distributed computation is to store it in one place, and allowing multiple agents at different locations to access this data. This kind of data is called centralized data and is how data is managed in classical relational databases. Coordination of access to the data and timely fulfilment of client requests relies on effective transaction management. Enlarging the database is costly, as it normally requires migrating to a larger, expensive database server.

An alternative to the single-server, centralized relational database is a distributed database, where as well as splitting the data across servers, some data items are replicated. Distribution is designed to optimize performance against expected client requirements, and extra processing is needed to ensure that replicated data remains consistent. In this way, we still keep the conceptual idea of centralized data, and leave detailed management of distributed, possibly replicated, data to the implementation. This is the place where the classical SQL databases are. From a users point of view, such a database should work as if the data was stored in one place. The famous ACID (atomicity, consistency, isolation, durability) rules for transaction processing ensure that this is the case.

The implementation itself will typically manage transactions so that a change is not committed before enough information is put into the system. This way, conflicting changes are avoided. Here, it is possible to choose whether the complexity should be on the read or on the write or shared between the two. It is important to notice that the read and write activities are finished when the database is in a consistent state and the returned value is correct. However, in case of much access and poor connectivity, client applications may find it slow or impossible to use the data.

Finally, based on the kind of application, we can relinquish the demand for absolute consistency. Now we are working with a truly distributed system, which is sometimes not connected, and which handles the data such that the user is not aware of connectivity problems. Of course, in this model, conflicting changes are possible, and they have to be sorted out at some point in time. The typical method for sorting out conflicting changes is timestamps, i.e. the later one of two changes is the more current one. Now the complexity of handling updates is moved partly out of the agents, and dealt with by their environment[1]. This allows for quick access to the database, but it means that there has to be an underlying process of cleaning up the database while the agents are doing something else.

The term *eventual consistency* is often used to describe how consistency is compromised in NoSQL databases, but its roots go back to the creation of the internet domain name system (DNS) created by Paul Mockapetris[2] in 1983.

Here is one definition of eventual consistency.

"Eventual consistency is a characteristic of distributed computing systems such that the value for a specific data item will, given enough time without updates, be consistent across all nodes[3]."

Eventual consistency compromises consistency in a distributed data store for availability and network partition tolerance. The need for compromise was famously articulated as the CAP Theorem or Brewer's Theorem [14] which states that you can have at most two of

- Consistency
- Availability
- Partition tolerance

---

[1] In the conceptually centralized model, the read and write handling is also moved out of the agent code, but it is still inside the agent activity, which is not completed until everything is sorted out.

[2] https://internethalloffame.org/official-biography-paul-mockapetris.

[3] https://whatis.techtarget.com/definition/eventual-consistency.

in a shared-data system. Conventional, relational database systems apply the ACID (atomicity, consistency, isolation, durability) rules for transaction processing to ensure consistency. They sacrifice partition tolerance or availability to ensure consistency.

Availability is not negotiable in the internet DNS, and distribution is also essential to ensure scalability, and so consistency is compromised in the DNS in order to ensure availability and network partition tolerance. Brewer [14] coined the term BASE (basic availability, soft state, eventual consistency) to describe the rules for transaction processing applied in the DNS and more recently in several NoSQL database systems.

This way, eventual consistency is tightly coupled with the concept of a soft state, i.e. a state that is changed even without user agent interactions. The soft state repairs consistency problems until the state becomes consistent.

2.2 Abstract State Machines

The basic definitions of locations and updates in abstract state machines (ASMs) are as follows. Variations of these definitions can be found in many sources, including, but not limited to [3,4,6–9].

At its most basic, an abstract state machine (ASM) consists of abstract states with a transition rule, or ASM program, that specifies how the ASM transitions through its states.

An ASM has a *signature* of symbols and a base set of values. The symbols of the signature are function symbols. Each function symbol has an arity. The symbols are interpreted over the base set so that a symbol with arity zero is interpreted as a single element of the base set, and a symbol with arity n is interpreted as an n-ary function over the base set. Expressions (terms) of the signature are constructed in the usual way, and are interpreted recursively over the base set.

Names can be classified with respect to change. Names like *True*, *False* and *undef*, whose interpretation is the same in all the states of an abstract state machine, are called *static names*, while all other names (called *dynamic* names) are subject to updates. Dynamic names can again be classified with respect to which agents are allowed to change them, which will be explained later. To support readability, new symbols can be defined as abbreviations for complex terms. In SDL such symbols are called *derived names* [18].

The signature includes the predefined names *True*, *False* and *Undefined*, and three distinct values of the base set serve as interpretations for these. The interpretations of *True* and *False* are called truth values. Function symbols whose interpretations deliver truth values are called predicate names.

Unary predicate names can serve as sort names, whose interpretations classify base set elements as belonging to the sort in question.

An interpretation of the symbols over the base set defines a *state* of the ASM.

An ASM program is composed of assignments, if statements, forall statements, and several more statement kinds. We will not formally introduce all the kinds, but rather refer to [8]. ASM is designed to look like pseudo-code and normally ASM programs can be read without further explanation.

The main means of change in a program is an assignment, taking the form $exp := e$, meaning that the value (object) represented in a given state by the expression exp is changed to the value (object) represented in the given state by the expression e. More generally, expressions at the left-hand side of an update can take the form $exp = f(e_1, \ldots, e_n)$, where f is an n-ary function symbol and e_i are expressions.

The ASM model is a dynamic model. Starting from an *initial state*, an abstract state machine repeatedly produces new states from existing states by *updating* the interpretation of its symbols. Such a sequence of states is called a *run* of the ASM. The *transition* (or *move* or *step*) from one state to the next is specified as a set of *updates* to *locations*, where an update is the change to the current state imposed by an assignment.

More precisely, a function symbol f with a tuple of elements $\bar{a}$ that serves as an argument of f identifies a *location*. The term $f(\bar{a})$ identifies a location and evaluates to a value in a state. In a subsequent state, the value of that location may have changed, and $f(\bar{a})$ may evaluate to a new value. In that case, an *update* indicates what the new value will be, and is expressed using the values of terms in the current state. Updates are written as triples $(f, \bar{a}, b)$, to indicate that $f(\bar{a}) = b$ will be true in the new state.

2.3   Distributed ASM

The abstract state machine model is very flexible and only asserts that state changes are given based on the current state. From here, a natural extension is to look into several ASM agents, each with an ASM program providing state changes. The agents share the (global) state and they start in a common initial state. Because the agents only use part of the state, they would normally not see the complete state, but only the part that is visible based on their signature. Therefore, we can distinguish different kinds of function names for a distributed agent: *monitored* functions are only read by the agent and updated by other agents or the environment, *controlled* functions are only visible to the agent itself and can be considered private, while *shared* functions are joint between different agents for reading and writing.

The execution model of ASM ensures that the agents do not clash in their updates of shared locations. The important idea here is that the underlying memory model is a global model with all locations being in principle available to all agents.

For the sake of the discussion in Sects. 3 and 5, we also assume the availability of a synchronized global time, which is accessed using the monitored function NOW. In reality, it is not possible to completely synchronize time in a distributed system, but here it is enough when time drift between two agents is smaller than their communication delay. This can be achieved using the NTP protocol [20]. There is also an assumption that time-stamps are never accidentally the same. Although that seems like a strong assumption, it is easily implemented by either sorting the servers issuing time-stamps and using this to sort out the time-stamp order, or to just use an ordering on the values to do the same. In practice, both these solutions, and others, are used [1]. This means we can safely assume that the time-stamps used by different agents are disjoint.

3   Abstract State Machine Model of Distributed State

3.1   Distributed, Duplicated Persistent Data

We start by looking at the user or client view of the database. The following definitions use the ASM method to model multiple agents that read, write, update and delete data that is duplicated, distributed and persistent. The definitions of communicating ASMs provided by Börger and Raschke [9], are modified to take account of duplicated data. This provides a basis for defining soft state as meaning that an update to a location is propagated to all copies. Based on this, several definitions of inconsistency are explored in Sect. 4.

Useful concepts that have already been developed, and that are relevant to consistency in a persistent data store with multiple ASM clients, include:

- persistent queries [5, 6]
- independent concurrent ASMs [27]
- communicating ASMs [9]
- communicating concurrent ASMs with shared memory [26]

Consider a distributed algorithm with several ASM agents, where the agents' persistent data is stored in a distributed database. The database management system (DBMS) can be a classical distributed SQL or a distributed NoSQL DBMS. The DBMS distributes its data across a number of servers, which can be viewed as nodes in a network. Data and functionality is replicated across server nodes, and storage is increased by adding more nodes, an approach called *horizontal scaling*. To optimise availability and partition tolerance, the requirement for consistency is relaxed to a requirement for eventual consistency.

Actions are performed by ASM agents following their ASM programs. Client agents issue requests to the DBMS, and DBMS server agents retrieve or update some of the replicated data in response to the client request. DBMS server agents also generate requests to other servers to propagate updates so as to make updated values available on those other servers.

Each location has multiple copies (replicas) on different DBMS servers. We consider servers to be agents themselves.

domain *Location*
domain *Server* ⊆ *Agent*
static *replicas: Location → $\mathcal{P}$ Server*
shared *value: Server, Location → Value*
shared *timestamp: Server, Location → Time*

We also define the latest timestamp amongst all the replicas of a location.

derived $maxTime(loc) \equiv max_{r \in replicas(loc)} timestamp(r, loc)$

We assume that different values for a location have different timestamps. This is obviously true when the different values come from different agents, as timestamps of different agents are disjoint. If the different values come from the same agent, then they have to come from different steps, as it is an inconsistency to assign two different values to the same location in the same step. However, because time advances, the timestamps of different steps of the same agent are different.

As discussed above, each location has a value that was allocated at a time that is universally comparable. Within a set of replicas, there will be a most recent update, defined as an update with the latest timestamp.

Server agents run a soft state update program which is detailed in the next subsection. The client programs run their code, which includes reads and writes of locations. This is the usual ASM handling, where for a given agent with its ASM program, an update set is determined. The update set is the set of writes, while the reading of values is given by the reads of locations. The replicas of shared variables are handled in the definition of read and write.

Connectivity between servers is of interest insofar as an update of a replica on one server is visible to another server. This is modelled using a monitored function *connected*.

monitored *connected* : *Agent, Agent* $\rightarrow$ *Boolean*

From the perspective of a client agent, database handling is an activity conducted by the environment, and the actions of DBMS agents are perceived as updates to shared or monitored locations.

Client agents can read values, where reading is a function providing a value. In reality, reading a value might be more than a function with an immediate outcome, and will rather have several steps that might or might not provide a result. For the discussion in this paper, it is sufficient to consider immediate results and keep a refinement into action sequences for later.

Reading in the presence of replicas means to read selected replicas and to use the value with the most recent time stamp among them. We abstract the possible replicas to be read with a predicate *ReadPolicyOK*, which represents an unspecified database policy that limits the subsets of replicas that need to be consulted for reading by a client agent.

static *ReadPolicyOK:* $\mathcal{P}$*Server, Location* $\rightarrow$ *Boolean*

$Read(loc) \equiv$
    choose $S \subseteq replicas(loc)$
    with $ReadPolicyOK(S, loc) \wedge \forall s \in S : connected(SELF, s)$
    do
        choose $s_0 \in S$
        with $max_{s \in S}(timestamp(loc, s)) = timestamp(loc, s_0)$

do
$$value(s_0, loc)$$

Client agents can also write a value, which means a state is changed. This way, writing is an activity. Again, writing will normally be an activity with many steps, which we abstract here to just one step. These updates bring all the replicas to the latest value. Like *ReadPolicyOK*, the function *WritePolicyOK* checks a subset of the replicas for validity to be updated, and allows write operations to be specified independently of the underlying database activity.

static *WritePolicyOK* : $\mathcal{P}$ *Server, Location* $\rightarrow$ *Boolean*

Write(loc,val) $\equiv$
    choose $S \subseteq$ *replicas(loc)*
    with *WritePolicyOK(S,loc)* $\wedge \forall s \in S :$ *ConnectedReplica(SELF,s)*
    do
    forall $s \in S$ **do**
        value(s,loc) := *val*
        timestamp(s,loc) := *NOW*

As an example, in a client program there might be an assignment $x := y+z$. This means, y and z are handled with *Read(y)* and *Read(z)*, respectively. The variable x gets a new value (lets assume 42) and this is handled with *Write(x,42)*.

An example for read and write policies could be that reading requires two replicas while writing requires all replicas. This would mean the following.

ReadPolicyOK_example(S,l) $\equiv S \subseteq$ *replicas(l)* $\wedge \mid S \mid \geq 2$
WritePolicyOK_example(S,l) $\equiv S =$ *replicas(l)*

3.2 Replicas and Updates

The DBMS has also an internal view on the data. DBMS agents handle the soft state and update locations in the background. The duplicates of the different locations are considered to be one from the client perspective, but the DBMS handles them individually and keeps consistency high. The state of the system and the different values present are later used to define eventual consistency.

We define a background process that improves consistency in the system by updating the values to newer versions. The abstract program that the DBMS agents are running in parallel to the client agents is as follows.

SoftStateUpdate $\equiv$
    choose $l \in$ *Location* **with** *SELF* $\in$ *replicas(l)* **do**
    choose $r \in$ *replicas(l)* **with** *SELF* $\neq a \wedge$ *connected(SELF,r)*
        $\wedge timestamp(r,l) >$ *timestamp(SELF,l)*
        do
            value(SELF,l) := *value(r,l)*
            timestamp(SELF,l) := *timestamp(r,l)*

4   Defining Inconsistency Formally

Eventual consistency means that from any starting state, in the absence of client-initiated updates, the system will reach a consistent state. Classical consistency is a qualitative measure, which can be true or false.

To model eventual consistency, we need a more quantitative measure of consistency as a way to express how far our system is from consistency. This will allow to express how a mechanism like *SoftStateUpdate* will, given sufficient time without client-initiated updates, cause the system to become consistent. Therefore, we do not measure consistency, but inconsistency.

In the following, we present alternative measures of inconsistency, some based on the count of outdated values, and others on the age of outdated values. To serve as a meaningful model of eventual consistency, a measure of inconsistency should have the following properties.

- P1: Inconsistency should decrease when values become less outdated. This could happen, for example, by a DBMS agent executing *SoftStateUpdate*.
- P2: Inconsistency should increase when a new value is introduced incompletely as a consequence of a client's request. In this case, the value is updated only in some replicas, which outdates the remaining values. Inconsistency should not change when consistent locations are updated consistently.
- P3: Changes to the network partitioning should not influence inconsistency. When replicas of a location become disconnected from one another, DBMS activities will not be able to reverse increases in inconsistency caused by client activities, such that the inconsistency does not decrease.

4.1   Total and Sufficient Consistency

Before defining measures of consistency, we first define total consistency, the ideal state which, given sufficient time, the system as a whole will reach in the absence of client-initiated updates. We then define sufficient consistency, a condition that means that each client read will yield the most recent value even though there might be inconsistencies in the data.

Total consistency is a state in which all the members in a set of replicas have equal values, and those equal values all have the latest timestamp. Please remember that the same timestamp implies the same value.

Definition 1 (Total consistency). *All replicas of a location have the same time stamp and the same value.*

$$TotallyConsistent(loc) \equiv$$
$$\forall s_0 \in replicas(loc) \bullet maxTime(loc) = timestamp(s_0, loc)$$

Sufficient consistency is then defined as stating that there might be different values for a location in the system, but these are not visible to clients due to the read policy.

Definition 2 ((Sufficient) consistency). *All possible reads of a location lead to the same, most recent, available value.*

$$Consistent(loc) \equiv$$
$$\forall S \subseteq replicas(loc) \bullet ReadPolicyOK(S,loc) \rightarrow$$
$$maxTime(loc) = max_{s \in S}(timestamp(s,loc))$$

4.2 Consistency as a Count of Inconsistent Replicas

In a distributed database system, consistency means having the same value for each location regardless of which server provides the value. For such a system, the number of extra, inconsistent replicated values in the system is a good measure of inconsistency. These extra values are the extra values that might be externally available to client agents. For distributed databases, there might be other hidden values in the system that are not yet presented to the users before their update operation is finished, but such values are at the level of the DBMS implementation and will not be considered further here.

Definition 3 (Outdated Values). *The measure of consistency in a distributed system is the total number of outdated values in the system. These are values that do not have the latest timestamp.*

$$OutdatedValueCount(loc) \equiv$$
$$\mid \{r \in replicas(loc) : timestamp(r,loc) \neq maxTime(loc)\} \mid$$

$$OutdatedValues \equiv \sum_{l \in Location} OutdatedValueCount(l)$$

When an old value is updated to the latest value, *OutdatedValues* decreases, as needed for P1. It does not decrease when the update goes to a new, but not the latest value. P2 is true as an incomplete client-initiated update will cause *OutdatedValues* to increase. The measure is independent of the network thus making P3 trivially true.

A second measure of consistency is presented below that takes account of the connectivity of the servers. It is not meaningful to expect nodes to be updated as long as they are disconnected from the current value.

Definition 4 (Outdated Reachable Values). *The measure of consistency in a distributed system is the number of outdated values that are reachable from the most up-to-date replicas but that are not (yet) up to date.*

$$OutdatedReachableValueCount(loc) \equiv$$
$$\mid \{r \in replicas(loc) : timestamp(r,loc) \neq maxTime(loc) \wedge$$
$$\exists \, r' \in replicas(loc) \bullet timestamp(r',loc) = maxTime(loc) \wedge$$
$$connected(r',r)\} \mid$$

$$OutdatedReachableValues \equiv$$
$$\sum_{l \in Location} OutdatedReachableValueCount(l)$$

Corollary 1.

$$OutdatedReachableValues \leq OutdatedValues$$

When everything is connected, this measure is the same as the previous one. When some parts are disconnected, then *OutdatedReachableValues* captures the connected part of the network. Again, P1 and P2 are true as long as they are in the connected parts, as we can assume that values cannot be updated in the unconnected parts. Still, *OutdatedReachableValues* is not a satisfactory measure of inconsistency because partitioning the network actually leads to increased consistency according to this measure, making P3 invalid.

Therefore we consider a measure that takes account of network partitioning.

Definition 5 (Outdated Isolated Values). *The measure of inconsistency in a distributed system is the number of outdated values that are isolated from the most recent update of a location, and so cannot be made consistent by the DBMS propagation mechanism characterized by SoftStateUpdate.*

$$OutdatedIsolatedValueCount(loc) \equiv$$
$$| \{r \in replicas(loc) : timestamp(r,loc) \neq maxTime(loc) \wedge$$
$$\exists r' \in replicas(loc) : timestamp(r',loc) = maxTime(loc) \wedge$$
$$\textbf{not } connected(r',r)\} |$$

$$OutdatedIsolatedValues \equiv \sum\nolimits_{l \in Location} OutdatedIsolatedValueCount(l)$$

Corollary 2.

$$OutdatedIsolatedValues \leq OutdatedValues$$

Corollary 3.

$$OutdatedIsolatedValues + OutdatedReachableValues = OutdatedValues$$

Inconsistency as measured by *OutdatedIsolatedValues* will not increase as a consequence of DBMS activities. However, the measure does not capture the fact that DBMS activities will increase consistency within connected parts of the system. Thus, P1 is not true. In fact, there are cases where also P2 and P3 are invalid for *OutdatedIsolatedValues*.

Combining *OutdatedIsolatedValues* with *OutdatedReachableValues* provides a measure that fulfils all three of the required properties of a meaningful measure of inconsistency. *OutdatedValues* is such a combination and therefore provides the most meaningful of the measures of inconsistency explored above.

4.3   Time-Based Measures of Inconsistency

Instead of counting inconsistent replicas of locations, the measures explored below describe inconsistency in terms of the time delay of the inconsistent replica values.

Definition 6 (Least Consistency Time). *For a location l, the consistency time is NOW in case the location is consistent. Otherwise, it is the latest timestamp with a value for this location. This leads to a measure of consistency that is the sum of distances between NOW and the consistency times of all the locations in the system.*

$$ConsistencyTime(loc) \equiv$$
$$\text{if } Consistent(loc) \text{ then } NOW \text{ else } maxTime(loc)$$

$$LeastConsistencyTime \equiv \sum_{l \in Location} (NOW - ConsistencyTime(l))$$

When an inconsistent location is made consistent, *LeastConsistencyTime* decreases, as needed for P1. It does not decrease when the update goes to a new, but not the latest value. It also does not decrease when there are still other outdated values around for the location. P2 is not true, because applying an incomplete client-initiated update to an inconsistent state will cause *LeastConsistencyTime* to decrease. As the measure is independent of the network, P3 is valid.

As this definition uses only the oldest update to a location, it does not take into account changes to other outdated values. An alternative time-based measure of inconsistency is the distance in time to the latest timestamp for all the replicas of a location. This is a measure of how out of date the replicas are.

Definition 7 (Delta Consistency Time). *The timestamp differences for all the replicas of a location.*

$$ConsistencyDelta(loc) \equiv$$
$$\sum_{r \in replicas(loc)} maxTime(loc) - timestamp(r, loc)$$

$$DeltaConsistencyTime \equiv \sum_{l \in Location} ConsistencyDelta(l)$$

DeltaConsistencyTime is a measure of the delay in propagating updates across all the replicas of a location. It improves with each improvement for any outdated value, such that P1 is true for all cases. It also fulfils P2 in all cases. Finally, as it is not considering the network, it also fulfils P3. *DeltaConsistencyTime* is more detailed than the other inconsistency measures.

5   Formal Definition of Eventual Consistency

5.1   Eventual Consistency

The previous definitions allow a formalization of eventual consistency as follows.

Definition 8 (Eventual Consistency). *A DBMS, in particular its soft state update functionality, is eventually consistent when its* DeltaConsistencyTime *is decreasing if there are no client-initiated updates and* OutdatedReachableValues *is not zero.*

This definition of eventual consistency demands that in the absence of other updates, the predicate *TotallyConsistent* will eventually hold for all locations in the system. In reality, the data is already consistent when the predicate *Consistent* holds, such that users will experience consistency earlier than that.

This is related to the other parts of the DBMS who provide as much as possible consistency already without the soft state.

The definition of eventual consistency and the use of *DeltaConsistencyTime* in particular also allows a comparison of different DBMS mechanisms and database configurations with respect to consistency.

Please note that this definition of eventual consistency does not define the consistency of a state, but the possible behaviours of a DBMS.

5.2 *SoftStateUpdate* Implies Eventual Consistency

Theorem 1. *The abstract soft state update functionality given in Sect. 3 provides eventual consistency. This means, in the absence of client-initiated updates,* DeltaConsistencyTime *decreases due to DBMS propagation of updated values across replicas.*

Proof. Let $OutdatedReachableValues > 0$[4]. This means that there is at least one location l_0 that has an outdated value. Let r_0 be a replica with the up-to-date value, and r_1 be the outdated replica. We can choose r_0 and r_1 such that $connected(r_0, r_1)$ because $OutdatedReachableValues > 0$.

Now the conditions for l, r, and $SELF$ in $SoftStateUpdate$ are fulfilled by l_0, r_0, and r_1. $SoftStateUpdate$ will run on r_1, because it is a DB server and keeps replicas. This means that $SoftStateUpdate$ for r_1 does not produce an empty update set, but changes the value of at least one location. This will decrease $DeltaConsistencyTime$ by the time difference between the old and the new value.   □

5.3 Example for Eventual Consistency

We consider the independent read - independent write (IRIW) algorithm A [10] with four agents $a_1, \ldots, a_4$ as follows.

$a_1 :$ $x := 1$
$a_2 :$ $y := 1$
$a_3 :$ $Read(x); Read(y)$
$a_4 :$ $Read(y); Read(x)$
initially $x = y = 0$

We consider three database servers db_1, db_2, db_3, keeping a replica of x and y each and running the *SoftStateUpdate* program. The user agents use the *Read* for reading values (a_3 and a_4) and the *Write* for storing the assignments of values

---

[4] Obviously, this also implies that $DeltaConsistencyTime > 0$.

(a_1 and a_2). We visualize the system state by the three replicated values for x and y, such that the initial state is $(x = (0,0,0), y = (0,0,0))$.

First, we look at a database policy where writing and reading are allowed already on just one replica. We run first a_1 and a_2 in parallel at time 1. They store the values for x and y in db_1 and db_2, respectively. This leads to the system state $(x = (1,0,0), y = (0,1,0))$ with $DeltaConsistencyTime = 4$. Now a_3 and a_4 read in parallel, where a_3 consults db_1 and a_4 consults db_2. This gives the result $x = 1, y = 0$ for a_3 and $x = 0, y = 1$ for a_4. As [10] argues, this is not sequentially consistent. However, still db_1, db_2, and db_3 are active with $SoftStateUpdate$. All of them can update at least one location, leading to $(x = (1,1,1), y = (1,1,0))$ and $DeltaConsistencyTime = 1$. The server db_3 can do one more update step, before everything is consistent.

Now we look at the case where two replicas are needed with reading and for writing. The previous scenario is not possible now, as now the system is sequentially consistent. Still, we run first a_1 and a_2 in parallel. They store the values for x and y as follows: $(x = (1,1,0), y = (0,1,1))$ with $DeltaConsistencyTime = 2$. Now a_3 and a_4 read in parallel, and independent of their choice of servers, they both get the result $x = 1$, $y = 1$. The server db_2 is already up-to-date, but db_1 and db_3 run $SoftStateUpdate$, leading to $(x = (1,1,1), y = (1,1,1))$ and $DeltaConsistencyTime = 0$.

Please observe that in the second case, the system is consistent all the time, even though $DeltaConsistencyTime$ is not 0. However, the soft state functionality does not stop before everything is updated to the latest value.

In the case of partitions, not all needed updates are possible and have to be delayed until the connection is restored.

6   Related Work

Bosneag and Brockmeyer [11] developed a formalism that enabled specification of different forms of consistency for a given data object. Like the work presented here, their approach is rooted in state machine models. Eventual consistency is defined as the fact that in the absence of updates, all replicas of a data item converge towards identical copies of each other. A history reduction operator is defined based on whether or not operations in a history can be reordered without affecting the end state that is reached, and a proof is given that any algorithm that respects the history reduction operator will achieve eventual consistency.

The definitions provided here differ from [11] in that they deal with a measure of distance from consistency rather than on dependencies between operations. We maintain that this more abstract view of eventual consistency, which does not need to refer to execution traces, provides a better basis for reasoning about whether or not a database management system can be said to ensure eventual consistency.

Burckhardt [15] provides ways to reason about the consistency of protocols in terms of consistency guarantees, ordering guarantees and convergence guarantees. Reasoning is in terms of states, where the current state is viewed as a graph of prior operations. Formal models are presented for protocol definitions and for executions in distributed systems, and proofs are provided to show that implementations meet consistency guarantees. This goes far beyond the definitions presented here, but has the disadvantage that it relies on a specially developed formalism for specifying the observable behaviour of a system. Our work has the advantage that it builds on the established ASM formalism, and so can be used immediately to reason about existing specifications.

Bouajjani, Enea and Hamza [12, 13] define eventual consistency as a property over traces observed by an external witness. Eventual consistency is grounded in the notions of safety and liveness, and is defined in terms of finite prefixes of a global interpretation of method calls in a system where the result of a call is well-defined (safety), and where there exists a global interpretation of all the method calls in an infinite trace. This facilitates reasoning about speculative updates and rollbacks, both of which are essential to a practically useful definition of eventual consistency. Again, our definitions do not refer to histories or execution traces, and so provide a more appropriate level of abstraction for reasoning about eventual consistency than was previously available.

In summary, the work presented here differs from previous work in that it builds on an existing ASM formalism and so can be used to reason about existing specifications without the need to translate those into a new formalism. It differs also in that it focuses on measures of distance from the desired state of consistency rather than on execution traces of a distributed system. This enables reasoning about consistency at a more appropriate level of abstraction than was previously possible. Finally, the ASM formalism also provides the semantic foundation for SDL [17], which provides an opportunity to provide automated support for verifying eventual consistency by building on existing tools.

7   Conclusion

Different definitions aimed at quantifying consistency in a distributed database with replicated data were presented above.

Some of the definitions are based on counts of inconsistent replicas of locations in the distributed system. These definitions capture the idea that client-initiated updates will make the database system less consistent, and that DBMS activities to propagate updates across replicas will make the system more consistent.

Other definitions are based on calculating how out-of-date some replicas are. Those definitions also capture the concept of a distributed database system that becomes less consistent with client updates and more consistent as updates are propagated by the DBMS.

However, none of the definitions fully captures the implications of network failure and partitioning. This is not necessarily a problem, but indicates that further metrics are needed to cover those aspects of distributed databases with eventual consistency.

For sure, distributed persistent data is essential to distributed computation, and the ASM formalism supports formal modelling of persistent distributed datastores with replicated values. Moreover, it enables such datastores to be seamlessly modelled alongside independent client and DBMS server agents.

Overall, a foundation has been laid to conduct deeper investigation of eventual consistency than has previously been possible.

References

1. Apache Software Foundation: Apache Cassandra 4.0 - Web Page and Documentation (2019). http://cassandra.apache.org/
2. Best, E.: Semantics of Sequential and Parallel Programs. Prentice Hall, Upper Saddle River (1996)
3. Blass, A., Gurevich, Y.: Ordinary interactive small-step algorithms I. ACM Trans. Comput. Logic **7**(2), 363–419 (2006)
4. Blass, A., Gurevich, Y., Rosenzweig, D., Rossman, B.: Interactive small-step algorithms II: abstract state machines and the characterization theorem. Logical Methods Comput. Sci. **3**(4) (2007). https://doi.org/10.2168/LMCS-3(4:4)2007
5. Blass, A., Gurevich, Y.: Persistent queries. CoRR abs/0811.0819 (2008). http://arxiv.org/abs/0811.0819
6. Blass, A., Gurevich, Y.: Persistent queries in the behavioral theory of algorithms. ACM Trans. Comput. Logic (TOCL) **12**(2), 16:1–16:43 (2011). https://doi.org/10.1145/1877714.1877722
7. Börger, E., Cisternino, A. (eds.): Advances in Software Engineering. LNCS, vol. 5316. Springer, Heidelberg (2008). https://doi.org/10.1007/978-3-540-89762-0
8. Börger, E., Stärk, R.: Abstract State Machines - A Method for High-Level System Design and Analysis. Springer, Berlin (2003). https://doi.org/10.1007/978-3-642-18216-7
9. Börger, E., Raschke, A.: Modelling Companion for Software Practitioners. Springer, Berlin (2018). https://doi.org/10.1007/978-3-662-56641-1
10. Börger, E., Schewe, K.D.: Concurrent abstract state machines. Acta Inf. **53**(5), 469–492 (2016). https://doi.org/10.1007/s00236-015-0249-7
11. Bosneag, A.M., Brockmeyer, M.: A unified formal specification for a multi-consistency replication system for DHTs. In: 12th IEEE International Conference and Workshops on the Engineering of Computer-Based Systems (ECBS 2005), pp. 33–40. IEEE (2005)
12. Bouajjani, A., Enea, C., Hamza, J.: Verifying eventual consistency of optimistic replication systems. In: Proceedings of the 41st ACM SIGPLAN-SIGACT Symposium on Principles of Programming Languages, POPL 2014, pp. 285–296. ACM, New York (2014). https://doi.org/10.1145/2535838.2535877
13. Bouajjani, A., Enea, C., Hamza, J.: Verifying eventual consistency of optimistic replication systems. ACM SIGPLAN Not. **49**(1), 285–296 (2014). https://doi.org/10.1145/2578855.2535877
14. Brewer, E.A.: Towards robust distributed systems (abstract). In: Proceedings of the Nineteenth Annual ACM Symposium on Principles of Distributed Computing, PODC 2000, p. 7. ACM, New York (2000). https://doi.org/10.1145/343477.343502
15. Burkhardt, S.: Principles of eventual consistency. Found. Trends Program. Lang. **1**, 1–150 (2014)
16. Hoare, C.A.R.: Communicating sequential processes. Commun. ACM **21**(8), 666–677 (1978). https://doi.org/10.1145/359576.359585

17. ITU-T: Specification And Description Language SDL (Z.100 Series). International standard, International Telecommunication Union, Telecommunication Standardization Sector (2016–2018)
18. ITU-T: Specification and Description Language – Overview of SDL-2010, Annex F1: SDL-2010 formal definition: General overview. International standard, International Telecommunication Union, Telecommunication Standardization Sector (2016–2018)
19. Manson, J., Pugh, W., Adve, S.V.: The Java memory model. SIGPLAN Not. **40**(1), 378–391 (2005). https://doi.org/10.1145/1047659.1040336
20. Mills, D.L.: A brief history of NTP time: memoirs of an internet timekeeper. SIGCOMM Comput. Commun. Rev. **33**(2), 9–21 (2003). https://doi.org/10.1145/956981.956983
21. Milner, R. (ed.): A Calculus of Communicating Systems. LNCS, vol. 92. Springer, Heidelberg (1980). https://doi.org/10.1007/3-540-10235-3
22. Mironov, A.M.: Theory of processes. CoRR abs/1009.2259 (2010). http://arxiv.org/abs/1009.2259
23. Object Management Group (OMG): OMG® Unified Modeling Language® (OMG UML®), Version 2.5.1. OMG Document Number formal, 05 December 2017. http://www.omg.org/spec/UML/2.5.1
24. Prinz, A.: Distributed computing on distributed memory. In: Khendek, F., Gotzhein, R. (eds.) SAM 2018. LNCS, vol. 11150, pp. 67–84. Springer, Cham (2018). https://doi.org/10.1007/978-3-030-01042-3_5
25. Prinz, A., Sherratt, E.: Distributed ASM - pitfalls and solutions. In: Aït-Ameur, Y., Schewe, K.D. (eds.) ABZ 2014. LNCS, vol. 8477, pp. 210–215. Springer, Berlin (2014). https://doi.org/10.1007/978-3-662-43652-3_18
26. Schewe, K., Prinz, A., Börger, E.: Concurrent computing with shared replicated memory. CoRR abs/1902.04789 (2019). http://arxiv.org/abs/1902.04789
27. Sherratt, E.: Relativity and abstract state machines. In: Haugen, Ø., Reed, R., Gotzhein, R. (eds.) SAM 2012. LNCS, vol. 7744, pp. 105–120. Springer, Heidelberg (2013). https://doi.org/10.1007/978-3-642-36757-1_7

Author Index

Printed in the United States
By Bookmasters

Printed in the United States
By Bookmasters